TREE STEVENS

ELEMENTARY ♥ ♥
MY DEAR ♥♥♥ ♥
& FABULOUSLY ♥
LOW FAT ♥ ♥ ♥ ♥

Sunstar
PUBLISHING LTD.

ELEMENTARY MY DEAR
& FABULOUSLY LOW FAT

Cover Design: Robert Shelley
Photo Credit: Don Carstens
Mark Swisher
Bill Anderson

Library of Congress Catalog Card Number: 96-069498
ISBN: 1-887472-12-6

Sunstar Publishing, Ltd.
116 North Court Street
Fairfield, Iowa 52556

Readers interested in obtaining further information on the
subject matter of this book are invited to correspond with
Tree Stevens, Author
PO Box 1017, Greenbelt MD 20768-1017

DEDICATION

To the one man with whom I'd rather do just about everything
(lowfat, naturally)...my David.
Thank you, for all of it!

ACKNOWLEDGEMENTS

My deepest appreciation to:

Marsha Friedman, for reminding me to keep it easy.
Kathy Giordano, for your support, your loyalty and your warmth...what a good friend is all about.
Karen Stefanik, for your tireless and timely editing...you're always on time and right on the mark.
Edythe Eisenberg, for being my "little" big sister...what a tough act to follow.
Julie Gray-Roller, for giving of your intellect and friendship.
Horacio Tijman, for your understanding and enduring patience.
Steve Stefanik, for getting me started...you'll get the hang of it, one of these days.
Meredith Bari Drescher, for being the first and turning out so fine.
Scott Drescher, for being the second and always trying to be first at everything else.
Kim Brette Rubin, for being the last and never coming in last at anything...just showing everyone else the way to do it right.
Kay Stefanik, without whom I wouldn't have my wonderful David...and for being my Mom, too.
Robert Shelley, for proving that it can be done, despite the pressure and fatigue...you are, truly, an artist.
Rodney Charles, for having the faith and making it happen this year.

CREDITS

Book design and art direction Robert Shelley, Baltimore, MD

Photography by Don Carstens and Mark Swisher, Baltimore, MD
Bill Anderson, College Park, MD

CONTENTS

FOREWORD
BY PAUL M. RIVAS, M.D.

Elementary My Dear & Fabulously Low Fat author Tree Stevens gives a very easy to follow and commonsense guide for healthy eating. Presently, at least one-third of all Americans are overweight and each decade the numbers keep rising. The causes of this are multifactorial and involve the close relationship between heredity and environment.

We have come to realize very clearly in the Bariatric field that the overweight condition has a strong genetic link. It appears that the tendency, or predisposition to fatness, is very hereditary. Studies on identical twins have clearly shown that heredity and not eating patterns is the predisposing factor most important in becoming overweight. Genetics seems to be the culprit behind food obsessions, cravings, compulsive eating and overeating.

This being said, the availability of high fat foods in western societies makes it very easy for someone who is genetically prone, to actually become overweight. For example, if one has a hereditary tendency to be fat, but is born in Ethiopia, where only lean foods are available, then that person will remain thin despite the genetic factors. If that same person moves to the United States where fast food chains are available in every neighborhood and chocolate bars in every store, then that individual will almost certainly become overweight.

While we have been making progress in combating the genetic influences, the importance of controlling diet and maintaining a good exercise program will always be there. This is where Tree Stevens has provided a very valuable service. In a very personal and readable style she gives practical advice on proper eating habits, exercise, low fat cooking and other pearls of her own struggles and experiences.

Most people will be able to easily relate to Tree's personal testimonies and will find her avenues to health and fitness to be refreshing and realistic. Her methods are geared for a lifetime of success and are not faddish or extremist. In other words, anyone can do it following her guidelines of exercise and tasty but easy recipes.

Paul M. Rivas, MD
Medical Director, Rivas Medical Weight Loss Program
Baltimore, Maryland

CHAPTER 1

LIVE IT!

S it back and make yourself comfortable. Take a deep breath and relax. Conjure up, in your mind's eye, a magnificent piece of juicy, crispy-crusted pizza. Inhale the rich basil tomato and the hint of garlic. Feel the chewy pull of the cheese as you sink your teeth into the mound of aromatic vegetables and tear off a mouthful. The flavors fill your cheeks and the spicy bouquet lifts up to your nostrils. Mmmmmm! You can feel it all the way back to your molars. There! You've got it!

Now gently embrace the cool, smooth feel of a spoonful of velvety ice cream melting in the back of your throat...the sweet, thick muskiness of the warm chocolate sauce curling around your tongue. Can you taste it? Can you feel it? Are you salivating and reveling in the ecstasy produced by these imaginings? Or are you craving the real thing, rushing to the phone for the nearest pizza delivery or diving into the freezer for a Ben & Jerry's fix?

Hold everything!

There are those out there who insist that we should "eat to live" not "live to eat." Pshaw! We are attacked by visual and verbal advertising salvos aimed at destroying any concentrated effort at self-control. Living in today's society is like life as a shuttlecock in a badminton game. On the one hand the temptations are over-whelming...you are force-fed gobs of goodies, professionally orchestrated to grab you during commercial breaks and at the supermarket, while, on the other hand, you are maligned for being the fattest American in history. You're told your diseases are a result of being too fat or eating too much fat, maybe both. You're besieged by fitness equipment and workout gimmicks, ton-ics and diet plans on 30-minute infomercials. And, let's be honest here — we *love* food! It's no wonder so many of us are on Prozac!

At the same time, there are much more common sense ways than ever before to alleviate the plight of the food-driven, over-fed guy on the street. Serious research findings have finaly found solu-tions for morbid obesity, which have proven to be very exciting in the area of hormonal and chemical imbalances and in genetic coding, as well. Researchers have even spent over $200 million dollars perfecting a fake fat, Olestra (that is not yet perfect), to satisfy the demands of the major noshers among us. The contro-versy has certainly been fervent, with the *Citizens for Science in the Public Interest* on one side claiming that Olestra absorbs and eliminates nutrients that are necessary for good health and causes the onset of loose stools, to Proctor & Gamble on the other side promoting this product as the panacea for the fat free folk. We have our Dean Ornishes to help bring a solid approach to a life-time of better health through wiser eating, and we have a pletho-ra of cookbooks out there based on the healthier, more satisfying, low fat lifestyle. Meanwhile, the food packagers are going wild claiming that their products are, indeed, low fat or no fat.

Some of the information is confusing and some of the simple facts have been tangled on purpose to make them confusing. Yet the major thread that runs through the sensible, intelligent, healthful food-talk, as well as some of the fodder, is the technique which fulfills our need for gastronomic gratification and yet provides the basics of wise eating for good health and weight control. You've got it! *THE LOW FAT LIFESTYLE* !

If you've already read my book, *LIVING & LOVING LOW FAT*, you know where I stand on this issue. If not, you'll certainly know by the time you finish this book. To present my theory in a nutshell: a diet has a beginning and an end. It is logical, therefore, that if you change your eating habits to fulfill the rules laid out in a particular diet...an eating regimen that is foreign to your tastes or obviously based on a short-term, quick weight loss, rather than long-term, lifestyle change...you will adhere to the diet for a particular period of time, after which you will revert back to your old way of eating. That's the whole point of "going on a diet." Right?

The only problem is that, invariably, the dieter will return to old routines, and eating as you did before, the old weight returns. It is also logical that if you embark on a new methodology when it comes to food, you must change your eating habits. If you enjoy the new way you eat so much that you never feel the need to regress to the old way, the "diet" is no longer a diet. It becomes a *lifestyle*. If this new lifestyle is not a matter of self-deprivation and hardship, but achieves all that you'd previously suffered so much to accomplish, you've really won! And that's the simple answer to sustaining weight loss...and continuing to eat healthfully whether the change was made for weight maintenance or if a medical problem prompted the changes in the first place.

Please let's not overlook the agonizing dilemma of the patient who's been advised that a change in lifestyle is necessary to prolong life! Did you know that heart disease patients are usually "good" for about six months or so after an attack, then they gradually slide back into old habits at the table, as the horror of the attack slips from an immediate fear to a distant memory? So what does it take, then, to achieve that feeling of robust good health and maintain it over the years, keeping the energy level up, the weight down, and the body humming like a perfectly tuned instrument? Eating the right foods and enjoying what we eat is only half the equation. Exercising regularly, enjoying the workout we choose, is the other necessary component of a truly healthful lifestyle. Before you say, "Yuk!" read on.

It's important for all of us who are concerned about living longer (and having a heck of a good time doing it), that we embrace those habits that are thoroughly gratifying and rewarding. That we feel better at the end of our years than we ever dreamed possible. And that the road to our golden years is paved with gold, as well. Can you think of a better way to grow old?

CHAPTER II

YOU'LL LOVE IT!

Food is such an important part of our lives that we can't possibly think of most occasions without it. What is the good of a get-together without the planning of the goodies that will be part of the party? In fact, the planning of the food is an integral component of the bash. It sets the tone.

Sometimes the celebration cannot be the celebration without the particular special support from the fridge! When you think of Thanksgiving, doesn't *turkey* come to mind? Or *hot dogs* on July 4th? Try to conceive of a child's birthday without the obligatory *ice cream* and *cake*. Heaven forbid! This would be a neglected child! And there's no question about it – it would be difficult to have that intimate, romantic dinner...without the *dinner!*

How, then, have we gotten ourselves into this fix? We love food! Much of our lives revolve around the planning for, the swallowing of, and the reminiscing over, the morsels we delicately savor or ravenously devour. Yet while we spend so much time on food, we hate ourselves or pride ourselves, on how much of it or how little of it, we've consumed. We fantasize over, binge on, feel guilty about, and reward ourselves with FOOD. A dichotomy, no question about it!

How many people do you know (and there's a strong possibility you're one) who are either on, about to start, or just finished a diet. Did they achieve their goal? And, if so, are they going to live on in the glory of this accomplishment, or are they going to have to redo the diet in the very near future to get back down to where they are now, because they've regained what they lost.

When I talk to groups about food, whether it's in relationship to weight control or health incentives, we always return to a few major questions:

• How does one eat what one enjoys without having to revert to a diet after the enjoyment? Is there really a way to live a diet-free life? Or at least feel like you are?

• What does a person do to maintain a weight loss, or maintain a regimen dictated by necessity, without boredom and abject misery?

• How does a busy, working individual have time to prepare the foods they should be eating at the end of a harrowing day? Or have the time to work out as they should, for that matter!

• Why does the food industry seem to complicate the labels and the packaging to make buying the right foods so difficult? How can we simplify shopping smart?

• Is it true that the percentage of fat in each food eaten must be measured?

• How does one order in a restaurant to maintain a healthy lifestyle?

Happiness is a driving force for most of us and the specter of being constantly on guard is not a happy thought. Food and the time we spend eating are so important to us. The conviviality, the camaraderie, and sometimes just the "feel-goods" are an integral part of our way of life. It's necessary that we find an answer to those questions that we can live with, happily.

For years weight-watchers were told that repetitive cycles of losing and regaining weight (the yo-yo syndrome) made the practice ever more difficult and led to poor health. Then an about-face in the world of obesity research occurred. Researchers decided that you not only won't suffer a heart attack from yo-yo dieting, but it's no more difficult for you to lose the next ten pounds than the last time you lost ten pounds. Yet dieters all over the world will dispute this finding.

Let's examine this for a moment. Experts in the field, such as George L. Blackburn, M.D., Ph.D., Harvard Medical School, point to a depression of the metabolic rate as a result of a restricted diet, since the body becomes more energy-efficient as the intake of calories is reduced. In addition, it is also agreed that the body feeds off protein as well as fat when food is denied, thereby depleting muscle tissue which can reduce the body's calorie-burning ability, since muscle is the most metabolically active tissue. Muscle burns more calories when the body is at rest than any other tissue in the human body.

Dr. Paul Rivas in his book, *If You're Fat It's Not Your Fault* (David-Paul Publishing), refers to a process that our body goes through called "lipogenesis," wherein the body manufactures *additional* fat cells to increase its storage capacity to avoid starvation...while we're trying valiantly to lose a pound or an inch! According to the *Tufts University Diet & Nutrition Letter*, December, 1994, if, in fact, the reasons for see-sawing may not be physiological, the emotional factors including the frustration, the irritability, the depression and the loss of self-esteem may all account for the lack of success in subsequent weight-loss after a first-time success. Add to these obstacles headaches from the reduced food intake and the basic discomfort caused by hunger, and it's no wonder that it's more difficult to lose weight during each subsequent attempt. Simply stated...*diets don't work!*

Ok! Diets don't work! Easy to say. But the doctor insists you change your eating habits or a heart attack is imminent! You are suffering from arthritic pain in your knees and less body weight will relieve pressure on your joints. You know that a high fat diet is a determining factor in cardiovascular diseases (heart disease, hypertension, stroke); cancers of the prostate, colon, uterus and skin; diabetes; and, of course, obesity. There are strong indications, according to Ronald Klein, professor of ophthalmology and visual sciences at the University of Wisconsin, that age-related macular degeneration (a disease causing blindness which occurs in later years) may be caused by fatty plaques accumulating in the arteries leading to the eyes or may even be a result of fatty deposits in the membrane behind the retina, itself, either of which may be a sign of too much fat in the diet. And here's one that will definitely get your attention. There is strong evidence that the buildup of fatty plaques in the arteries of the brain reduces the amount of blood that feeds the brain cells and may very well cause a deterioration of memory and thought processes.

You can maintain and yes, even improve, your sex life as a result of switching to a low fat diet!

Aha! I got your attention! The same principle applies here as with the blood vessels in the brain. An unrestricted blood flow is necessary for proper sexual function and sensuality in both the male and female sex organs: a concentration of fat in the arteries may adversely affect this physiological functon. In other words...too much fat in your diet can really mess up your love life!

That's over the long run. What about the immediate effect a high fat meal has on your sexual function? A study published in *Metabolism*, September, 1990, showed that four hours after having consumed a high fat shake, a group of men experienced a 30% reduction in testosterone. After a low-fat drink of carbohydrates and protein the control group experienced no change in testosterone levels. Since testosterone affects the sex drive of both men and women, it appears that eating high fat food is a definite detriment to a high-flying romance.

We haven't even talked about the difference in the way you feel when you're lean and mean, ready to take on the world, feeling so good about yourself and the way you look that you glow! This fabulous feeling of having the world by the tail is strictly emotional, but what an emotion!

Is it worth an adjustment in your lifestyle? You bet! Will it take a long time to become accustomed to this new lifestyle?

Relax...you can approach this new way of living without trepidation. Behavioral scientists maintain that it takes only four to six weeks to form a new habit. The same amount of time applies to changing an old one. With the right motivation (you can't deny you've just been exposed to a few motivating factors!) the modifications I'm going to introduce to you should be really easy to make and then enjoy for the rest of your life.

Please don't consider this a short-term foray into the world of low fat and treat the changes you make as temporary...the end of which is in sight. Instead, if you accept all the information in the media hype about the effects of a low fat lifestyle and moderate exercise, consider this a road to a fuller and longer life.

Why do I say "fuller" life when I'm obviously demanding you change the way you live now...a life with which you have no doubt become very comfortable...a life that provides for you the warm fuzzies when you need them, whether they be in the form of hugs or hot fudge sundaes? The answer is easy. If you react with the joie de vivre we see in others as they have attuned themselves to this way of living, you'll be amazed by the results. See if it works. If not, you'll really enjoy the recipes in the rest of the book, anyway. They taste good!

When you feel *good*, whether it's because you're healthy, because you've just accomplished something important, or you know you look great, the world is a happier place. By living differently, if you can be healthier, have more energy, look better and feel better, wouldn't that do it for you?

That's my challenge to you!

Give this lifestyle six weeks and you'll be in a happier place. Try it...you'll love it!

CHAPTER III

EVERYONE'S DOIN' IT

There has been a bombardment of information about fat. Fat on your body, fat in your body, and fat in your food. The problem is that much of the information is complicated, contradictory and confusing. Even the experts on the *diet* way of life have moved over to the *low fat diet* way of life. It's a fascinating bandwagon, joined by many who see it as a gravy train. The truth is obvious. An approach to food that is based on low fat is the intelligent answer to good health. The only question is how to assemble the information available, and make it fit your needs. And it's got to be a comfortable fit!

The major opposition I've received to the logic of embracing this lifestyle is the difficulty most people *imagine* they'll encounter in changing. Changing the way they think about food, changing the food they eat, changing the way they cook and changing the food they enjoy. Who likes change? We become so stuck in routine, we can't even imagine breaking out. And that's what I'm recommending you do!

So it had darned well better be easy!

And it will be, I promise.

To begin with, I'll fill you in on a quick little story about how I got started living this way. It may help you to see how simple it is. The payoff has been much greater than I ever expected. That's how *good* I feel!

I've been spending about forty-five minutes to an hour working out five to six days a week since about 1975. I'd started exercising as an adjunct to dieting to help control my weight. My mother was a magnificent Reubens nude. And Reubens was definitely in my genes. As a child I was slim and grew like a weed until I was ten years old. Then all of a sudden, at 5'7", I stopped growing up. Since I continued to eat as I had before, I started growing around, instead. Dieting started for me when I was twelve years old. It stopped for me in 1985, when I learned I needn't diet ever again!

While working out one morning, one of the guys who was always there at the crack of dawn, returned from an extended business trip. I hadn't seen him for about a month and was astounded by what I saw. He was gorgeous! At least he was compared to the round fellow he'd been when last I'd seen him. Wow! I ran over to him and begged him for the secret. That secret changed my eating habits forever! And I've never dieted a day since!

He told me that his doctor had suggested that he *stop counting calories.* Instead, he was told to *count fat grams!* He was advised to confine himself to 20 grams of fat, or less, a day.

Now, that was a new one. Well, what the heck. I'd done it all...the grapefruit diet, the water diet, the high-protein low-carb diet, the every-other-day diet, the all-week and off-weekend diet, the liquid-meal diet and the fasting diet. Why not the low fat diet? Little did I know then that I would end up living and loving the low fat lifestyle.

Back in 1986, there were no fat free cheeses, sour creams, mayonnaises or ice creams. It was necessary to "guts" it up and do without. But the years of longing for a baked potato or a bowl of spaghetti (the word "pasta" was just becoming the *in* thing), a bagel...oh, what I would have given for a bagel! There were so many goodies I could enjoy that had previously been taboo. Foods that help you feel full: potatoes, beans, bread, corn, rice. I remember sitting before a lunch of grilled hamburger with a scoop of cottage cheese, gagging it down and wondering how much longer it would be until I'd lost ten pounds so I could *eat* again! Of course, I lost that same ten pounds at least one hundred and fifty times! And here I was, contemplating spending the rest of my life without being forced to eat that cottage cheese. Joy to the world!

Since, back in 1985, the government hadn't yet demanded that every packaged food produced in the United States carry a nutritional label, I was on my own. The first thing I did was purchase a paperback with nutritional breakdowns including fat grams and calories for most fresh foods and a number of packaged products. As you will see, this is a must, and we'll get into this in more detail, later. There are books available now that list fat grams and calories for almost all national brands, some private label products and chain restaurant foods as well. The important point is that as difficult as gram-counting was for me originally, gram-counting was still a whole lot easier than any of the diet regimens I'd suffered from before.

Oh, by the way, I love what I eat! And you'll love what I eat, too, if you prepare some of the recipes I've collected for you in the *Fabulous Food* section of this book! Then you'll wonder why you've been fighting making this change. The lucky break for you is that there are now loads of wonderful products, available to you in your supermarket, catering to the low fat lifestyle. You wanted easy? This is easy!

There has been, in this major evolution to a low fat world, one problem I didn't have to contend with years ago. Since the producers had not yet become imbued with the low fat spirit, differentiating between a healthy, tasty low fat food and a *high calorie*, low fat food was not cause for the intense scrutiny necessary in today's supermarket. There are definitely products to steer away from. The consumption of more calories than you burn will lead to weight gain. Even if they are fat free calories, if they are easily convertible calories, such as simple sugars, they are easily assimilated into your system and stored as fat. Complex carbohydrates are the foods to load up on!

The greatest advantage to eating low fat is that you won't feel as though you are depriving yourself. A gram of carbohydrate is 4 calories, a gram of fat is 9 calories. You can eat twice the carb grams for the same caloric intake as a gram of fat. At the same time, it takes more calories to burn carbs as energy than fat. Since the fat is utilized more efficiently, it takes more grams of carbohydrates to store the same amount of fat in places like the tummy, hips and tush. In his book *Eat More, Weigh Less* (HarperCollins), Dr. Dean Ornish alludes to the fact that the body uses ten times the amount of calories storing carb calories as it does storing fat calories. The blessing is that carbohydrates are foods that satisfy the feel-good and taste-good needs and are still in your calorie range for losing or maintaining weight. Simply stated: go with complex carbs...you get more burn for the buck!

A simple example might help to show you how easily this works: a small bag of M&M's Peanuts, 1.74 ounces, contains 250 calories. A pound of apples contains 242 calories. Talk about a difference in the "feel full" equation, this one is a pip, isn't it? But that's the "feel *full*," what about the "feel *good?*"

A tablespoon of real butter has 11 grams of fat and 100 calories. A tablespoon of Fleischmann's Fat Free Low Calorie squeeze margarine has 0 fat and 5 calories. A 3.1 ounce Sara Lee frozen onion bagel with a tablespoon of Fleischmann's has 1 gram of fat and 235 calories as compared to the same bagel with the butter sporting 330 calories and 12 grams of fat. Same full, satisfied feeling but a tremendous difference on your love handles.

There's always a choice, isn't there? And the choice is yours. Fat in, fat on! Food in, maybe no fat on! Oooh, that sounds pretty good. But I mentioned that there are two parts to this play. The second part is exercise. We'll get back to food after a short workout.

CHAPTER IV

BREAK A SWEAT

T here is no way to talk about good health without spending some time in the gym. You may very well say, "I wanted to know about low fat and food and she's giving me exercise!"

Whether it's a health thing or a matter of weight, increasing your energy and well-being as the result of exercising less than an hour a day, cannot be ignored. That time will bring additional vitality and gusto to your life, not only now, but also in the last of those extra years you'll add to your life, as a result of the gym.

This may be your own gym, at home. It may be one of those fancy, equipment-jammed spas that has racquetball courts and tennis, or it may just be the whole outdoors. However you do it, you just *gotta* do it!

"There's no time." "It never worked for me." "Working out made me gain weight." "I hurt myself." "It's never done any good."

There are as many excuses as there are unused lifetime athletic club memberships! Despite the excuses, however, the reasons *for* exercising truly overshadow any and all of the most ingenious rationalizations *not* to exercise.

When you consider the benefits of a regular exercise program, both physically and mentally, you will find a way to devote some time to being good to yourself. That's exactly what exercise is...a commitment to your own well-being! Let's see if any of the following data will get you into a pair of sweats or maybe a pair of shorts and t-shirt.

A good workout kick-starts the engine. It revs up the motor and keeps it going. There are two kinds of workout. Aerobic and strength training.

Aerobic exercise is good for the heart and lungs. It also increases the metabolic rate during the workout and for hours afterward, thereby helping to burn calories for a much longer period than the duration of the workout itself. A thirty minute energetic dance routine or brisk walk will give you from four to six hours of extra calorie-burn. The aerobics you enjoy can be anything from jumping and jogging with the TV on in your bedroom, to a stair-stepper. A great workout is thirty minutes using an aerobic step, with or without a video tape for instruction, maybe a bit of Madonna for a beat, or an old movie on TV. You'll never notice the time spent and in thirty minutes you'll have stepped the equivalent of fifty flights on a fourteen step stairway. That was easy, huh?

There's always the aerobic dance class (low impact or high impact), or bicycling (indoors or out), maybe cross-country skiing (indoors or on the slopes). There's a class in New York, and I just caught one on cable TV, that combines aerobics with Karate. Pretty neat to get your aerobics in while you're learning how to defend yourself! If that's not your bag, perhaps a brisk walk in the park or mall will do it. And since variety is the spice of life, try doing it one way for a week or two and then do a change-up routine. Take a hike or go square dancing. It's a healthy change for your body and certainly a mental plus, too.

If you have a problem tucking thirty minutes away in a neat package, do a quick, brisk ten minute walk before breakfast, then another ten minutes during your morning break, another ten at lunch, or while dinner's cooking. In fact, do all four sets of ten and you'll go forty minutes instead of thirty. That was easy, wasn't it?

We've known about the benefits of aerobics for years, since they were first introduced to us in Dallas by Dr. Kenneth Cooper. The increased capacity of the heart and lungs is important, but have you considered the increased blood flow to the skin, which keeps your face looking younger. And if that's not enough to turn you on, in addition to the extra calorie burn, think of the higher levels of endorphins (the natural mood-elevator in your brain), delivering a natural high.

You may decide you feel so good exercising for thirty minutes, three times a week, that you end up spending thirty minutes, six days a week. Once you get a routine going, you may find it easier to stick with if you work out every day. Usually it's a good idea to take off at least one day a week. This helps to avoid fatigue and burnout. Take time to warm up and cool down each time you work out. If you're just starting, take your time. Your body will dictate the intensity best for you, as you gradually increase time and effort.

While we all know how beneficial aerobic exercises are, the last few years a great deal of research has proven that weight resistance exercises, or strength training, have a separate and equally compelling list of benefits for those who believe that living longer is better, if you're *enjoying* those extra years.

A Tufts University study, in 1995, showed that a small group of participants undertook a twelve-week strength training program that gradually increased in intensity. They worked out for thirty minutes, three times a week. Although their weight was unchanged, they averaged a strength increase from 20% to 92%, and their amount of body fat reduced by 3%! They were gaining muscle to take the place of the fat they burned. That's in only twelve weeks! Their resting metabolic rate increased by an average of 8%. The muscles gained burn more efficiently, even at rest. That means the participants are burning more calories all day, every day, because they spent ninety minutes a week performing weight resistance exercises. This study showed these people were able to consume an additional 300 calories per day without gaining weight.

With all that good news, believe it or not, that's not all strength training does for you. While the sedentary are losing bone, pumping iron increases bone density, helping to ward off osteoporosis. It decreases the risk of developing diabetes because more muscle mass helps the body utilize insulin more efficiently. It improves the ratio of HDL (the good cholesterol) to LDL (the bad cholesterol). It helps to build the muscles that surround the joints supporting the joints and eliminating or easing arthritis pain.

In another, truly extraordinary study conducted by the researchers at Tufts, men and women in their 70's, 80's and 90's, who were suffering the frailty and weakness typical of the aged, increased their daily activity by 35%, on average, after starting a weight resistance regimen. Their renewed strength enabled them to climb stairs, walk faster and suffer less fatigue. In other words, they could derive more joy from life. Some of the individuals in the program were able to trade their walker for a cane! These folks had been sedentary for years. Just think of the rewards a couple of dumbbells deliver, if you start when you're younger!

In addition, the extra muscle-tone provides increased energy, along with better balance, and the firmer, more youthful appearance a well-muscled body presents. Tell me, how can you say "no" to weight training?

It needn't be a costly affair, although a membership at a swank health club is nifty. A set of dumbbells with additional weights (to increase the challenge, and therefore, your strength); ankle and wrist weights; an aerobic step (if a stairway is not readily available); a large towel for floor work, and a positive attitude are all you need. If the positive attitude is not yet readily available, the aerobic and weight resistance routines will help you develop one! The workout at home may be most convenient for you. You can roll out of bed into the sweats that are lying on the floor (readied the night before) for you to pop into, stick the piece of chewing gum (sugar-free) you left on the night table into your mouth, fill a glass with water, stumble into your workout area (the equipment mentioned stores in a space two feet by three feet), turn on some music ala Michael Jackson (or that show you taped last night) and begin your warmup.

Never perform strength training on the same area (lower body or upper body) two days in a row. Give that part of your body at least forty-eight hours to rest. It's just as good to work out the lower portion of your body (hips, thighs, legs) one day, and upper part of your body (shoulders, arms, chest, upper back) the next, as it is to use the weights and spend thirty to forty-five minutes on the whole body two times per week. The tummy can take a workout every day. How you divvy up the time and the body parts is totally up to you and your schedule. Whether you prefer sweats or a coordinated thong and cutoff top is strictly your own thing. How, when, and what equipment you use won't matter...just do it!

If you have not been working out, consult your physician before beginning. To get a really fine handle on how and what to do, a few sessions with a certified fitness consultant is a very wise investment. Whichever way you decide to start, *please start*. The additional one hundred and eighty minutes a week will reward you with an additional fifteen to twenty years! And they'll be more productive, vigorous years at that!

CHAPTER V

BECOME AWARE

Some of the information you find here may surprise you. How about this...eat *more*. Huh? Eat more times a day...not more food! Change the concept of three big meals a day to five or six small meals a day. Maybe even seven or eight mini-meals each day. This is certainly something you haven't considered before but the logic, and the research to back it up, is simple. Do you remember the reference earlier to the feelings of denial and deprivation that doomed every "sensible" diet ever recommended? If you've ever had the need to restrict yourself, because of weight or health, you know that awesome feeling of *can't* have. We are going to give that feeling a fond farewell.

Here's how it works. When you're skipping meals or eating when you're not only hungry but *very* hungry, you set yourself up to overeat. The nutritionists call the principle of eating small meals many times a day, rather than the traditional knockout meals, two or three times a day...grazing. Tests have been conducted on the consumption of up to seventeen meals a day, eating every hour. There's a major problem with that, especially if you work eight or nine of those hours. But consider the advantages of nibbling five or six mini-meals...total cholesterol levels dropped 7% when the men and women in a study in New Zealand nibbled the same nutritional intake as men who ate three squares. People in a Canadian study reduced the blood sugar levels and insulin levels when eating thirteen times a day as opposed to the control group eating three times a day and grazers tended to lose weight when compared to those eating the same amount of calories in two or three meals. These results were reported in the *American Journal of Clinical Nutrition* and point to the benefits of eating more frequently. The only problem, which may cause a reverse in the positive findings cited, would be the reference to "the same amount of calories." All that means is that if your consuming 1500 calories, and eat those calories in small increments throughout the day, you'll appreciate the benefits reported. If, on the other hand, you pop Milky Ways and jelly beans throughout the day, making up those five or six "meals," your calorie and fat intake will be high enough to defeat any benefits of grazing.

It's important to compare these studies with one conducted at the City University of New York. You've heard for years that food consumed after dark will cause weight gain since the calories consumed at night are not burned off. Yet the study groups, one including women who ate nothing after dark and one with those who ate the same calories, but who consumed a major percentage of them after dark, showed no difference in weight gain or loss regardless of the time of day the calories were ingested. The women left on their own, for whom the food was not predetermined, ate more high calorie and high fat foods and, of course, did gain weight. It's what you eat, not when, that matters.

Combining the findings of these two research projects, a pattern which makes the most sense is frequently eating low fat foods during the day and into the evening. It seems that if you eat properly many times, rather than just three times a day, your body likes it better. The most important factor is the total amount of calories and fat you consume. Our own study has shown that the primary advantage of grazing (eating five or six times a day), is the absence of hunger. The relentless gnawing of hunger pangs finally erupt in an overpowering urge to devour anything and everything in sight...and the devil with the consequences. The fact that there are some positive side affects, such as the lowering of cholesterol and weight, only makes the rationale for nibbling that much more attractive!

Here's one for all of you who skip breakfast. As you've heard for years, this is not extremely clever nutritional planning. In fact, it's a definite detriment to weight-loss. In 1992, the *American Journal of Clinical Nutrition* reported a study in which obese women who ate breakfast lost more weight than obese women who skipped breakfast, when the same amount of calories were consumed in a day. More verification of the value of eating less, more often. This indicates that a calorie isn't always just a calorie...it appears there is something to be said for timing, but it's not timing alone. Eating small meals, starting early in the day and continuing into evening, seems to help the body burn calories more efficiently.

The need for discriminatory grazing can't be emphasized enough. It's got to be satisfying and smart. I like to call it a nibble-nourish or an authorized nosh. By eating food at the onset of hunger pangs, you don't allow it to become a reason for overeating or eating something high in calories, high in fat, and high in guilts. Just think, if the combined nibbling has taken the edge off your hunger and curbed overeating at dinner you'll have loads of room for a delicious, well-thought-out, low fat dessert or nosh. You now know it won't add weight merely because it's consumed after dark.

Another plus to eating often, and staving off that famished feeling, is that you will no longer get to the point where you are so hungry that you wolf down your food, not allowing your brain the twenty minutes it takes to realize you're satisfied. You've already eaten more than you wanted, before you even know you've had enough to eat! Has that ever happened to you? You get up from the table and you know you've eaten more than you should have. That's one of those times you rub your tummy and mutter, I can't believe I ate the *whole thing!*

Later, in Chapter IX, you will find an extensive list of over fifty snacks or noshes. I call them the authorized nosh. You'll see exactly what I'm talking about when I say that it's easy and satisfying to eat this way.

Being aware of the amount of fat grams you consume in a day is not difficult although, at first glance, it may appear to be. We're going to make it simple. You know what you normally eat during the day. According to many studies, most people underestimate these numbers by at least half. But that won't adversely affect what we're about to do. The average American consumes about 65 to 85 grams of fat a day. That means, in fat grams alone, you're probably consuming 585 to 765 calories. Reduce that fat intake to just 20 grams and you've got only 180 calories in fat. You've just effectively reduced the caloric intake by about 400! If it's easy to reduce the fat grams ingested in a day to 20 (and I'll show you how) you will easily begin to shed pounds *without counting the calories!* If you don't want to lose weight, simply increase the complex carbohydrates in your diet to make up for the calories you're cutting in fat, and you'll end up with a healthier lifestyle without the weight loss.

Before we begin, let's address the extremely low (by FDA standards) amount of fat to which we're going to limit ourselves, daily: the number (20 grams) given to me in the gym in 1985. I've had no problem accepting and adhering to this fat gram count, nor have a vast number of people I know. Dr. Dean Ornish, famed as a proponent of preventing and reversing heart disease, and Nathan Pritikin, who started The Pritikin Center for Longevity, recommend 10% of calories in the day be fat calories. That's 15 to 20 fat grams a day for a normal adult consuming 1500 to 2000 calories a day. It only takes about 5 grams of fat a day to properly utilize the fat-soluble nutrients: vitamins K, E, D, A and beta-carotene.

Biochemist Colin Campbell, Cornell University, has conducted research comparing the incidence of heart disease, diabetes and various cancers in this country and diverse areas in China, where the diet varies. In certain locales where the diet is primarily vegetables and grains, the fat consumption hovers at 15%. The findings point to a much lower rate of the above diseases in these areas. The lower the concentration of meat and dairy in the diet, the lower the blood cholesterol levels and incidence of these diseases.

Why, then, does the government recommend 2000 calories, 30% of which should be fat calories? Perhaps because of pressure from the meat and dairy industries, since those two foods are among the greatest sources of fat in the American diet. Dr. Steven Swartz, a surgeon, and expert in geriatric nutrition and formerly with the United States Navy, says the 2000 calories recommended as the "average" diet is enough to sustain a marine in basic training! And you know the strenuous calorie-burning workout they get!

I've heard that an individual should determine the ideal weight, adjust the caloric intake to fuel that weight and consume 30% of those calories in fat. If you're a woman who wants to weigh 130 pounds you would consume 1600 calories a day, 54 grams of which would be fat calories (30%). My caloric intake is about 1600 to 1800 a day (maybe more on some days). My fat gram count is about 12 to 18, and I am maintaining my weight. And, no, I will not tell you my weight! I will tell you I wear a size 10, and that's all the info you'll get from me! At 54 grams a day, I'd no longer be a size 10.

Determining how many grams of fat a day you want to consume is paramount to making the decisions about how you are going to consume them. Start with 20 grams a day and then make any adjustment you feel best for you. Certainly, if heart health is involved, 20 grams of fat should do it for you. If that sounds tough, relax! The foods you will eat are going to continue to give you the warm fuzzies, without the binge/guilt/punish cycle so often suffered in the past. Trust me, and follow these simple methods for creating the new you.

What about calories? Some say you should count, some say you shouldn't! You will probably find that with this change in the fat gram intake (as pointed out earlier in this chapter), your caloric intake will drop dramatically, all by itself. Remember this is *not a diet*, this is not something you'll do for a while and then go back to "normal" eating. This *is* normal for you from now on. A slow, gradual weight loss is much healthier and will last. What's the sense of drastically cutting calories, if you gain back what you've lost because the drastic change is not long-term? Remember that drastic calorie-cutting will cause a slowdown in the metabolism of the "hunter-gatherer" body that we still sport. The metabolic system will think you're starving causing a slowdown to conserve your energy. At the same time, you can't go crazy with fat free, high calorie snack foods. That's just fooling yourself. Good sense is still important. This way of eating has worked for so many without calorie-counting. But the calories are there for you to measure, if you feel the need.

The major question is still, "How difficult is this going to be?" Now on to these simple methods for becoming a part of the low fat movement.

READ LABELS

There are very few products which are on the grocer's shelves without the mandated nutritional labeling. Although there may be a bit of "bending the rules" by the packagers, you'll find these labels are a great help in making your purchasing decisions. We'll talk about the tricks you'll see some of the food giants playing as we go along. And you'll find some of these yourself as you walk the aisles of your favorite supermarket. The important adjustment in your life is that until you become totally familiar with the products you'll be using all the time, you will become a label-reader of each product you consider buying. Some will end up back on the shelf after you see the grams of fat you would have consumed.

As you see, in the illustration we're using a can of Campbell's Condensed Soup (truly an American favorite) as an example. The nutritional labels usually follow this format, however, I have seen some, where the information is listed in paragraph form, and I always wonder what they're trying to hide, since it makes it so much harder to read and decipher. The diagram you see us using here is a copy of the nutritional label on Cream of Chicken soup. We'll concentrate on the numbers which are most important to us: A) the *serving size*; B) the *amount of servings* in the package; C) the *calories in each serving*; D) the *total fat per serving*; E) the *saturated fat in each serving*; F) the *amount of sodium in each serving*; and G) the *fiber content in each serving*.

| | A | B | | D | | | G | |

Nutrition Facts
Serv. Size 1/2 cup (120 ml.)
condensed soup
Servings About 2.5
Calories 30
  Fat Cal. 70
Percent Daily Values
(DV are based on a 2,000 calorie diet.

Amount / serving	%DV*	Amount / serving	%DV*
Total Fat 8g	12%	**Total Carb.** 11g	4%
Sat. Fat 3g	15%	Fiber 1g	4%
Cholest. 10mg	3%	Sugars 1g	
Sodium 890mg	37%	**Protein** 3g	
Vitamin A 10%	**Vitamin C 0%**	**Calcium 2%**	**Iron 2%**

Satisfaction guaranteed or money back. If you have any questions or comments, write Soup Cosumer Center, Campbell Soup Company, Campbell Place, Camden, NJ 08103-1703
Include information on can end.   1031-312-408

| C | | E | | F | | | |

The first detail to check is A) the *serving size*. How much of the can, after dilution, do you consume when you're eating Campbell's soup? Whenever I ask this question in workshops, the answer is almost always, *the whole can*. And those who don't eat the whole can, certainly eat at least half. But the accurate measure of a serving of soup is only 8 ounces, so there are *2 1/2 serv-*

ings in the can. When you're figuring out how many grams of fat you're consuming you'd better darn well know what the packager thinks a serving is, rather than what you think a serving is! When you consider that a coffee mug is usually 12 ounces, you're looking at only 2/3 of that for your serving of soup. In other words...where's the soup? If you make a habit of looking at the labels before you take the product home, you'll save yourself the aggravation of cooking it anyway, or taking the time to return it. For example: you're planning to make a vegetable stir-fry and you need 1/2 cup of the bottled stir-fry sauce you've been buying from the supermarket to properly flavor the dish. The serving size is a tablespoon which delivers 3 grams of fat. There are 8 tablespoons in 1/2 cup so you multiply the 3 grams by the 8 tablespoons you must use and your total is 24 grams of fat! Not the 3 grams that first caught your eye. The *serving size* is important!

B) Knowing the amount of servings in the container is a great help when you're planning on using the whole thing. This can of Cream of Chicken soup, while it has 8 grams of fat in each serving, will give you a hefty 20 grams if you eat all the soup in the can (8 times 2 1/2). That's a whole day's worth of fat and you haven't eaten the crackers yet!

C) The calories count when you're eating sweet snacks much more than when you're eating concoctions from the frozen food department. If the fat grams are high in a frozen or canned food, it's usually from creams, cheeses and oils and you won't buy these products once you look at the fat gram count. Campbell's Manhattan Clam Chowder has only 1/2 fat gram per serving (a total of 1 1/4 grams per can) and 60 calories per serving as opposed to 130 in the Cream of Chicken soup. That's how removing the fat removes a bunch of calories, too. When you buy fat free cookies...*beware!* The sugar is increased significantly and can cause the calorie count to skyrocket. One or two cookies is fine. If you eat the whole box, you'll wonder why the low fat lifestyle doesn't work!

D) The total fat grams *per serving*, not per package, matter a great deal. As you've noticed, we pay no attention to the line giving us fat calories. Divide that number by 9 and you end up with the gram count. If you were figuring out the percentage of fat calories, as compared to total calories of the serving, then your math would show you that this product is 54% fat in calories and doesn't even fit the Surgeon General's inflated estimation of how much fat you should consume. This is a no-no food. It just went back to the shelf.

E) Saturated fat, or Sat. Fat as shown here, is important to you if you're trying to lower your cholesterol count. Of course, if you eat as we're discussing in this book, you'll cut your sat. fat by eating much less flesh food and much more of the stuff that will help to lower that rate, anyway. Then "grazing" and working out will do the rest for you! Stay away from palm or coconut oils, both of which are saturated even though they are plant foods.

F) Sodium is a factor if you've been advised to reduce sodium intake by your physician. Although we don't make a fuss about sodium in this book, it will adversely affect the blood pressure of those individuals who show a sensitivity to it, making this listing very important for them. Consult your own doctor for the necessary guidelines for you. It appears, from preliminary testing, that a high sodium diet may have an effect on bone density. A conservative approach to sodium consumption may be wise.

G) Fiber is one of those components of our diet that most Americans ignore and shouldn't. The recommended fiber intake is 30 grams per day, rather than the 3 to 5 grams in the typical American diet. The incidence of colon cancer is greatly reduced with a high fiber diet. With a switch to a diet emphasizing fruits, veggies, grains, beans and peas, you will greatly enhance your fiber consumption. Use this line on the label to monitor the fiber content in packaged foods. Here again, the Manhattan Clam Chowder is a better bet than the Cream of Chicken soup because it doubles the fiber intake per serving. It's not as tasty or as good for you as Progresso's Black Bean soup which has 10 grams of fiber, 170 calories and 1 1/2 grams of fat per serving (8 1/2 ounces). When you're in the supermarket pick up the two cans of soup and make a side-by-side comparison, you'll notice the difference very quickly. See how easy label reading is?

The balance of the label is all about the percentage of daily values (DV) which really has no affect on us at all. Just think how helpful this number would be for those living the "fat calories as a percent of total calories" if this number related to each food. They could then keep track during the day, using the percentage of each product's fat calories, calculating in accordance with their own total daily calorie quota. Instead, these numbers are based on the 2000 calorie a day average we discussed before.

While we're talking about labeling I would be remiss not to mention the "percentage labeling" shouting 97% Fat Free or a like number that means absolutely nothing to any of us who are "fat gram" counters or the "percentage of fat in calorie" watchers. Why? Because the percentage of fat they're claiming refers to *weight*! And who cares how much a part of the product the fat weighs? 2% milk is 2% fat in weight as compared to the rest of the milk, not 2% calories in fat or 2 grams of fat. There are 4.7 fat grams in an 8 ounce glass of 2% milk, which is 37.2% of the total calories.

Learn to make the labels work for you. If you know you usually eat the whole box of SnackWell's Cheese crackers and there are 11 grams of fat in the box...take half out and put the rest away for another snack. That way you know you've got 5 1/2 grams of fat. Add it to your day. It's easier to figure that out than to carry around a scale to measure the ounces. The problem arises when you look at a label on a product that states it's "fat free." The government allows a claim of fat free on any product with a serving size lower than 1/2 gram. But what if you're eating more than a serving size? And there's a good chance you are. What then? We usually figure that the serving size just makes the cut and so it's probably about 1/3 gram. If you consume 3 "servings" you can assume 1 gram of fat. It's close enough for government work.

At that rate, if one measly cookie is fat free, you can give yourself credit for 5 grams of fat, if the box had 15 cookies and you ate the whole thing. That ought to get you thinking differently about those high calorie, fat free sweets!

Another point to check is the game of shrinking the serving size to come under the 1/2 gram rule. In 1992, Pam, the no-stick spray had a measure of 2 1/2 seconds' spray at less than 1 gram of fat. After the mandated labeling went into effect the label changed to 1/3 of a second spray...0 fat. Have you ever accomplished anything in a third of a second? It usually takes about 2 to 4 seconds to spray a baking pan. Figure a gram or 2 for this procedure. Divided by the entire recipe, that gram or so won't add up to much and is still a great way to prepare a surface to avoid sticking.

USE A FAT COUNTER BOOK

I can't say enough about the usefulness of a good fat-counter book. There are fresh products on the market that are not labeled, and there are recipes you'll convert from old favorites, for which these numbers will come in darned handy. These books also include fat grams in popular chain and fast-food restaurants. Take it with you the next time you go on a trip. You'll be amazed at how fast you'll remember the grams of fat in your favorite foods and how quickly you'll only have to check the book occasionally, for verification. My favorite is *The Complete & Up-To-Date Fat Book* by Karen J. Bellerson, Avery Publishing Group. For at-home use I've found *The NutriBase Nutrition Facts Desk Reference* by Dr. Art Ulene, also by Avery, extremely helpful. Bellerson's book has 15,000 foods...Ulene's has over 40,000 listings. It's a bit difficult to carry Ulene's book into a Wendy's with you!

EAT MORE FRUITS, VEGETABLES, GRAINS, BEANS AND PEAS

There's not enough that can be said about increasing the amount and variety of veggies, fruits, beans and grains you eat. They are so healthy for you. And the more you eat of these foods the less you'll eat of the others. For years the answer to diet was to go easy on the potatoes, corn, beans and rice. Now it's evident that a truly well-rounded regimen, including the beans and grains, will provide you with all the protein you need for healthy living.

Vegetarianism, once frowned upon by nutritionists, is enjoying great and growing popularity, fueled by the likes of Dean Ornish. The FDA has, at last, agreed that a vegetarian diet is a healthy diet. Beans, peas, grains and a variety of green vegetables will supply the necessary protein as well as some of the flesh foods that so many people feel are a must. If you are reluctant to switch to a strict vegetarian diet, think about utilizing some of the leaner flesh foods, such as poultry (turkey and chicken) and seafood. Using these foods as a condiment, rather than as the entrée with a smattering of veggies as a side dish, will avail you a better fiber intake and you'll still realize the flavor of the meats. The fiber factor, the major component of most of the food you'll be adding to your diet, is responsible for helping to regulate the bowels, eliminating the need for laxatives, as well as fighting colon cancer. As it passes through the intestines the fiber picks up, and carries out with it, some of the fat you may have consumed, but not yet digested...an extra benefit.

Think of this not as an adjustment in *your* habits, alone...whether it's for health or weight loss, take the family with you. Take a little more time in the supermarket now and you'll see the changes accumulate, from your higher energy level to your family's improved health, as you get further along in the low fat lifestyle.

CHAPTER VI

THE WAY THINGS USED TO BE

One day, years from now, you'll try to remember what it was like before you started eating this way and you'll have to squint and do a number with your hand to your forehead. Nah...you never ate 120 grams of fat for *breakfast*! Of course that was only when you ate out on a Sunday, never during the week, when you skipped breakfast all together!

No more of that, right? We're "grazing!"

What exactly does that mean in terms of breakfast? Most people don't have time to prepare a sit-down, cooked breakfast. Breakfast is either some dry cereal with milk (skim, of course) and a dash out the door, or just the dash out the door with the wide-bottomed coffee mug, to sip from, in the car. It's easy enough to cut up an apple (mere traces) and nibble on it while applying your makeup or shaving. Maybe it's just a banana (1 gram) you grab with that bagel (1 to 2 grams depending on size) you threw into the toaster before you jump into your hose or socks. You like a shmear of cream cheese? Give the Philly Free a go. You won't miss the original after you've used it for a week or so. Try to get some of the fiber and nutrients from fruit first thing in the morning. It may be your only opportunity. If you do have some time for a bit of cereal, choose one of the high fiber, low fat, low sugar cereals to avoid a raging high and a free fall in an hour or two. Use one of the great butter substitutes on your bread. They may be as low as 0 for I Can't Believe It's Not Butter Spray and Fleischmann's Fat Free Low Calorie squeeze margarine to Weight Watchers Buttery Spray (1 gram for a 3 second spray). Watch out for the low fat spreads. Some of them are higher than you might think at a first glance because the measure is 1 teaspoon instead of 1 tablespoon. That increases your fat intake three-fold. Check the fat grams of the sliced bread. An English muffin (1 gram), with a touch of preserves that will not add any fat, is a great change of pace. If you're cooking your breakfast cereal, try oatmeal which is high in fiber (about 2 grams of fat in 2/3 of a cup), Farina, Cream of Wheat or Cream of Rice (fat free).

As you exit the kitchen, grab the package you left in the freezer for your nibbles today. You can use the microwave at work to reheat them when you're ready for a snack. If you're going to be making calls outside and will be running about in the car today, take that Marvelous Carrot Muffin, some raisins, the Health Valley Fat Free Granola Bar or some carrot and celery sticks in a bag...maybe all of them!

While you were limiting yourself to about a gram or two for breakfast, your next-door neighbor had a 3-egg omelet with cheese, 3 sausages, home fries, a croissant with real butter and cream in his coffee. He's packed away about 125 grams of fat! You'll be cooking on all burners with slow carbohydrate-sustained energy, while he's still working on digesting his breakfast, three hours later.

What about a Sunday morning special when you have plenty of time to sit back, relax and eat breakfast over the funny papers? How about the Mexican Omelet with Mission fat free flour tortillas and Jim's Beans and Red Rice. Total fat in the whole breakfast is 3 grams.

Getting back to the work week is important because when you're at home, nibbling is easier than at the job. Of course, there is nibbling smart and then there's the kind of all-day snacking that turns to fat. It gets back, again, to grazing on the right foods, not junk. The right foods just have to be foods you enjoy and want to eat...not some goofy combination of foods you "gotta" eat. I remember when everyone thought alfalfa sprouts were healthy and you just *had* to eat them. I couldn't eat them then, and I won't eat them now. Same thing goes for cottage cheese. I used to eat the stuff because it was on the "required" diet. Forget it! Now I eat only what I want and enjoy.

So, it's about three hours after breakfast and it's time for a nosh. This can be anything from an English muffin pizza made with fat free cheese (yes, there are some out there that taste good!) and a bit of leftover marinara sauce, to a turkey-breast-salad half-pita pocket and a pickle. The trick is to have a plan. Microwaved popcorn is a favorite in the office and when that aroma permeates the air, it's brilliant to have your own micro-air-popper in which you can pop your own, fat free. Then hit it with some I Can't Believe It's Not Butter Spray and a touch of salt, garlic or seasoned pepper. You end up with less fat than the 3 available in packaged "lite" microwave popcorn. It doesn't take long (six weeks, is it?) for you to prefer the popcorn you make, to that old buttery stuff the movies scoop up.

Lunchtime is upon you in no time and it's a no-brainer. Dee's acquired the habit of cooking a low or no fat dinner in quantities that are much greater than the family can consume. She started taking what was left over to the office and sharing it with her associates so that they could see how good this low fat life can be. They ate her fantastic food for a couple of weeks and then began to feel a bit guilty about only being on the receiving end. Her associates were moved to repay her kindness and now they all enjoy a round-robin. Each day is someone else's turn to supply the low fat lunch. The lunches have varied from Shrimp Creole to Greek Lentil Soup. They're saving a bunch of money while sharing the camaraderie and therapy of eating together, low fat.

There are so many ways to make this low fat lifestyle work for you.

There's no question that almost any form of restriction can be accepted when you're in total control. If you're brown-bagging it, or sharing lunch with friends that have the same convictions, it's a darn sight easier than joyfully following your own rules while surrounded by those whose program is totally different.

You've got a business lunch scheduled. This is a challenge. It's in a fine restaurant that you've known and loved. This is not one of those situations that will return you to the peanut butter jar afterwards feeling you've blown it. I promise.

Remember that you are in control! There are three ways to handle this. One way is to request the waiter recommend any of the low fat dishes the chef might prepare for you, explaining that you prefer to eat low fat whenever possible. Another way, to simplify matters, is to look for dishes on the menu that you know are prepared with less fat than others: go for the red, not the white. Order the sauce that has a tomato base, rather than a cream base...a marinara sauce, instead of the Fettucini Alfredo. Request that the pasta be served without tossing it first in olive oil. This is a common practice in restaurants to avoid the pasta sticking together.

Ask for more of the vegetables and maybe skip the roast. Ask for the salad dressing on the side, and when you're eating the salad, dip your fork in the dressing and then take a mouthful of greens, instead of spooning the dressing all over the salad (you end up with about 2 grams of fat, whereas the spooning method can deliver up to 15!). The third way to get what you want is to choose the dish and ask that it be prepared without any added oils or butters. A perfect example of this is to request that a bunch of the vegetables be poached in broth rather than seared in butter or ask that the seafood be broiled without the butter-based sauce and use lemon, pepper and perhaps some grated Parmesan cheese to dress it up. The flavor of grated Parmesan on seafood is delightful and the cheese has 1 1/2 grams of fat per tablespoon. Use a teaspoon and you've got only 1/2 gram of fat on top of the fat in the fish. If you go with grouper (1 1/2 grams, 4 ounces), perch or redfish (2 1/2 grams, 4 ounces), sole (2 grams, 4 ounces), flounder (1 1/2 grams, 4 ounces), shrimp (less than 1 1/2 grams, 4 ounces), scallops (1 gram, 4 ounces). Order these fried or stuffed and you're buying 14 to 18 grams for the same 4 ounces. How much does 4 ounces look like? About the size of a deck of cards!

Of course, restaurants don't serve portions that look like what the nutritionists say we *should* be eating! You'd complain heartily. In fact, portion sizes are getting larger and larger. Well, shucks, what's a striving fat-counter to do? My answer when I eat out, which is just about every lunch and two or three dinners a week, is so simple. My mother insisted that I be a charter member of the clean-plate club. There are children starving somewhere in the world. When I was growing up it was Europe. There is still a continent or country where kids are starving, I guarantee, and my mother would find it. It never dawned on me that finishing the food on *my* plate would not help these kids! The same sentiment of "waste not, want not" is ingrained in my "born of depression survivors" upbringing. My simple solution to the "eating out" problem works beautifully with my background. *I eat half…I take the rest home in an "eat-later" container!* I know I will eat no more than half…sometimes less. It works for me. It will probably work for you.

If you are in the driver's seat and can determine the restaurant, there are a few national chains that make ordering a snap. Ruby

Tuesday's is great for a salad at their salad bar with one or two of their fat free dressings. Try some of the fat free ranch and then top it with the fat free honey mustard. A really tasty combo. Skip the mayonnaise-based potato salad and cole slaw. You're looking at about 9 to 15 grams of fat per 1/2 cup, depending on the recipe. TGIF is a good choice, too, offering their low fat menu. Read carefully, you may want to make some adjustments and lower the grams per serving even more by ordering steamed veggies with the sauce on the side instead of stir-fry. Ask for any sauces or dressings on the side, so that you remain in control of what you eat. The Olive Garden is doable if you order the salad with the dressing on the side and stick with the red sauce on pasta that has not been tossed with olive oil.

At some of these places you really have to push that. The mine-strone is a better bet than the pasta e fagiole which has meat and the attendant fat. The wait-person will be happy to serve you the breadsticks sans the buttery garlic topping. Restaurants like Fresh Choice are popping up here and there and make it really easy for the likes of us. Ryan's is a place where you can enjoy a great meal, if you stick to the salad and the baked potato, without butter, and use salsa and some of their veggies or beans to flavor it up. The only problem with Ryan's is you'll need lots of will power to stay away from their home-baked chocolate chip cookies. Have the fat free frozen yogurt, instead. You'll feel so proud of yourself when you walk out of there, knowing how brave you were! Bennigan's has been a disappointment. The so-called low fat menu offers a low fat lasagna at 17 grams of fat! C'mon Bennigan's, you can do better than that!

Since you ate a very light lunch (we're "grazing," remember?), about two to three hours later, it's time to have a nosh. Now a fat free slice of bread with a banana mashed on it, sprinkled with raisins, might satisfy your sweet tooth. And if the sweet tooth is raging, how about a Sweet Rewards Double Fudge Supreme Snack Bar? If you can't leave your desk, or you're running around in your car, those pretzels will come in mighty handy. I always carry a plastic container of bottled water with me in the car. It's healthy to drink lots of water and it certainly helps when the pretzels make me thirsty. The boy scouts said it best, "Be prepared!"

Sometimes the other half of this morning's bagel is a neat fill-in. You've got the idea. When you start preparing dinner you won't be famished and ready to raid the refrigerator or eat half the dinner while you're standing at the stove. Have you ever done that? For some reason it's natural (oh, yes, I've done it, too) to think that what you eat standing, before it's on a plate at the table, simply doesn't count! It does!

It's dinner time, or supper time, that meal that *was* the largest repast of the day. It's not that tough to reduce the size of dinner if you're not terribly hungry because you had a snack just three hours ago. If this is a one-dish dinner it may be extremely low in fat and calories. There are a whole bunch of recipes that are easy (thirty minutes or less) to prepare, and taste heavenly, later on in the book. Many times, when you walk in the door, if the traffic was bad or the last-minute glitch at the office held you up, there may not only be little time to make dinner but little motivation, as well. Take out a container of Vegetarian Chili, or a Restuffed Baked Potato, or the leftover Broccoli Rice Casserole, stick it in the microwave, and let your own frozen dinner defrost and cook, while you're getting into something more comfortable.

Oh, you're going out to dinner! Throw off that office getup, slip into a hot, perfumed bath, and relax. When you get to the restaurant you've got it made. Any of the tricks we talked about at lunch will do nicely here. If you feel you want variety, order a couple of appetizers. Or if there's only one that fits the bill...share it and take the other half of your entrée home for nibbling another time. Don't trick yourself with the Caesar Salad. There hasn't been one devised yet that's not high in fat. If you cannot resist, have a small amount, not the salad as the entrée. You're only kidding yourself, and you'll still know! Treat dessert as the treat it is and if you *must* have some of that Chocolate Decadence, share it. We're not even going to talk about the damage in grams. It's not important. It's certainly more than you want to eat as a regular routine...so enjoy. Tomorrow is another day to resume the same manner of eating as today. No guilts about overdoing, no binges because you've blown it "anyway"...and no fasting to make up for it.

Chinese or Asian food is always fun and easy to eat low fat. Whatever you order, request it be prepared with little or no fat. After the razzing Chinese restaurants got from the CSPI (*Center for Science in the Public Interest*) for the high fat content of most foods on their menu, the restaurants are now happy to prepare for folks like us. One eggroll has 11 grams of fat. 4 cups of House Fried Rice deliver 50 grams, and Sweet and Sour Pork has 71! But it's not any more difficult to get what you want in an Asian restaurant than anywhere else if you do it smart.

Keep in mind that more meat is used in these Americanized versions than in the country of origin. Think veggies! They are prepared so crispy and fresh. Order your vegetables steamed, with the sauce on the side. Then you place the rice on your plate and dip the veggies one by one, as you eat. If they won't do that for you, order extra rice. Make a small pile of rice on the side of your plate. Take the vegetables individually before you put them in your mouth, and tap the excess sauce on the little bit of rice you've set aside. This way you're eliminating most of the sauce and you're not losing the flavor because the vegetables have already been flavored from cooking in it. If you eat only about half the dish with all the rice, you'll be more than satisfied and you'll have another meal to take home with you. Stay away from those fried, cashew, or peanut mixed dishes. The fat skyrockets and there are so many wonderful tastes you can enjoy without it.

Don't be hesitant to make requests or to demand what you wish. You're in control. You're paying for the service. There are restaurants we haven't returned to because they chose to ignore my request. I have found it easier to visit another restaurant, instead. One of the finest eateries in D.C. is the Coeur de Lion at the Henley Park Hotel. Ralph Fredericks is the Maitre D' and is one of us. One evening, while I was ordering, he picked up on my request for a low fat, chef's "brainstorm." The restaurant is without question a favorite of ours, perhaps because I've been served a platter of wild, meaty mushrooms, asparagus and sweet potato pâté, with the same flourish reserved for Chateaubriand. Some of the finest, most interesting dinners have been presented to me, in the name of *low fat*, in that lovely place. And, served with panache. After all, even though we eat low fat, we deserve to be treated like we count, too!

Find your favorite places like The Coeur de Lion and restaurant managers like Ralph, who make eating our kind of food *a celebration*. Thank you, Ralph! And thanks, too, to the genius in the kitchen.

If you're in an American style restaurant, you're one of many in a group, and your friends badger you to "go on, order something good, just this once!" just remember that they mean well...and then ignore them. If you're enjoying the lifestyle and you're loving the food, what's "good" to them may no longer taste good to you. This has already happened to lots of folks I know. They really thought they'd love that hamburger and decided to splurge, just this time. What a surprise when they ended up trying to find a genteel way of disposing of the second mouthful!

You can order a baked potato, hold the butter (11 grams of fat per tablespoon), with a tablespoon of sour cream (2 1/2 grams) and some salsa. The salsa is, usually, totally fat free and brightens up the flavor of the potato which is virtually fat free, too. A pound of potatoes has less than 1/2 gram of fat! In the year 1995 more salsa was sold in this country than ketchup. This stuff is getting very popular.

If it's a barbecue joint, they always have a baked potato for you to order and there it's great with the barbecued or baked beans as a topping.

My dear friend, Kathy, joins me at a few restaurants where, when we start to order, they say, "and NO OIL," before we have the opportunity. It certainly keeps us going back for more. And there's something to be said for training the service people in places you frequent. It helps to keep you on your best behavior. The neat part about eating this way all the time is that you'll begin to dislike the mouthfeel of fat. The first time you're served a dish with too much oil or butter, and you feel as though you'd just melted a tablespoon of Crisco on your tongue, you'll know you've arrived. You'll never have to worry about returning to that old fat-crammed life again! With the popularity of our lifestyle, it's getting easier and easier to get a bit of personal fat conservation wherever you go.

If you're going to a party, the same rules apply. Life is always satisfying and fun. Don't punish yourself. Have a nibble before you go, so you take the edge off your hunger. Choose red, not white, when you peek into the chafing dishes and as the hors d'oeuvre tray passes under your nose. Stick to the boiled shrimp rather than the fried. Stay away from the cheese. 1 1/2 ounces of cheese is about the size of three dominoes, and has 12 grams of fat and 150 calories. It adds up fast!

By now, you may have noticed I'm not big on flesh foods. Perhaps the reason is the sunny, exciting, and robust flavors that I find in vegetables. Maybe it's the chew – sometimes crispy and crunchy, sometimes a fluffy mouthful of goodness. Then, again, it may be the high fat gram count in most meats that takes away the fun from eating them. Lean flank steak (that deck of cards, remember?), braised, has 15 grams for 4 ounces; 4 ounces ground beef, extra lean, 19 grams; 8 ounces corned beef hash, 25 grams; one 4 ounce pork loin chop (fat trimmed), 17 grams. Compare that with skinless turkey breast meat, 4 ounces, 1 gram; skinless chicken breast meat, 4 ounces, 4 grams; canned tuna packed in water has 1 gram in each 2 ounces; 4 large shrimp, 1 gram. Doesn't that set up a case for eating turkey, chicken and certain seafood?

Watch out for packaged ground turkey and prepared turkey, like sausage and franks. There is skin and fat in the mix and it's a good idea to read the fat grams per ounce. Salmon and mackerel are higher in fat than some of the other seafoods I've mentioned. Use your fat gram counter book.

If you're one who loves to entertain, you need not fret. This way of life lends itself so well to entertaining that your guests will never know how much healthier they'll be, after one of your festivities, as opposed to one of their own! A marvelous seven-course dinner may be served with less than 12 grams of fat per person. Our Thanksgiving dinner, with the turkey, mashed potatoes, candied sweets, broccoli casserole, string beans with mushrooms, rolls, fruit salad and the pumpkin pie, totaled less than 6 grams per person...and no one knew but the cooks!

To give you an idea of how effortless this is, follow me. Start out with some hors d'oeuvres. The Artichoke Spread, Black Bean Dip, and Janice Marshall's Spinach Balls will present a tasty array of nibbles before dinner with a wine spritzer. The appetizer could be the Boiled Shrimp with the Red Cocktail Sauce or Remoulade Sauce. Follow this with Onion Tomato Soup and toast points sprayed with I Can't Believe It's Not Butter Spray and a sprinkle of garlic powder and some fat free grated Parmesan, then baked until bubbly. Then serve a light salad, primarily romaine lettuce, a touch of radiccio and watercress, topped with a vinaigrette of balsamic vinegar, a touch of olive oil (1 teaspoon), honey, mustard and garlic.

A fruity sorbet would be perfect right now to clear the palate and to give the guests a breather between courses. It's a good time for the chef to take a moment to add the finishing touches to the main course.

The entrée is Turkey Tetrazzini or Chicken Cacciatore and the ingredients, which had been prepared earlier, were combined and have been simmering for the last 6 to 8 minutes during the sorbet break. Fresh asparagus has been set in a microwave dish, ready to steam to crispy perfection. The asparagus is sprayed with buttery spray and the turkey casserole, or chicken and sauce, is heated through. They are ready to serve.

Fat free dinner rolls or fat free sourdough bread is served with the entrée. The guests are overwhelmed and you are aglow. But what about dessert?

This can be an elegant array of berries, perhaps some pineapple and orange slices with deep purple grapes. How about a layer of fat free chocolate cake covered with Healthy Choice Cappuccino Chocolate Chunk Ice Cream with a drizzle of fat free chocolate sauce? Fresh ground coffee is served with the dessert. That ought to do it!

There are only 4 grams of fat in all of the hors d'oeuvres, combined. You can therefore assume traces of fat for each individual. The shrimp cocktail would add about 1 gram of fat per person. Soup, salad, sorbet and bread points add mere traces.

The entrée has no more than 4 grams of fat per person with less than 1 additional gram each for the buttery spray. The dessert has about 2 grams of fat per person. The dinner delivers a skinny total of 8 grams of fat per person. Prepared without thought to the fat grams, the total would be closer to 30 or more per person. And they never knew! They thought they were eating *normal* food!

That's good eating! The wonder of this method of preparing foods is that you can go ethnic with Mexican, Italian, or Asian. A palate-pleasing Mexican buffet can start with a warm Artichoke Spread and a bowl of Black Bean Dip with baked corn chips. The Chili Con Queso is a must, while everyone is sitting around the margarita pitcher. A bright salad with chopped green, red and yellow bell pepper, followed by Mission flour tortillas (fat free) and Red Rice with Vegetarian Chili or David's Famous Chili. Dessert is an assortment of fresh berries, nestled in fresh pineapple triangles.

The Italian dinner begins with an Antipasto, of course, followed by Aunt Rose's Minestrone or Pasta E Fagiole. Then, the entrée, a magnificent Simple Spinach Lasagna with Lentils, sourdough bread and breadsticks.

You can convert old-time favorites and traditional foods as well, without a lot of fanfare, except the applause you'll receive from your guests. Join us as we convert your kitchen and your life into low fat.

CHAPTER VII

GET READY
GET SET

Before you begin this adventure into low fat living, take a
long look at your pantry. Chuck any of the high fat canned
goods and boxed edibles, that are no longer part of your
life, into a big paper bag or plastic bag and run them over
to the nearest food bank, where these items will be appreciated.
They certainly are no longer appreciated in your home. Check your
cooking utensils. There may be a few things you'll want to be sure
to have on hand to make cooking low fat easier.

A set of pots with a non-stick surface is ever so important.
Without these, performing oil-free cooking is a nightmare, and
we're doing this the simple, easy way. The investment is worth it.
Just think of the clean-up time you'll save. A very large soup pot,
(8 or 10 quarts) is a must, because you'll be preparing foods in
large amounts for freezing to defrost on too-tired-to-cook nights
and for making your own frozen dinner entrées. A crock pot is a
lifesaver in the busy cook's kitchen. You cut up the ingredients,
throw them in the pot (no oil), go off to work and let the pot do
all the cooking for you. You may be able to live without it, but
once you get started cooking with one, you'll love it.

You'll want to have a muffin tin (I like to bake the jumbo muffins) with a non-stick surface, to be sure you're eating muffins that really are fat free. Wooden spoons and a plastic spatula avoid marring the non-stick finishes. Be sure to have a colander for rinsing the pasta, and a salad spinner for getting the water off the greens, so your salads won't be soggy!

Pyrex makes some wonderful glass dishes for freezing which can go right into the microwave. I prefer the rectangular ones so they can be stacked, with little loss of space in the freezer. Have gallon-sized and quart-sized freezer bags on hand for storage in the fridge and the freezer.

The benefits of using extremely good knives that are kept honed to a very sharp edge are multi-faceted. A sharp knife is easier to use. It speeds up the cutting and chopping, and there'll be quite a bit of that since your meals will be a reflection of a cuisine depending on a greater variety of vegetables. In addition, it is safer to use a knife that cuts clean and on the mark, the first time. More cooks hurt themselves in the kitchen with dull and worn utensils than with tools that are kept in top-notch condition.

A wood or plastic cutting board is essential. We have both. We use the wood for vegetable and fruit cutting and the plastic one, which can go in the dishwasher, for the poultry and fish. Both get scrubbed with a stiff brush after each use. The stiff brush gets into the scratches and gouges of the boards and introduces detergent to the bacteria which can then be rinsed away. Always be extremely careful with any juices from poultry or fish. If a sponge is used to wipe the counter clean, place it in the dishwasher in the silverware holder and give it a spin through a wash cycle. Keep your workplace protected from the strains of bacteria carried by flesh foods that can make you very sick and might even kill you.

A very sharp, firm-handled vegetable peeler is necessary for peeling the hard, fibrous skin on the stalks of the asparagus, celery and broccoli, as much as for peeling potatoes, carrots and cucumbers.

A mandolin (utensil for slicing, grating and chopping vegetables and cheeses) comes in very handy, as does a Salad Shooter. The Salad Shooter is a luxury...the mandolin is more of a necessity. A potato masher or ricer will serve you well for, of course, mashing potatoes, and mashing other veggies like beans. A blender does an excellent job whipping different liquids and purées for soups and sauces. It also does wonders with a compliment of fruits and a dollop of non-fat yogurt for a delicious shake! While a food processor (Cuisinart type) will do all things for all dishes, ours broke down about three years ago and we've not found the one we're sure we want to replace it. Interestingly, we've made do with the mandolin, the potato masher, the Salad Shooter and the blender. One day, we'll decide which of the food processors we want and use one appliance to do it all.

A pair of tongs for pulling rolls out of the oven, turning foods you're grilling, and dishing out slaw or pasta will be in daily use. As will, of course, the measuring cups (at least a 2-cup, a 4-cup and an 8-cup), and a set of measuring spoons. You'll want at least one set of graduated mixing bowls. Pyrex is good because they can go from the fridge into the microwave or the oven.

Try to find some bowls, for your soups and stews, that can be used in the microwave and won't be adversely affected by the dishwasher, for defrosting and reheating some of the wonderful one-dish dinners you'll be freezing or refrigerating. A great disappointment recently was the purchase of some nifty plastic bowls, in the colors we wanted, which were produced by Rubbermaid. Always a reliable brand, we noticed the label assurance that this was a dishwasher-safe bowl. Upon reheating some soup shortly after the purchase, the finish on the bowl charred and melted. We made the foolish assumption that a product obviously made for the kitchen in the '90's would be microwave-safe. Shame on us. They're in the back of the shelf, now, and are used only occasionally when we've prepared food stove-top.

You'll find certain recipes in this book that will really turn you on. Others may not appeal to you when you look at the ingredients, and I'll wager you'll never even give those a try. That's what makes for horse-racing, and I promise you that my feelings will not be hurt. It therefore makes sense that there are some seasonings or spices you'll never ever use, while some will be on the front of the shelf, where you won't have to reach over other bottles to get to them. A perfect example of this is my garlic powder. David always uses fresh, minced garlic when he cooks. He does the big cooking...chowders, soups, chilies and stews. I mess around more with the hors d'oeuvres and quick-fix meals that can be thrown together at a moment's notice. If someone unexpectedly walks in the door, and I can't convince them that dinner out would be the way to go, I'm the one who gets to check the fridge for odds and ends, and a one-two, in the wok for you! That's when my garlic powder comes in handy and you can always tell who's done the cooking last, depending on where in the cabinet that powder is stashed...front or back.

When I talk about staples there are certain products we all use in this lifestyle, to impart flavor and give us the mouthfeel we appreciate from the old days. I promised you your tastes would change but there are certain triggers we need pulled, regardless of how much we change, and we intend to pull them to keep us happy. When I talk about staples, I'm referring to products you may have seen in the marketplace and some products you've always used in your kitchen.

Of course, you need onions and garlic. Every good cook's kitchen must have fresh onions and garlic. Years ago our buddy, Jim Mann, was shopping with me for a dinner we were going to prepare, when he gave me this gem of information about picking onions at the supermarket. He grew up in Arkansas (you'll see a recipe or two of his, later on) and knows a bunch about growing things. He told me to try, always, to find the flat onions. They're sweeter. It was about 1979 when he told me that, and I'm still picking the flat ones. They should also be firm, with no soft spots, and the skin must be dry. There are different kinds of onions which we'll talk about in the recipe section, but here, we're talking about the basic yellow onion.

Garlic heads consist of several cloves joined at the ends and held together with a thin outer skin. Look for a firm, compact head with no sprouts. If stored in a cool, dry, airy place it can last a relatively long time, up to six months, but hopefully you'll be using it up faster than that.

Don't ever store onions or garlic in a plastic bag because they get mushy and rot. Onions that have been kept in the refrigerator are easier on the tears, as you chop. You can chop up a bunch of onion, or slice it for future recipes, and freeze it in a freezer bag for up to three months. Garlic, already minced, is available in the stores and is just as good as fresh. You must refrigerate it after opening. Polinar and Spice World sell minced garlic, in jars, without the addition of oil. Again, check labels.

I like to use garlic powder when sprinkling spinach leaves or bok choy as these vegetables are wilting in defatted stock. You'll see other examples of garlic powder and fresh garlic's use in the recipe section.

Garlic adds a pungent, sweet flavor and, when cooked, lends a hearty aroma to the dish, along with the zesty taste. Health nuts are known to eat garlic raw for its disease preventative powers and cholesterol-lowering properties. Some believe it prevents the common cold. It appears to help reduce the incidence of stomach cancer and may be associated with the reduction of the risk of colon cancer. The verdict on the veracity of these claims is still out, but enjoy the bulb for what it does for a hunk of French bread!

There are a number of vinegars that add delightful flavors to salads, but when talking about basics, regular white vinegar, red wine and white wine vinegars, balsamic vinegar and rice wine vinegar should all have a place on your shelf. You'll end up using them all, at one time or another. Honey is another product that comes in handy, as will some preserves like marmalade. They can be used from time to time to sweeten a dish that needs a richer flavor than you get from sugar, alone. Applesauce is important if you're going to bake any goodies that call for oil. It's a great substitute, measure for measure.

Chicken bouillon, preferably granular (the cubes are harder to use), and vegetable bouillon, are in use all the time. Sautéing is done with the bouillon or defatted chicken stock. We use wine for sautéing, either white or red, but some of the folks don't like to use any alcoholic beverage and the bouillon or stock works very well, too. If you do use wine, the alcohol content of the liquid burns off so you need not fear serving a dish in which wine or liquor was cooked.

Without question, the salvation of the low fat kitchen is the herbs and spices that give the foods you prepare the magic that it takes to make your guests or family ask for seconds. If you have some spices or herbs in your pantry that have been there for six months or more, do yourself a favor. Toss them. The full impact of the spice is gone. When you consider the low cost of these products, and the importance of their use to bring up the flavor of a dish you've worked so hard to put together, you want it to be full strength. Not a whisper of what it once was.

The supermarket is loaded with different manufacturers' spices and they will manage to do the job for you. Prices run fairly close for one product line or another. However, when you get to the point where you know you're consistently using certain condiments and you're using a sufficient quantity to make it beneficial to "go gourmet"...do yourself a favor. Get in touch with one of the spice mail order houses and get the stuff freshly ground. You won't believe the difference in the quality. And every six months, restock!

Making the adjustment to this lifestyle is so much easier with the wise use of the wonderful condiments from all over the world. The other day, David and I had opened our delivery from Penzeys, Ltd. They bill themselves as "merchants of quality spices." As we pulled the plastic bags of goodies out of the box, our dining room was permeated with the scents of these aromatic herbs and spices. This shipment was the Italian herb mix, dried basil, thyme, tarragon and curry powder. It's very possible that the true warmth and comfort of a household is the scent of the spices used. No question about it: the best room freshener I have ever been exposed to must be those heavenly perfumes surrounding us the other day.

Bill Penzey's catalog includes some recipes right along with the spice listings and some interesting information on each spice or herb, as well. He's even included some gift packages. Their address is P.O. Box 1448, Waukesha WI 53187; or telephone 414-574-0277; fax 414-574-0278. See what I'm talking about. Tell him Tree sent you!

As you build a repertoire of your own favorite dishes, you'll find the herbs and spices you will come to depend upon. Start your own spice rack. We would be lost without the Italian mix, dried thyme and oregano, dill, and whole peppercorns. Gracious! Once I start listing them, I realize how many we use. Rather than bore you with a list, check out the recipes and you'll see for yourself.

Another taste-lifter is cayenne pepper liquified in vinegar, known in the bottle as Louisiana Hot Sauce. Just a splash or two of the right hot sauce can move the flavor from boring to oooooeeeee, good eatin'. We like Crystal Louisiana Hot Sauce. Tabasco is the granddaddy of them all and imparts its very own flavor that you're either going to love or find distasteful. You might like to try a number of different hot sauces and chilies if you like it hot, since each is different.

There are a few other products that fill out your pantry on the ingredients shelf. Cornstarch is a very important helper in the low fat kitchen. A few tablespoons dissolved in cold water and added to the pot thickens and clears the sauce, imparting a shine that is reminiscent of that stuff we used to use: oil. It's a necessary ingredient in Chinese food and important in stews and gravies.

Right next to the cornstarch we find the Molly McButter and Butter Buds. Molly, sprinkled on a baked potato or on steamed veggies, is great and adds a salty taste, too. If you're reducing salt in your diet, stick with the Butter Buds or refrigerated butter substitutes. Butter Buds adds a good butter flavor to a recipe and it works very well in baking, too. Try a few of these different products and come up with your own preferences.

To round out the pantry you'll need a spray-on low fat oil for sear-ing and to render pans non-stick for baking. The old standby Pam, has been joined by Mazola, Weight Watchers and Wesson. Any of these is fine and then, for specialty purposes there are Olive Oil Pam, which we like to use on occasion for an extra olive oil flavor, Weight Watchers Buttery Spray for popcorn, along with some other flavored spray-on oils that are suddenly appearing in the stores. The Buttery Spray now has some competition from I Can't Believe It's Not Butter Spray. We've stocked both and use them intermittently. The advantage of using the Weight Watchers is it takes up pantry space, not refrigerator space. With all the fresh fruits and vegetables in the fridge, the shelf space is very dear, indeed.

Speaking of refrigerator space...let's take a look in there! Since we were talking about butter substitutes, how about one that I mentioned earlier in the book: Fleischmann's Fat Free Low Calorie squeeze bottle margarine that does well on a toasted bagel or in the oven. The flavor's comparable to butter and most of the tasters I've surveyed think that Fleischmann's and I Can't Believe It's Not Butter Spray are neck and neck. Fleischmann's also has a squeeze cheese (Fleischmann's Fat Free Cheddar) that does the job for kids with a cracker and a hankering for something to chew on, without the saturated fat of real cheese. The ingredients include hydrogenated vegetable oil, which does have trans fatty acids, but that's after the water, skim milk and salt, making them both a darn sight better than stick margarine or even tub margarine. There are certainly a variety of good-tasting substitutes to choose from to take the place of butter.

Another refrigerator staple is skim milk. For years I've heard people say they can't take the gray, thin look of skim milk. Better to have 2%. In an earlier chapter I described what you're really getting in 2% milk...5 grams of fat in 8 ounces. I've heard that adding some powdered skim milk to the liquid skim milk helps thicken it up some, and relieves the ickiness, and Butter Buds recommends adding 1 tablespoon to an 8 ounce glass to make it taste "richer." Interestingly enough, most people who go the skim milk route for a few weeks become accustomed to it and can no longer accept the goopy thickness of the original, whole fat stuff. Isn't that neat?

Alongside the skim milk, we have a pitcher of herb tea. I just read recently that sun and moon teas may build harmful bacteria so we use an iced-tea maker and refrigerate the stuff immediately. Almond-flavored, orange-flavored, apple cinnamon or mint is always sitting there for a refreshing break.

There is Philly Free Cream Cheese for a "bagel with a schmear" and it's great as a base for dips. When it comes to non-fat sour creams, we have two favorites: Naturally Yours No Fat and Land O' Lakes nonfat. Both work well in place of the real thing. We can't even tell the difference, anymore. Meg MacDonald was visiting recently, stuck her finger in the sour cream, tasted it and made a face. I was incensed! "Give it a few weeks, Meg!" I cried. "You'll see!" I can't wait to check back with her on the sour cream to see if her taste buds have appropriately adjusted.

One of the most common complaints I field is the flat taste of fat free mayonnaise. We prefer Smart Beat. Add a touch of Dijon mustard and it will lift the flavor. Hellman's Low Fat with 1 gram per tablespoon, has good mayo flavor, too, but I like mine fat free.

A discussion of a fat free refrigerator would be incomplete without a rundown on fat free salad dressings. We have a few recipes listed in the book for you, but when it comes to the prepared-in-a-bottle kind our vote goes to Hidden Valley Ranch Fat Free and the Hidden Valley Honey Dijon Ranch Fat Free. In fact, you will find, in the recipe section of this book, my own version of the honey-Dijon ranch, which I think you'll like.

There's Sorrento's Fat Free Ricotta Cheese which we use in our lasagna and it's a winner. Speaking of cheeses, we always have a 2 pound loaf of Healthy Choice Pasteurized Process Cheese Product in the fridge, just waiting for guests to ask for my famous Chili Con Queso. At 0 fat grams, this cheese melts just like Velveeta and will do a number in a baked potato or melted on some beans. It works just beautifully in casseroles, too. Remember the Green Bean Casserole or the Broccoli Rice Casserole? These casseroles were prepared with Cream of Mushroom soup and Velveeta. The cost of fat for the cheese and Cream of Mushroom soup, alone, when fixing the large casserole is 124 grams! The same casserole, prepared with Healthy Request Cream of Mushroom soup and Healthy Choice processed cheese food, is about 20. And that's for the *whole* casserole! Anywhere you've used Velveeta (6 grams per ounce) you can melt this cheese and you'll be overjoyed with the results. We use Healthy Choice shredded Mozzarella and Cheddar, too, because they melt uniformly. Some of the other brands have failed us in the flavor or melt category. Again, if you're one of those who's said it just doesn't taste the same...give it some time. It's *not the same* but you'll find it works as well, and you'll grow accustomed to the taste, even if it is different.

The ketchup, salsa, mustard, the pickles and that vast array of vegetables in the crisper have always been fat free or have only mere traces of fat not worth measuring. You'll enjoy the veggies and beans more and more as you become accustomed to preparing them and find your own favorites among them. And then, as you continue to try out new recipes in this book and others, you'll start adding to this basic rundown of products and utensils.

Chapter VIII

Go

Our kitchen is coming together right before our eyes!

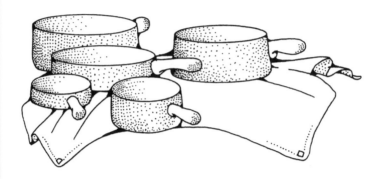

One of the simplest techniques to apply in switching to this healthier lifestyle is taking an old, truly loved recipe and rendering it low in fat. In performing this ritual, the measurements and their equivalents, become vital information. Here then are the most commonly used measurements and equivalents, to make this simple chore even simpler for you.

MEASUREMENTS AND EQUIVALENTS

LIQUID MEASURE

A pinch or dash	Less than 1/8 teaspoon	
1 teaspoon	1/3 tablespoon	
1 tablespoon	3 teaspoons	1/2 fluid ounce
2 tablespoons	1/8 cup	1 fluid ounce
3 tablespoons	1 jigger	1 1/2 fluid ounces
4 tablespoons	1/4 cup	2 fluid ounces
5 tablespoons + 1 tsp.	1/3 cup	

8 tablespoons	1/2 cup	4 fluid ounces
16 tablespoons	1 cup	1/2 pint
2 cups	1 pint	1/2 quart
4 cups	2 pints	1 quart
16 cups	4 quarts	1 gallon

WEIGHT MEASURE

1 gram	0.035 ounce
1 ounce	28.35 grams
100 grams	3.57 ounces
4 ounces	1/4 pound
8 ounces	1/2 pound
16 ounces	1 pound

ABBREVIATIONS

Tbs. = tablespoon
tsp. = teaspoon
oz. = ounce
lb. = pound
BTW = By the way

COOKING TERMINOLOGY

Bake: Cook in a heated oven at a prescribed temperature, usually referring to muffins, breads or casseroles. When the masses fry potatoes, we bake them. The term "roasted" is interchangeable with "bake."

Baste: Moisten food by spooning liquid over it while cooking, a practice common with roasting, such as the Thanksgiving turkey. A brown-in bag "self-bastes" the turkey for you.

Beat: Using a beater or spoon, mix ingredients until smooth, or until stiff, as in the case of egg whites. Stiff egg whites are used in meringues and angel food cakes.

Blend: Combine two or more ingredients with a spoon or an electric blender. This may be accomplished with a food processor. An electric blender may be used for "whipping" drinks to make them greater in volume.

Boil: Bring liquid to a heat high enough (212° F) for bubbles to appear and break at the surface of the liquid. The high temperature of the liquid will reduce when additional foods are introduced, which may necessitate bringing the liquid "back to a boil."

Blanch: Bring liquid to a boil and dip the vegetable or fruit into the water just long enough for the skin to crinkle. This takes about a minute or two and is a method used for skinning tomatoes.

Broil: Cook in oven under top heat of broiler or between two hot surfaces. This direct heat and broiling "toasts" the food on the outside, while the lower, indirect heat of baking heats the food through more evenly.

Chill: Place in refrigerator to cool. Certain foods may need to be chilled before continuing with the recipe. Ingredients used for a whipped drink will increase in volume and retain that volume longer, if chilled before blending. Lasagna will slice more uniformly for storage after being chilled.

Chop: Cut in squares with knife, chopper or food processor, in 1/4 inch to 1/2 inch squares or cubes. The proper way to chop is with a wooden or plastic cutting board and a sharp, wide knife. Food choppers are available to facilitate this procedure, as well as food processors.

Coat: Roll in flour or bread crumbs, or shake in a bag, until coated. The most common method of coating is to roll the food in an egg substitute and then in some sort of seasoned flour or crumbs prior to baking.

Cool: Let stand at room temperature until no longer hot to the touch. This is especially important before placing cooked foods in the freezer, since the heat may affect the other frozen foods.

Defat: A liquid, such as a broth or gravy, is refrigerated so that the fat congeals on the top and can be spooned off, leaving the broth fat free.

Dice: Chop in cubes about 1/4 inch in size. This size is smaller than chopping and larger than mincing.

Dissolve: Mix dry ingredient with a liquid until the two are smooth and the dry ingredient has melted. This is important when adding cornstarch to a recipe. If not first dissolved in cold water, the heat of the cooking food (usually a sauce) may cause the cornstarch to form lumps.

Dot: Place small pieces, such as bits of cheese, over surface of the food. Often cheese is "dotted" on the top of a casserole during the last 15 minutes of baking to facilitate even melting.

Fold in: By placing spatula or wide spoon into mixture, under the mixture and then turning the mixture over, until ingredients are blended. This procedure is used most often when there is a need to retain the airiness of a food. Beating the ingredients would be destructive to delicate ingredients like egg whites or whipped topping.

Grate: Using a mandolin, a grater or food processor, reduce food to fine, medium or coarse particles. Carrots and cabbage are grated for slaw, as are cheeses for enhancing a dish at the table or before baking.

Marinate: Allow food to sit in mixture or sauce for a set period of time to acquire flavors or seasonings. Chicken and fish may be marinated before stir-frying or grilling.

Mince: Dice or chop very fine, about 1/8 inch or less. The size of a minced food is smaller than diced.

Parboil: Place food in boiling water until almost, but not fully, cooked. Usually done to continue cooking in a recipe, such as parboiling potatoes, before adding ingredients that require shorter cooking time.

Peel: Remove the outer skin of a vegetable or fruit such as a carrot, potato or apple. Sometimes the vegetable, perhaps a tomato, requires blanching to loosen the skin, which then peels off when the tomato cools.

Pit: Remove the pit or seed from a fruit such as a prune.

Preheat: Set oven at a particular temperature prior to preparation of the food that will be baked.

Purée: Mash food to make a paste either in a food processor, with a spoon against the side of the pot, pushed through a strainer or sieve, or in an electric blender. Cooked tomatoes may be puréed before using them in a sauce.

Sauté: Soften foods in a defatted broth or defatted stock, wine or spray-on oil, usually prior to adding the other ingredients of the recipe.

Sear: Brown quickly over high heat in non-stick pan with or without the use of spray-on oil.

Season: Flavor or marinate with spices and/or herbs prior to, during, or after cooking.

Simmer: Cook just below boiling, a slow roll (185° F). Most soups and stews are simmered to meld the flavors.

Skewer: Place on metal or wooden sticks for cooking. Common on a grill or under the broiler in an oven.

Slice: Cut into long, narrow pieces about 1/4 inch thick. A tomato may be sliced "on the round" across the fruit, whereas a bell pepper may be sliced either in thin sticks or in rounds across the vegetable.

Sliver: Cut in long, thin pieces. This process may be accomplished with a mandolin or a food processor.

Snip: Cut into small pieces, usually with kitchen shears. Parsley is often snipped, as are a number of fresh herbs, to retain more of the flavor. It keeps the leaves from bruising.

Steam: Cook over steaming water, either in a bamboo steamer, a steamer tray or a metal strainer set atop boiling water. Another method of steaming is in the microwave, in a covered dish, with 1 or 2 tablespoons of water. It's common to steam vegetables to just the crispy-cooked stage to retain more nutrients in the food. A fresher flavor is a result of steaming rather than placing the vegetables into boiling water.

Steep: Allow to stand in hot liquid, such as tea leaves to brew tea.

Stir: Blend ingredients with a spoon until well-mixed.

Stir-fry: Quickly toss foods in hot liquid to heat through, while the foods remain crispy, retaining more flavor and nutrients. Especially popular with an assortment of vegetables, with chicken or seafood used as a condiment for flavoring, if at all.

Thicken: Add thickening mixture (such as cornstarch dissolved in water) and stir until the liquid is thickened. Very popular method of thickening sauces or gravies.

Toast: Brown in a toaster, broiler or oven.

Toss: Mix lightly with the use of 2 spoons, or fork and spoon, such as salad in a large bowl or vegetables through a pasta dish.

Whip: Mix rapidly, usually with an electric mixer, eggbeater or blender to introduce air and increase volume, such as egg whites for a meringue or a frothy drink.

CHAPTER IX

FABULOUS LOW FAT FOOD

The kitchen awaits the tender ministrations of the chef extraordinaire who is going to whip up tender morsels of culinary magic. The wonder of this achievement is that the basis for all wizardry in this particular kitchen is intrinsically tied to the phenomenon of low fat cookery.

Can this be? Delectable, delightful, delicious edibles that are prepared in accordance with the strictest rules in the low fat arena? Yes!

If you've never cooked before you'll be amazed at how simple these recipes are to put together, and there's no better time, than when you're learning how to cook, to learn how to cook low fat. If you're an old hand in a chef's hat and apron, you'll be learning some new ways to prepare familiar and beloved foods and you'll have the opportunity of trying a number of exciting new recipes you've not had a go at before. Either way we're all in for some good eats and fun foods that won't take a certificate from the Cordon Bleu to produce.

The recipes that you are about to explore are, for the most part, large enough for serving to company or to the family. Large recipes assure sufficient portion variances and leftovers. One of the greatest fears of my life is inviting guests to dinner and overestimating the amount prepared, serving the diners skimpy portions and having them leave my table hungry. If there are no leftovers, I know I didn't prepare enough food for everyone. Someone must have left the table wanting more!

When reading recipes in cookbooks and magazines, I'm always amazed at the yield designated as "6 servings" with no total volume listed, so that you never really know how much food you'll end up with until you fix the recipe. Oh, my goodness, the six servings they recommend are for toddlers...not grown people!

The number of serving sizes predetermined by someone whom you don't know, who has no idea how much you eat, doesn't make a whole lot of sense. Even following the tenets of living on mini-meals, instead of packing your edibles into two or three big sit-downs, still leaves room for differences in portion size. You might eat six tiny mini-meals in comparison with your best friend who has thirty more pounds of muscle to support than you have. In this book, following each of the recipe instructions, the information you see states *YIELD* and *FAT GRAMS IN ENTIRE RECIPE*. If the fat grams for the dish total 20, and eight people have the pleasure of enjoying it, the fat grams (if they each eat an equal amount) would be about 2 1/2 grams per serving. On the other hand, if you prepare the entire recipe and you are splitting the total amount into ten frozen dinners for yourself, you know exactly how many grams per serving you will consume each time. And, of course, if you and a friend are having dinner, finish off about half the recipe and your friend eats twice what you do, the math is really easy to perform (you've consumed 1/6 of the total recipe and your friend has consumed 1/3). In most cases, you'll find the total fat grams for each recipe so low, you'll average only 1 or 2 fat grams per meal, unless there is some seafood or poultry included in the recipe.

How do I keep the fat grams at such a low number when you read all these recipes in other books, or in magazines, that are so much higher? It's simply a matter of depending on vegetables, grains, beans and peas to make up the greatest part of every recipe, leaving the flesh foods to a minimum, and using special oils, occasionally, only as a flavoring, rather than as a part of the preparation of the dish. Fat free sour creams, cheeses and mayonnaise work just as well, when used properly, as the low fat varieties, leaving out a bunch of fat grams.

MUNCH-A-BUNCH

There's no need to get stuck in a rut when it comes to ideas for the nibbles or the minimeals. Since you've probably never had the permission, from yourself or anyone else, to nosh a number of times a day, we'll start out the food and recipes with a list of easy edibles to fill the snack attack at no more than 1 gram to 1 1/2 grams of fat per munch. In fact, a good number of them are fat free.

Microwave ovens vary in power and the time a food requires in the oven may vary as well. Please keep this in mind when figuring the cook times for these snacks.

THE AUTHORIZED NOSH

1. 1/2 toasted English muffin with a slice of fat free Swiss and a slice of tomato, microwaved for 2 to 3 minutes.

2. A fat free tortilla (Mission brand is great) with some fat free bean dip (or refried beans) and fat free cheese, perhaps a dollop of salsa, rolled into a burrito.

3. 3 fat free sourdough pretzels.

4. 1/2 bagel with Philly Free or Healthy Choice Cream Cheese and a dab of your favorite preserves.

5. Grapefruit and orange sections with a dash of honey.

6. A pita pocket stuffed with chopped tomato, onion and bell pepper along with grated fat free cheddar, microwaved until the cheese melts.

7. An apple, sliced in half, cored and topped with sugar and cinnamon, microwaved for 3 or 4 minutes...a quickie baked apple!

8. A scrubbed potato, baked in the microwave for 7 minutes, topped with fat free sour cream and salsa.

9. A scrubbed potato, baked in the microwave for 7 minutes, topped with Chili Con Queso.

10. A handful of Utz or Tostito brand baked corn chips with salsa or Chili Con Queso...or both!

11. A cup of cooked twisted macaroni with chopped tomato, bell pepper and peas, tossed with fat free Italian dressing.

12. A slice of fat free pound cake topped with strawberry preserves.

13. A slice of fat free chocolate pound cake topped with fat free vanilla ice cream and fat free chocolate sauce (Hershey's and Smuckers each have one; read the label).

14. A handful of Mr. Phipps Fat-Free Pretzel Chips with Land O' Lakes Fat Free Onion Dip.

15. 2 tablespoons of water-packed tuna salad, fixed with fat free mayo and chopped celery with lemon juice, on melba toast.

16. A toasted English muffin with I Can't Believe It's Not Butter Spray and blueberry preserves.

17. A cup of pasta tossed with 4 tablespoons of The Marinara Sauce.

18. A cup of applesauce sprinkled with cinnamon.

19. A fat free carrot muffin.

20. A toasted cinnamon bagel with Fleischmann's Fat Free Low Calorie squeeze margarine.

21. 1/2 cup Philly Free blended with 1 to 2 tablespoons salsa on Utz Baked Corn Chips.

22. A scrubbed potato, baked in the microwave for 7 minutes, topped with fat free sour cream, chopped chives and BacO's.

23. A pita pocket stuffed with Red Rice and Jim's Beans.

24. A banana, mashed, on a slice of fat free white or wheat bread, with raisins sprinkled on top.

25. A kosher dill pickle.

26. A slice of smoked turkey (Louis Rich Low Fat Luncheon Meats) with mustard, folded in a slice of fat free rye bread.

27. A slice of fat free French bread, with I Can't Believe It's Not Butter Spray, sprinkled with garlic powder and broiled until bubbly. Add some chopped parsley or basil, if handy.

28. Celery and carrot sticks with fat free Thousand Island dressing or Ranch dressing.

29. Fresh apple chunks dipped in sugar and cinnamon.

30. A cup of Campbell's Tomato Soup, made with skim milk or water.

31. Air-popped popcorn with a spray of imitation butter flavor mixed with water.

32. A glass of Bloody Mary Mix with a stick of celery.

33. 2 fat free Fig Newtons or reasonable facsimile.

34. A skewer of onion, bell pepper and mushrooms, grilled or broiled.

35. A toasted English muffin with The Marinara Sauce, covered with shredded fat free mozzarella, baked until the cheese melts (an English pizza).

36. 1/2 cup of Progresso Black Bean Soup on 1/2 cup steamed rice (white or brown), heated through in the microwave. A dollop of fat free sour cream may be added after removing from the oven.

37. Some chopped Romaine lettuce with tomato, celery, bell pepper and carrot, topped with fat free salad dressing.

38. A handful of Lay's Original Baked Potato Crisps.

39. A Hostess Low Fat Crumb Cake.

40. A handful of dried fruits: 2 apricots, 2 dates, 2 figs and 2 prunes.

41. A cup of pasta with 2 tablespoons of defatted chicken stock and a slice of fat free Swiss cheese, heated together in the microwave until the cheese melts. Sprinkle a tablespoon of fat free grated Parmesan on it, after removing from the oven and tossing it.

42. Stir some sliced zucchini with onion and mushrooms, some of The Marinara Sauce and bake on a toasted English muffin or half of a pita bread. Any kind of fat free cheese is good on top.

43. An Archway Fat Free Oatmeal Raisin Cookie or two.

44. 1/2 cup of fat free ice cream in a cone.

45. A Health Valley Fat Free Granola Bar.

46. A cup of Campbell's Manhattan Clam Chowder.

47. A Special K Eggo Waffle with some Lite Maple Syrup.

48. A frozen Dole Fruit & Juice Bar.

49. A handful of Rold Gold Fat Free Pretzels.

50. 2/3 of a cup of Richard Simmons Fat Free Caramel Popcorn.

51. A cup of Wheat Chex sprinkled with Cajun seasoning and baked until crispy.

52. 5 Quaker Oats White Cheddar Mini Rice Cakes.

53. A heated cinnamon raisin bagel spread with orange marmalade.

54. Utz Baked Corn Chips dotted with Healthy Choice Processed Cheese Food and baked until the cheese melts.

55. A bowl of melon chunks (honeydew, cantaloupe and watermelon) with grapes or raisins. Throw in some orange sections and banana and you've got a fruit salad.

56. A SnackWell's Double Chocolate Nonfat Yogurt.

57. A banana rolled in Grape Nuts.

58. A container of Fantastic Foods dehydrated soups or one-dish mixes.

This list of munchies is only a beginning. Don't forget the leftovers from previous dinners for a snack or lunch.

THE SPICE OF LIFE

As you become more familiar with preparing delicious recipes for low fat delivery, using spices and herbs to enhance the natural flavor of these foods will become an integral part of your cooking efforts. You'll see a number of different herbs and spices throughout the recipes, some which you're accustomed to using and some which may look new to you. I say "may" look new to you because you are probably already enjoying some of them in the restaurants you frequent. You just never made the connection before. This list will help you to find these goodies in the supermarket and may take some of the mystery out of using them.

After a while you'll be able to taste a newly prepared creation and with a smack of your tongue against your palate you'll recognize a gap that only fresh basil or, perhaps, some crushed, dried thyme leaf can fill.

You'll notice that when listing dried herbs and spices in recipes I usually add the term *crushed*. The dried herbs and spices radiate the aroma and flavor better after crushing between your palm and the heel of your other hand.

Basil
A sweet, heady flavor, especially when used fresh, basil enhances everything from Italian dishes to Thai foods. The beauty of this herb is the mellow, aromatic tones it introduces, even when used dried. Tomato with basil is a marriage made in heaven. Some recipes demand the fresh leaves whereas in some the dried will do. The Shrimp with Basil and Hot Chilies requires the fresh leaf while the fresh leaf would be overwhelming in the Ratatouille and either one will do in the Split Pea Soup.

Bay Leaf
Frequently used in tomato sauces, stews, soups and marinades, the laurel or bay leaf is used dry and whole. Do not break up the leaf and always remove the leaves from the dish, since the leaf doesn't bend and pieces have been known to lodge in an unsuspecting diner's throat. You'll find the bay in The Marinara Sauce and the Greens With Beans Soup.

Cajun Seasoning
A blend of different peppers, such as cayenne and black, along with Italian herbs, onion, cumin, curry, cardamom, turmeric and other assorted spices that can be purchased already mixed. We know that Penzey's Ltd. carries a Cajun blend already put together for you.

Cardamom
A seed that is aromatic and used, ground, in curries and some-times, bruised, in after-dinner coffee.

Cayenne
Cayenne powder is peppery, ground from seeds and pods of various peppers. It is used in the powder form and also as a base for Louisiana hot sauce. You'll use this pepper in Judy's Red Beans 'N Rice.

Celery Seed
A light, fresh flavor, this seed can be added to dressings, sauces and stews, almost any dish that would be better with the fresh taste of celery. We recommend celery seed in the Spinach and Cappellini.

Chili Powder
We all know that chili powder makes it hot, whatever it is. The powder may be from one type chili pepper, numerous peppers or may be a combination of chili pepper powders with cumin and other spices or herbs added for flavoring. Read the label. You'll find chili powder called for in the recipe for Spicy Baked Beans.

Chinese Five Spice Powder
A combination of cinnamon, ginger, star anise, anise seed and clove, this spice is an addition to Oriental stir-fry. Try adding it to any of the stir-fry recipes to see if it's a flavor that does it for you.

Cilantro
This herb is available fresh in most supermarkets. It looks like flat-leaf parsley. The leaf of the coriander plant, it has a delicate per-fume that truly enhances bean dishes and is a necessary part of most salsas. The dried version just doesn't do it. To be sure you're getting a fresh cilantro, squeeze a leaf or two between your fingers and take a sniff. The aroma will stick to your fingers and you know you've got it. You'll fall in love with this herb in the Black Bean recipes and it's a must in the Salsa.

Cinnamon
Either as sticks, to stir a hot drink or powdered, to enhance apples and raisins, or in chunks, for grating, it's difficult to imagine so

many foods without this aromatic spice. It's also used in scents of candles and sachet. See how it works its magic on Karen's Candied Yams with Apples.

Cloves
Another aromatic spice that is also used for incense, as well as in cooking, this spice has a very strong flavor and is often used whole (example: stuck in onions) and then removed from the pot. Cloves are used medicinally, as many herbs and spices are.

Coriander
The seed of the same plant that gives us cilantro, coriander has a light lemony flavor and needs either high heat or a long cook-time for the full impact of the spice to develop. There's coriander in the Curried Vegetable Stew.

Crushed Red Pepper
For those who like it hot, it's a good idea to have some crushed red pepper handy. Throw some into Italian dishes and Szechuan or Thai food for that warm after-glow. You'll enjoy this pepper in the Marinara Sauce.

Cumin
Cumin is an important part of recipes from Mexico to India. Cooking with this spice is an art, since a bit too much and the flavor of the dish goes flat. With just the right touch, it enhances bean dishes and is a must in chili. Try your hand at using this spice in The Vegetarian Chili .

Curry Powder
So familiar to you as an Indian spice, in India "curry powder" is not used at all. Instead, the individual spices are chosen whole, for a particular dish, and then hand-ground. We are not quite so well attuned to our curry. We buy the powder that is a result of a mix of turmeric, ginger, cumin, different peppers, cardamom, nutmeg, coriander, cloves and other spices. There are many different types available. Start out with a simple sweet curry and experiment from there. The Curried Rice is a perfect example of how curry makes a dish special.

Dill

Available as seed and weed. The seed is used, primarily, in pickling. We enjoy dill weed in potato salad, vegetable stock, chicken soup, and with salmon and shrimp. It's available fresh, at most supermarkets, or can be purchased dried. It's a cinch you'll appreciate this fresh flavor in Potato Salad and Jewish Penicillin.

Fennel

A bulb with wispy leaves, fennel has a taste similar to licorice and the leaves are used to enhance soups and salads. It's available fresh and dried. Try it in the Potato, Leek and Fennel Soup.

Garlic Powder

This bulb is highlighted, along with onions, in our recipes because of its importance as an ingredient in so many dishes...almost every ethnicity. The powder does have its purposes and can be found in the spice section of your supermarket. This powder is used in the recipe for Baked Herbed Fish.

Ginger

An important part of Asian cooking, fresh ginger root, a gnarled root you've seen in your neighborhood market, is used by peeling and then grating the amount of root you need. The powder is a welcome addition to salads (add a pinch!) or to add an extra zip to sauces and marinades. It is an important part of the curry mix. We use ginger in a number of our Asian recipes, such as Broccoli and Cauliflower Stir-fry.

Gumbo Filé Powder

Sassafras leaves, dried and powdered, give us the inimitable subtle flavor of Creole and Cajun cooking. We use this herb for thickening as well as flavoring the stew or soup. Take a look at the Shrimp and Okra Gumbo.

Mace

The outer coating or aril of the nutmeg fruit, dried, delivers a milder flavor than the nutmeg does and can be used interchangeably with nutmeg. It's a flavor we're familiar with in pumpkin pie.

Marjoram
A fragrant spice, marjoram enhances stews, soups, stuffings and sauces. Somewhat similar to oregano, the flavor is more delicate. Try the Potatoes and Black-eyed Peas.

Mixed Italian Herbs
A combination of our favorite Italian spices, this makes seasoning sauces and soups a snap. Basil, oregano, marjoram, thyme and rosemary are all part of this mix. Try stirring this into some Fleischmann's Fat Free Low Calorie squeeze margarine, add garlic powder and fat free grated Parmesan, spread it on French bread slices and bake until the bread begins to turn golden brown. This is heaven, with or without a meal. You'll find so many of our recipes require this mix of herbs and spices from the Lasagnas to the Squash and Onion Cheese Bake.

Mustard
The powder and the seed are both available. The powder can be used to make the prepared mustard that we are all familiar with but the amount of time the mustard is allowed to mature before refrigerating will determine how hot it is. Water, white wine or beer can be used to make the paste, changing the flavor. The seed is used in pickling and can also add an interesting flavor to barbecue sauces and marinades. You'll find mustard powder in Cajun Black-Eyed Pea Casserole.

Nutmeg
This is one of the finest aromatic additions to so many foods. Think of Eggnog without nutmeg. It's unthinkable. Even a simple café au lait is dramatic with a touch of nutmeg. All the experts remind us that the way to truly enjoy this spice is to freshly hand-grate it on the small side of a four-sided grater. If you happen to have some fresh, to add to any spice-based muffin or cake (made with applesauce instead of oil, of course), you'll see the impact it makes. A little bit will do it. You'll enjoy a taste of nutmeg in Jim's Honey Vinaigrette.

Oregano
Called for in so many recipes, it's hard to consider cooking with-

out oregano. Italian, Mexican, Greek, all cuisines use oregano for that extra roundness of flavor. Dried oregano leaf does the job and we always crush it between the palm of one hand and heel of the other to get the full flavor. Take a look at any of our Italian dishes and you'll find this herb, such as the Rice and Beans Italiano.

Paprika
There are two kinds of paprika: the hot and the sweet. The herbalists insist that our stores carry a non-descript, tasteless imitation of real paprika, which comes from Hungary and without which no Hungarian recipe is worth its salt! You will note the difference in the flavor if you buy your paprika from a specialty store or catalog provider. The recipe for Vegetarian Chili includes paprika.

Parsley
Like basil, fresh is better. I even enjoy throwing sprigs in at the end of a cook-time to relish eating this herb that most people throw away. Yes, those decorative parsley leaves on the side of a plate are edible! If you don't have the fresh on hand, crush the dried. There are two parsleys available in your market: the Italian flat and the curly variety. The Italian is a milder version. You'll have a need for parsley in the Black Bean Soup.

Pepper
There are a variety of peppercorns available from the black or white to green, pink and red. The feeling in our kitchen is: go with freshly ground Tellicherry peppercorns from India. Seasoned pepper and lemon pepper are two of many flavored peppers also available. Almost every recipe we prepare calls for some freshly ground pepper.

Rosemary
An aromatic herb that delivers a sweet, pungent flavor, used in tomato-based sauces, poultry stuffing and it's great with or without the usual accompaniment of oregano and thyme. Try rosemary in Salad With Beans.

Saffron
This has been known as the most prized spice...and well it should

be considering that 75,000 blossoms must be hand-picked to produce one pound. The threads or stigmas of the flowering crocus, three to a flower, are the pieces we use to impart the golden color and the saffron flavor. The quantity necessary to flavor a dish is so limited that it is not terribly expensive to use, although it is the most expensive spice available in the world. There are 450 to 500 stigma in a gram. The most famous dish requiring saffron is paella and nothing else will do. And what better place to use this marvelous spice but our own Paella.

Sage
Best known for stuffing and sausage, sage presents an unmistakable flavor and can be used to pep up stews and soups. Sage is most often purchased dried. Try the Sage Potatoes.

Savory
The name of this herb says it quite simply. The flavor is recommended for chilled vegetable juices, soups, stews, beans and peas.

Tarragon
A robust seasoning that reminds me of anise or licorice, tarragon is the herb of France. Fresh is the way to go and use sparingly, at first, until you determine the amount for a particular dish. This flavor is found in Duxelles.

Thyme
Ah, one of the herbs without which Italian food just couldn't make it. Fresh is wonderful. Dried will do. I like the dried leaf, crushed. It brings a heartiness to tomato-based dishes that no other herb can deliver as in Black Beans with Thyme and The Marinara Sauce.

Turmeric
This herb is used as a substitute for saffron in many dishes and lends a yellow hue to foods in a manner similar to saffron. You'll find this spice in most curries, in pickles and American mustard. The Curried Vegetable Stew includes this herb.

BEANS AND CERTAIN PEAS

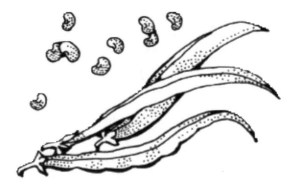

There are so many absolutely marvelous, and hearty recipes with beans that you won't even realize you're not eating meat. The bean is packed with complex carbohydrates. Bite for bite they are tummy-filling beyond the calories they deliver. There are few foods as versatile as the bean in a recipe. I've been known to "just throw a can of them in" to a recipe that never thought of having beans before and thereby converting a side-dish into a one-dish meal.

I've heard numerous times, from different folks, that although they love the flavor and consistency of beans and peas, they are embarrassed by the meal for hours, and for this reason simply don't eat them. When you consider the nutritional value of the bean and the fiber content, that is so very important to good health, skipping this food would be truly a shame.

There are complex sugars, called oligosaccharides, that cannot be digested by human enzymes. These sugars are consumed by the intestinal bacteria and in the process produce the gas we know so well. Here are a few ways to alleviate the flatulence problem. See if they don't change your opinion of the luscious legume.

When preparing dried beans, be sure to discard the water used for soaking. In fact, change the water often (about three to four times) to keep flushing out as much of these sugars as possible. If you're intent on getting out as much of the oligosaccharides as possible, you might try this formula: soak 1 cup of beans in 9 cups of water for 4 to 5 hours; discard the water, add 9 cups of fresh water and cook for 1/2 hour; drain the beans again. If the beans are not completely cooked, add 9 cups of fresh water and repeat the scenario until the beans are completely cooked. This method is very time-consuming and there are easier ways to prepare dried beans, but the more you rinse, the less gas you experience. When using canned beans, be sure to rinse them very well, also. This helps to get much of the offending sugars out of your food and down the drain. Never cook your beans in the liquid in which they soaked or eat the liquid in the can.

Another solution to the problem is a product you've probably seen advertised in a number of health-oriented magazines. It's called *beano* and they have a number for you to call if you have any questions, 800- 257-8650. This product is a food enzyme and introduces the enzyme we lack that helps to break down the oligosaccharides.

As you eat more of these high fiber foods, such as legumes, cruciferous veggies like broccoli and cabbage, brans and whole wheats, your system will become more accustomed to the high fiber you're consuming. In the meantime the *beano* folks say their pills or liquid will help with the digestion of any of these foods.

There is, on average, about 1 gram of fat in a cup of cooked beans along with about 100 calories. The bean can reflect so many different ethnic flavors because it is a staple all over the world. The cannellini bean is a Tuscan favorite; the garbanzo (also known as the chick-pea) is a staple in Mid-Eastern cooking; the soybean is an important part of the protein in the diet in the Far East; the red kidney is the backbone of our beloved chili, here in the U. S. of A.; the pinto bean is the refried love of our neighbor, Mexico; the lentil with a touch of olive oil and lemon is a touch of Greece; and who can do New Year's Eve without the black-eyed pea of our own southern states? The lima bean gets its name from the capital city of the country where it first grew, Peru. There are so many other varieties but we simply don't have enough space. Until recently, the bean has certainly not been a star in our country, but it is finally beginning to receive the acclaim it deserves as the low fat lifestyle becomes more accepted.

Whether you eat the beans you prepare yourself from dried, or you open a can, you're in for a treat. The greatest advantage to buying them dried, and spending the time soaking and cooking, is a tremendous savings in dollars. The dried beans are so inexpensive!

BUYING BEANS: Try to buy your beans in stores where the business in beans is brisk. Older beans cook more slowly and need lots of soak time. Check to be sure the color is bright, not dulled by age. Try to buy see-through packaging so you know what you're getting. There should be few broken or cracked beans and the skin should be smooth, not shriveled.

STORAGE: Dried beans can be stored in the packaging as purchased until you cook them. If you open a package and remove a portion, or if you buy them in bulk, store the balance of the beans in air-tight glass jars. They look great on display in the kitchen. Remember that beans continue to age as they sit on the shelf and the older they are, the longer you have to soak them to reconstitute them.

Always pick through beans and peas before rinsing and cooking. Although most packaged product merely has broken beans you want to discard and dust you want to rinse off, loose or bulk beans and peas may have stones and other debris. You want to be sure and remove any tree limbs and boulders *before* cooking. The easiest way to soak the beans, after picking and rinsing, is overnight, although eight hours will do it for most beans if it must be a daytime affair. Be sure to use about three to four times as much water as beans or cover with water about 3 inches above the beans. Remember to change the water from time to time as you're soaking them, during your waking hours, to eliminate oligosaccharides.

Precooking is accomplished with the addition of some seasonings, depending upon the recipe or the flavor you're trying to achieve, but *never add salt or a tomato product to the beans before they reach the desired tenderness.* The salt or any acidic additive will interact with the seed coat and cause the bean to halt tenderizing. This reaction of the bean's seed coat is great once they've reached the tenderness you want because you can then cook them all day and they'll retain that firmness you desire. Many a meal was inedible before we learned this lesson in bean cookery. Lentils, split peas and black-eyed peas do not usually require soaking before cooking.

After soaking, the beans need only about 20 minutes cook-time (older beans may require more time) in fresh water, with or without seasonings (obviously, not salt), test them for tenderness, and you're ready to add them to a recipe or a salad.

We use canned beans when we're in a hurry and they do the job, beautifully. The nutrients in both kinds of beans will benefit you equally as well. Some of us simply do not have the time, nor the inclination, to soak! In the recipes that follow, where cooked beans, or canned, are called for...make your own choice. If sodium is a problem for you, buy the salt-free canned beans.

FREEZING: After cooking and cooling, the beans can be placed in plastic freezer bags and frozen for future use when you need them at a moment's notice. Place the beans in individual meal-size containers flattened for uniform freezing or use large bags and follow these instructions for easy separation. Here's how: when you put the beans in the bag, squeeze out the air and seal the bag. Lay the bag flat on a table or counter top and flatten the beans so that they're only one layer thick, evenly distributed in the bag. Store them in the freezer flat, one on top of the other, so that they freeze like a board. When you're ready to use them, you needn't thaw out the whole bag. Gently hit the bag on the edge of a counter and the beans will break up so that you can remove only the amount you want. Return the unused portion to the freezer. To thaw, simply place the beans in a colander under cold running water or throw them into a pot of cooking ingredients. They'll thaw in a hurry that way.

BLACK BEANS

(Turtle Beans)

1 cup dried makes 1 1/4 cups cooked.
1 cup cooked beans will deliver 1 gram of fat.

From the Caribbean, South and Central America, black beans are versatile and cook up well with other beans. The canned black bean can be substituted for the home-soaked-and-cooked bean with no flavor loss and there are some good canned black bean soups available, as well.

BLACK BEAN DIP WITH CILANTRO

This dip will simply disappear when you serve it. It's great, too, heated, topped with some Healthy Choice Shredded Cheddar, rolled up in a Mission Fat Free Flour Tortilla.

Preparation utensil: A medium-sized bowl

---

2 cups cooked black beans or 1 can (16 oz.) black beans, drained
1 Tbs. fresh cilantro, snipped
1 Tbs. fresh lime juice (about 1/2 lime should produce it)
3 Tbs. Salsa

---

1. Mix all ingredients.
2. Use a potato masher to mash some of the mixture, so that you have a mix of paste
   and whole beans.
3. Heat in the microwave for about 1 minute to enhance flavors.
4. Serve with Utz or Tostito Baked Corn Chips.

YIELD: About 2 cups
FAT GRAMS IN ENTIRE RECIPE: 4

BTW: There are numerous ways to use this dip. It's a great topper for a taco salad or a baked potato. If you don't have time to prepare the salsa from scratch, Old El Paso and Pace Chunky can fill in for your own, homemade.

BLACK BEANS WITH PEPPERS

This is a dish with all the heartiness of a Cuban dinner but takes just minutes if the beans and the rice are already prepared. Have the rice frozen ready to go at a moment's notice. And a can or two of beans should always be in the pantry. This is good enough to serve to unexpected guests!

Cooking utensil: A non-stick 3 quart saucepan

1/4 cup dry red or white wine, or defatted stock
1 medium onion, sliced
1 green bell pepper, sliced in strips
1 red bell pepper, sliced in strips
4 medium garlic cloves, minced
1 tsp. ground cumin
1 large ripe tomato or 2 canned plum tomatoes, diced
2 cups cooked or 1 (15 oz.) can black beans
1/2 cup water or juice from canned tomato
Salt and pepper to taste
3 cups steamed white or brown rice
2 to 3 Tbs. chopped fresh cilantro, divided
Louisiana Hot Sauce to taste

---

1. Heat the wine or stock and add the onion and peppers; sauté until soft.
2. Add the garlic and cumin; stir over low heat for about 1 minute.
3. Add the tomato, beans and liquid; bring to a boil; reduce to a simmer; cover and cook for 5 minutes or until peppers are tender.
4. Season with salt and pepper to taste.
5. Add rice and toss mixture; cover and cook over low heat until heated through.
6. Add half of the cilantro; toss again; cover and let stand for about 2 minutes.
7. Serve with additional cilantro sprinkled on top and hot sauce for flavoring.

YIELD: 6 to 7 cups
FAT GRAMS IN ENTIRE RECIPE: 5

BTW: If you're out of black beans but you've got a couple of cans of red kidney beans, you can make the switch with no fear of failure.

BLACK BEANS WITH THYME

Although this recipe may appear to be just another black bean combo, the flavors surprised us. The thyme and oregano add a different flavor to the beans and perform wonders. You must try this dish once...it's a winner.

Cooking utensil: A 6 to 8 quart non-stick pot

---

4 cups black beans, canned or cooked
1 cup onions, chopped
1 cup green peppers, chopped
2 cloves garlic, minced
1 1/2 tsp. dried thyme, crushed
1 tsp. oregano
1 tsp. white pepper
1/4 tsp. black pepper
1/4 tsp. cayenne pepper
1 tsp. chicken bouillon granules
2 bay leaves
1 tsp. dried basil
1 can (8 oz.) tomato sauce
1 can (16 Oz.) stewed tomatoes

---

1. Combine all ingredients; cover and cook on low heat for 2 hours.
2. Remove bay leaves.

YIELD: About 6 cups
FAT GRAMS IN ENTIRE RECIPE: 4

BTW: This is delicious served as is. Put it over steamed white rice and see what you think!

Notes:

_____

_____

_____

Black Beans 'N Rice In A Hurry

This one recipe has saved us from going hungry many times. When the question, "What's for dinner?" comes up after a busy day we're prepared.

Cooking utensil: A 3 quart non-stick saucepan

1/4 cup dry wine or defatted chicken stock
1 small onion, chopped
1 tsp. garlic, minced
1 can (16 oz.) black beans, drained
1 can (14.5 oz.) tomatoes and juice
1 Tbs. fresh cilantro, chopped
Salt and pepper to taste
Louisiana hot sauce to taste
Steamed white or brown rice

---

1. Sauté the onion and garlic in the wine or stock until soft.
2. Add the beans, tomatoes and cilantro. Break up the tomatoes with a spoon; simmer about 10 to 15 minutes.
3. Serve on rice with the seasonings on the side.

YIELD: About 2 1/2 cups, without the rice
FAT GRAMS IN ENTIRE RECIPE: 2

BTW: Some chopped onion sprinkled on top, or a dollop of sour cream, is a nice touch when serving.

Notes:

THE BEST BLACK BEANS

This is another quick-fix recipe that is amazingly good. It takes 5 minutes to put together, 5 minutes of attention during cooking time, and 25 minutes to finish cooking, while you get into something more comfortable.

Cooking utensil: A 3 quart non-stick saucepan or a large non-stick skillet

---

1/4 cup white wine
1 medium onion, chopped
1 jar (8 oz.) pimiento, drained and sliced
2 cans (16 oz. ea.) black beans, partially drained
1/4 cup white wine, additional
1/2 tsp. dried oregano, crushed
1/2 tsp. sugar
Salt and hot pepper sauce to taste
Steamed rice, cooked without oil or margarine

---

1. Sauté onion in white wine until tender.
2. Add the pimiento and cook for about 2 minutes.
3. Add the beans, the additional wine, oregano and sugar; simmer, uncovered, until somewhat creamy looking, about 25 minutes.
4. Serve over steamed rice. Salt and hot pepper sauce to be added to taste.

YIELD: 5 cups
FAT GRAMS IN ENTIRE RECIPE: 5

Notes:

BLACK BEAN SOUP

It's a classic. Soups usually don't cook in 30 minutes or less, so bear with me. Try it once. You'll love it and you'll see why I included this recipe (and a few others like it) even though it takes a while to prepare. Most of the time you can enjoy a novel and just "throw an eye" on it from time to time.

Cooking utensils: An 8 quart non-stick pot and a non-stick skillet

---

2 cups dried black beans, soaked and drained
1/4 cup dry wine or defatted chicken stock
4 medium onions, coarsely chopped
5 cloves garlic, minced
2 carrots, peeled and chopped
1 Tbs. ground cumin
4 celery ribs with leaves, coarsely chopped
2 bay leaves
1 Tbs. chopped fresh parsley
1 Tbs. liquid smoke
Salt and freshly ground pepper to taste
2/3 cup sherry (optional)

---

1. Bring 8 cups of water to boil in your large soup pot; add the beans; lower heat to a simmer, cover, and cook for 1 hour.
2. While the beans are cooking, sauté the onion in the wine or stock until soft.
3. Add the garlic, carrot, cumin and celery; sauté until vegetables are slightly soft; about 3 minutes; turn the heat down to medium/low; add about 1/2 cup liquid from beans; cook for 20 minutes. Check occasionally to add more liquid if it's drying out...about a tablespoon or so.
4. Combine vegetables with the pot of beans and liquid; add the bay leaves, parsley and liquid smoke; cover and cook for 2 hours. Check if drying out...add hot water from time to time.
5. Purée half the bean mixture in a blender or food processor. Return to the pot.
6. Add the sherry; cook until hot.

YIELD: About 12 cups
FAT GRAMS IN ENTIRE RECIPE: 8

BTW: This soup may be served with grated Parmesan, chopped onion or a dollop of sour cream. If serving to company, put out the pretty bowls and let them help themselves.

BLACK BEAN CHILI

This dish cooks by itself after you get the ingredients together. It's very hearty and a super one-dish meal.

Cooking utensil: An 8 to 10 quart non-stick pot

1/2 cup dry sherry
2 cups onion, chopped
1/2 cup celery, chopped
1/2 cup carrot, chopped
1/2 cup red bell pepper, chopped
4 cups black beans, cooked or canned
2 cups defatted chicken stock
2 Tbs. garlic, minced
1 cup tomato, chopped
1 tsp. ground cumin
4 tsp. chili powder, or to taste
1/2 tsp. dried oregano, crushed
1/4 cup fresh cilantro, chopped
2 Tbs. honey
2 Tbs. tomato paste
Fat free sour cream garnish
Grated onion for garnish
Fat free shredded cheddar for garnish

---

1. In the large, heavy pot, sauté the onions in the wine until soft.
2. Add the celery, carrot and bell pepper; sauté 5 minutes, stirring often.
3. Add remaining ingredients except garnishes; bring to a boil; lower heat, cover and simmer for 1 hour.
4. Serve with the sour cream, onion and cheese on the side for each individual to use as a garnish.

YIELD: 8 cups
FAT GRAMS IN ENTIRE RECIPE: 6

BTW: Baked corn chips go well alongside this dish.

PROGRESSO TO THE RESCUE BLACK BEANS 'N RICE

Cooking utensil: A 3 quart non-stick saucepan

1 can (19 oz.) Progresso Hearty Black Bean Soup
2 Tbs. fresh cilantro, chopped or minced
1/2 fresh tomato, chopped
Steamed rice
Louisiana hot sauce to taste
Chopped fresh onion as garnish

1. Open the can of soup and pour into the saucepan.
2. Add the cilantro and the tomato; heat until bubbly, or until the tomato is softened.
3. Pour over steamed rice; season with the hot sauce and garnish with the onion.

YIELD: 2 cups soup
FAT GRAMS IN ENTIRE RECIPE: 3

BTW: You are the decision maker as to the amount of rice you want to use. I usually end up with a cup of steamed rice, white or brown.

Notes:

BLACK-EYED PEAS

1 cup dried makes 2 cups cooked.
1 cup, cooked, will add up to about 1/2 gram

Also known as cow-peas, these peas are creamy in color with a black spot on one side. Black-eyed peas do not need pre-soaking before cooking. A favorite in the south, they've always been prepared with lots of fatback for flavoring...but not here!

HOPPIN' JOHN

Cooking utensils: An 8 quart non-stick pot and a non-stick skillet

---

5 cups water or vegetable broth
1 cup dried black-eyed peas, rinsed
1/4 cup white wine or defatted stock
1 medium onion, chopped
1 tsp. garlic, minced
1 cup unconverted white rice, uncooked
1 small green bell pepper, cut in 1/2 inch pieces
1 Tbs. liquid smoke
1/2 tsp. Tobasco or other pepper sauce
1 bay leaf
1/2 tsp. thyme, crushed
Salt and pepper to taste

---

1. Bring the water or broth to a boil; add the peas.
2. Reduce heat to simmer; cook for about 40 minutes or until tender, but not mushy.
3. In another pan, sauté the onion and garlic in the wine or stock until soft; set aside.
4. When beans are done, pour out all but 2 1/2 cups of liquid. If there is less than 2 1/2 cups of liquid, add broth to make that amount.
5. Add the rice, bell pepper, liquid smoke, hot pepper sauce, the onion and garlic that were set aside, bay leaf and the thyme; stir to combine all ingredients.
6. Cover and cook for 20 minutes or until the rice is done.
7. Season with salt and pepper to taste. Let stand 15 minutes.
8. Remove bay leaf and serve.

YIELD: 6 cups
FAT GRAMS IN ENTIRE RECIPE: 4

BLACK-EYED PEAS AND POTATOES

This recipe changed my feelings about the black-eyed pea. The pork-doctored stuff never tasted good to me and I thought it was the fault of the bean. Try this combination. You won't believe your taste buds.

Cooking utensils: A large non-stick skillet treated with spray-on oil and an 8 quart non-stick pot

---

1 pound potatoes, boiled
2 cups black-eyed peas, canned or cooked, drained
1 very large onion, sliced in 1/8 inch rounds
1 1/2 tsp. marjoram
1 1/2 Tbs. tomato paste, mixed with 2 Tbs. water
Salt and pepper to taste

---

1. When a fork can pierce the potatoes, drain, cool and slice them into 1/4 inch rounds; set aside.
2. Spray about a 5-second spray of Pam or Mazola in the large non-stick skillet.
3. Sauté the onion in the pan until translucent.
4. Add the potatoes and fry for 5 minutes.
5. Add the peas and continue to fry until heated through. If too dry add some of the tomato paste mixture.
6. Sprinkle with marjoram and add the rest of the tomato paste mix; toss all these ingredients until heated through.
7. Season with salt and pepper and serve.

YIELD: 8 cups
FAT GRAMS IN ENTIRE RECIPE: 4

BTW: A crispy salad and some crusty bread make this a meal.

Notes:

_____

_____

_____

CAJUN BLACK-EYED PEA CASSEROLE

Just a little "ole'" taste of Louisiana here, should show you how the folks in Louisiana like their black-eyed peas.

Cooking utensils: A small non-stick skillet, a 6 quart non-stick pot and a baking dish about 8 x 8 or 9 x 13

1/4 cup white wine or defatted stock
1 medium onion, chopped
2 ribs celery, sliced
2 cloves garlic, mashed
1/2 cup tomato sauce
1/4 cup honey
1/2 cup wine, additional
Salt and pepper to taste
1 to 5 splashes hot pepper sauce, to taste
1 to 2 tsp. dry mustard
8 cups cooked black-eyed peas

Preheat oven to 350°

1. In a small skillet, sauté the onion, celery and garlic in the 1/4 cup wine or stock, until translucent; set aside.
2. In a bowl, combine the tomato sauce, honey, 1/2 cup wine, salt, pepper, hot sauce and mustard; add the onion/celery/garlic mixture.
3. In a baking dish, toss together the peas and the mixture until coated, using care not to mash the peas.
4. Bake, uncovered, for 35 minutes or until bubbling. Stir before serving.

YIELD: 10 cups
FAT GRAMS IN ENTIRE RECIPE: 8

Notes:

CANNELLINI BEANS

1 cup dried makes 2 1/2 cups cooked.
1 cup of cooked cannellini beans brings you less than 1 fat gram.

These beans are also called white kidney beans. They are a little larger than a navy bean. It's a hearty bean that is originally from South America, but is a factor in French, Greek and especially, Italian cuisine. Once you cook with them you'll use them again and again.

CANNELLINI BEANS AND ONIONS

Try this dish on the side with grilled fish or chicken, or toss this mix with some cooked pasta. Pasta and beans make a great combination, and comprise a perfect protein.

Cooking utensil: A non-stick skillet

1/4 cup white wine
2 cups cannellini beans, cooked or canned
1 medium onion, sliced
2 tsp. garlic powder
1/4 cup white wine, additional
Hot sauce to taste

---

1. Soften the onion in 1/4 cup wine.
2. Add the remaining ingredients and cook until heated through.

YIELD: About 2 cups
FAT GRAMS IN ENTIRE RECIPE: 2

BTW: Take a look at the next recipe that adds some chicken to this dish if you need to satisfy a flesh food fiend.

Notes:

CANNELLINI-CHICKEN DINNER

This is a 10 minute cook-up. As easy as it looks it will satisfy the heartier appetite.

Cooking utensi: A large non-stick skillet or non-stick wok, treated with spray-on oil

---

2 boneless, skinless chicken breasts (about 4 oz. each)
1 to 2 tsp. garlic powder
4 oz. white wine
1 medium onion, sliced
2 tsp. mixed dried Italian seasonings, crushed
2 cups cannellini beans, cooked or canned
1 tsp. garlic powder, additional
1/4 white wine, additional

---

1. Place chicken breasts in the pan and sprinkle with the garlic powder.
2. Sear the chicken breasts on both sides.
3. Remove the chicken from the pan and slice in 1/2 inch strips.
4. Return the chicken to the pan and add the wine, onions, and Italian seasonings; sauté until the chicken is cooked through and the onions are translucent.
5. Add the rest of the ingredients and heat through.

YIELD: About 4 cups
FAT GRAMS IN ENTIRE RECIPE: 10

BTW: This combination can be served on rice or pasta, cooked without oil or margarine.

Notes:

A Tuscan Bean Soup

A favorite in Tuscany, this robust soup is sometimes called Pasta E Fagiole. In areas of New York, I've heard it called Pasta Fazool. Whatever you call it, it's good eating.

Cooking utensil: An 8 quart non-stick pot

1/4 cup white wine or defatted stock
1 small onion, chopped
1 small carrot, chopped
1/2 rib celery, minced
2 tsp. garlic, minced
1 cup tomatoes, chopped
4 cups defatted chicken stock, additional
1/2 tsp. dried oregano, crushed
2 Tbs. fresh basil, chopped or 1 tsp. dried basil, crushed
2 cups cannellini beans, cooked or canned
1 cup elbow macaroni, uncooked
1/4 cup fresh parsley, chopped
Freshly ground black pepper
Fat free grated Parmesan, to taste

---

1. Sauté the onion, carrot, celery and garlic in the wine or 1/4 cup stock until very soft.
2. Add the 4 cups chicken stock, tomatoes, oregano and basil; simmer, covered, about 5 minutes.
3. Add the beans and parsley; simmer another 10 minutes.
4. Mash some of the beans against the side of the pot with a flat spoon.
5. Add the macaroni; simmer an additional 10 minutes or until the pasta is cooked.
6. Season to taste with the black pepper. Sprinkle with Parmesan to taste.

YIELD: 6 cups
FAT GRAMS IN ENTIRE RECIPE: 7

BTW: When adding the macaroni, you can add a head of escarole, cleaned and coarsely cut. It more closely mimics the way the soup was originally designed to be eaten.

Cannellini Beans With Tomatoes

One of the benefits of having beans around the house is the instant meals you can fix that are healthy and satisfying. With this dish you can add some additional vegetables if the spirit moves you and certainly, you can serve this on steamed rice, brown or white.

Cooking utensil: A large non-stick skillet

1/4 cup white wine or defatted stock
2 cloves garlic, minced
1 small to medium onion
1 1/2 cups tomatoes, chopped
1 tsp. dried or 1 Tbs. fresh parsley, snipped
1 can (19 oz.) or 2 cups cannellini beans
Salt and pepper to taste

---

1. Sauté the onion and garlic in the wine or stock.
2. Add the tomatoes and parsley; simmer 5 minutes.
3. Add the beans and heat through.
4. Season to taste.
5. Serve as is or on rice.

YIELD: About 4 cups
FAT GRAMS IN ENTIRE RECIPE: 2

BTW: Some dried basil or oregano, crushed, adds a bit more gusto to the flavor.

Notes:

CANNELLINI BEAN HUMMUS

If you have a food processor, use it. If not, use a potato masher. A take-off on the hummus original which is garbanzo bean, this flavor is a bit more delicate.

Preparation utensil: A medium-sized bowl

---

1 can (19 oz.) cannellini beans, drained
1/4 cup dried basil leaves, crushed
1/4 cup dried parsley, crushed
1/2 tsp. freshly ground black pepper
4 cloves garlic, peeled
1 tsp. extra virgin olive oil
1/4 cup defatted chicken stock, as needed
Hot sauce to taste

---

1. Place beans in the food processor or mash with the masher.
2. Add all the ingredients except the broth and hot sauce; process 30 seconds, scrape sides as needed; add chicken stock to desired consistency.
3. Continue to process or mash until the hummus is smooth.
4. Season to taste with the hot sauce.

YIELD: About 2 cups
FAT GRAMS IN ENTIRE RECIPE: 7

Notes:

_____

_____

_____

_____

_____

_____

GARBANZO BEANS
(Chickpeas)

These beans date back to the Middle East and Northern Africa, in the area known as Mesopotamia. Also known as a chickpea, it came to Europe through Spain and was originally described as "ramlike" because of its resemblance to a ram's head with curling horns.

Cultivated by man since 5000 B.C., garbanzos have a texture reminiscent of water chestnuts, enjoying popularity all over Europe and the Western Hemisphere for its hearty mouthfeel and versatility. One of the most familiar dishes made with the garbanzo bean, or chickpea, is in a paste as Hummus.

1 cup dried makes 2 cups, cooked.
1 cup of cooked chick peas is 2 to 3 grams of fat.

These peas are very easy to use. They taste better cooked from dried beans than canned.

Soak overnight. Rinse. Cook for 1 hour.
If using canned beans, rinse well and refrigerate for a few hours or overnight to freshen the taste.

JOAN'S HUMMUS DIP

If you've ever had Hummus prepared in the original manner in a Lebanese or Syrian restaurant, you're aware of the amount of tahini (sesame butter) that's used. Since 2 tablespoons of tahini is 16 fat grams. Joan converted the recipe for us. You can make the hummus and refrigerate it in a large bowl, tightly covered, for up to three days.

Preparation utensil: A food processor

---

2 cans (15 1/2 oz. each) chickpeas
4 garlic cloves
1 Tbs. fat free mayonnaise
1 Tbs. cumin
1/2 Tbs. fresh lemon juice
1/4 cup vegetable broth, divided
Hot sauce to taste
Toasted fat free pita triangles

---

1. Place the chickpeas in the food processor or use a masher.
2. Add the garlic, mayonnaise, cumin and lemon juice.
3. Add about 1 Tbs. of the broth and process or mash; if too thick, add some broth, a bit at a time, to approximate a paste.
4. Add a shake of hot sauce and adjust taste with more if desired.
5. Cut 4 pita breads in quarters and toast until crispy.
6. Serve the hummus in a small bowl set on a larger plate; place pita triangles around the hummus.
7. To toast the pita: separate the pita into two rounds. Cut each round into quarters. Place on ungreased cookie sheet. Bake at 350° about 10 to 15 minutes or until golden.

YIELD: About 3 cups
FAT GRAMS OF ENTIRE RECIPE: 6

Notes:

_____

_____

CHICKPEA MACARONI

Here again the beans are cooked right along with the pasta. A delightful, filling meal in a dish.

Cooking utensil: A 6 quart non-stick pot

1/4 cup white wine or defatted stock
1 medium onion, chopped
1 tsp. garlic, minced
1 can (16 oz.) tomatoes with juice
2 cups chickpeas (garbanzo beans), cooked or canned, drained
3 cups large shell macaroni, cooked
2 Tbs. fresh parsley, chopped
1 tsp. ground cumin
Salt and pepper to taste

1. Sauté the onion and garlic in the wine or stock until tender.
2. Add the tomatoes and the chickpeas, breaking up the tomatoes with a spoon.
3. Simmer, uncovered for 10 minutes.
4. Add macaroni; mix through.
5. Add seasonings and simmer an additional 4 to 5 minutes.

YIELD: 8 cups
FAT GRAMS IN ENTIRE RECIPE: 3

Notes:

AUNT ROSE'S MINESTRONE

Everyone has an Aunt Rose. Well, ours is wonderful, bless her, and wherever she goes everyone begs her to fix this soup. It's easy and you'll love her, too, after you taste it.

Cooking utensil: An 8 quart non-stick pot

1/4 cup white wine or defatted stock
1 large onion, chopped
2 ribs celery, sliced
1/4 head cabbage, shredded
2 cans (15 oz. ea.) stewed tomatoes
1 tsp. dried mixed Italian seasonings
1 can (10 1/2 oz.) garbanzo beans, with liquid
1 can (7 oz.) whole kernel corn, with liquid
2 zucchini, sliced
1 1/2 tsp. chicken bouillon granules
1/2 tsp. dried basil, crushed
1 1/2 cups defatted chicken stock, additional
3/4 cup small, eggless pasta

---

1. Sauté the onion, celery and cabbage in the wine or stock for 3 to 4 minutes.
2. Add all remaining ingredients, except the pasta.
3. Bring to a boil; reduce to a simmer and cook for 30 minutes, stirring occasionally.
4. Add the pasta and cook for about 8 minutes or until the pasta is done.

YIELD: About 8 to 10 cups
FAT GRAMS IN ENTIRE RECIPE: 2

Notes:

_____

_____

_____

KIDNEY BEANS

1 cup dried makes 2 1/4 cups cooked.
1 cup, cooked, delivers a little over 1 gram of fat.

There are two kinds of kidney beans, the white called Cannellini, and the red. The red are either dark or light red and are the beans of the red beans 'n rice our Cajun brethren in Louisiana are famous for. These beans are the beans of our Texas Chili and are great thrown into a salad.

There are so many uses for this colorful bean. It was first cultivated 7000 years ago in Mexico, for which we give our neighbors to the south a hearty "Thank you!" It took thousands of years before the Europeans were exposed to the kidney bean when the Spanish explorers brought it back to the continent.

Get to know the kidney bean in dishes other than those you automatically think of, setting the flavor off with rice. We always keep a couple of cans available in the pantry for adding to salads, soups, stews and other bean dishes. The firmness of this bean, along with its wonderful, robust flavor, is what makes it a natural add-on.

SPICY BAKED BEANS

This recipe is a cross between a baked bean and a chili bean dish.

Baking utensil: A 4 quart oven-proof casserole

---

2 cans (15 oz. ea.) dark red kidney beans
1 can (16 oz.) black beans
1 can (16 oz.) white kidney beans
1 large can (28 oz.) plum tomatoes, drained and chopped
1 large onion, chopped
3 cloves garlic, minced
1/4 cup dark molasses
1/4 cup cider vinegar
2 Tbs. light honey
2 tsp. dried oregano, crushed
2 tsp. dry mustard
2 tsp. ground cumin
1 1/2 tsp. ground ginger
1 tsp. chili powder
1/8 tsp. red pepper flakes
Salt to taste

Preheat oven to 350°

1. Remove the beans from the cans, rinse and drain.
2. Place all ingredients in an oven-proof casserole dish; gently toss to mix without breaking up the beans.
3. Bake, covered, for 45 minutes.
4. Remove cover; stir and bake, uncovered, for an additional 30 minutes, or until hot and bubbly.

YIELD: About 12 cups
FAT GRAMS IN ENTIRE RECIPE: 10

Notes:

VEGETARIAN CHILI

We've fixed up this chili for many a meat-lover and they had to admit they didn't miss the meat! It takes time to cut up all these vegetables, but it cooks itself after the cleaning and the chopping is finished. You'll have lots to freeze for those no-time-to-make-dinner nights.

Cooking utensil: An 8 quart non-stick pot

1/4 cup white wine or defatted stock
1 large onion, chopped
4 cloves garlic, minced
1/2 pound mushrooms, cut in quarters
2 cups frozen cauliflower pieces
1 large potato, peeled, chopped in 1/2 inch pieces
1 large green bell pepper, chopped
2 large carrots, chopped
3 cups frozen corn kernels
1 can (28 oz.) plum tomatoes, chopped, include juice
1 pound kidney beans, cooked or 1 large can (52 oz.)
1 cup Bloody Mary Mix or Spicy V-8 Juice
1 Tbs. ground cumin
2 Tbs. chili powder
1 tsp. paprika 1/2 tsp. salt
1/8 tsp. ground red pepper
2 Tbs. tomato paste
3 Tbs. dry red wine

1. Sauté the onion and garlic in the wine or stock for about 5 minutes.
2. Add mushrooms and cook for 10 minutes.
3. Stir in all additional ingredients and bring to a boil.
4. Reduce to simmer; cover and cook for about 30 minutes or until the veggies are done.

YIELD: About 12 cups
FAT GRAMS IN ENTIRE RECIPE: 6

BTW: This chili is delicious all by itself or you can eat it on Red Rice. Shredded fat free cheddar is good sprinkled on top, too.

DAVID'S FAMOUS CHILI

There's something brilliant about loving food and loving a guy who is a great cook. I'm brilliant because my David is the *greatest cook*! This little gem is David's and he's wowed them all over D.C. with this chili.

Cooking utensil: An 8 quart non-stick pot

1/4 cup white wine or defatted stock
2 large onions, coarsely chopped
2 pounds butcher-ground turkey breast
4 cans (16 oz. ea.) whole tomatoes with juice, chopped
1/2 cup tomato sauce
1 package Wick Fowler's 2-Alarm Chili Kit
1 jumbo can (64 oz.) red kidney beans, drained and rinsed

---

1. Sauté the onion in the wine or stock until translucent.
2. Add the turkey; cook over medium-high heat, breaking up the meat, until all the meat is browned and no pink color remains.
3. Add the tomatoes, the tomato sauce and the seasonings from the chili kit; adjust the red pepper packet to taste, using it all if you like it *medium hot*; omit the masa flour if you like your chili juicy. The masa will thicken up the chili.
4. Simmer, covered, for 45 minutes, stirring occasionally.
5. Add the kidney beans; cover, simmer 45 minutes more, stirring occasionally.
6. Serve at once.

YIELD: About 14 cups
FAT GRAMS IN ENTIRE RECIPE: 40

BTW: If you use regular tube-packaged ground turkey: after browning the meat, drain it well, rinse with hot water, and then drain again. Be sure to add about 18 to 20 additional grams of fat if this is the turkey you choose. If you don't drain at all, add 32 grams to the 40 indicated above. This chili is delicious without the turkey if you like to go without. The fat gram count is then down to 10.

Notes:

JUDY'S RED BEANS AND RICE

This is it! Judy Walz, thank you for this recipe. It's a taste of Louisiana without the air fare.

Cooking utensil: An 8 to 10 quart non-stick pot

---

2 pounds dried red kidney beans, presoaked overnight
2 cups onions, chopped
1/2 cup green onion tops, thinly sliced
4 tsp. garlic, minced
2 Tbs. fresh parsley, minced
1/8 tsp. cayenne pepper or to taste
1/2 tsp. black pepper or to taste
2 bay leaves
1/2 tsp. dried thyme leaves, crushed
1/8 tsp. dried basil, crushed
1 Tbs. liquid smoke
1/2 cup celery tops, chopped
1 Tbs. salt or to taste
Steamed rice, cooked without oil or margarine

---

1. Drain the beans; combine with all other ingredients, except the salt, in a heavy 8 to 10 quart pot.
2. Add cold water just to cover.
3. Bring to a boil over high heat; lower heat and simmer, uncovered, 2 1/2 to 3 hours, or until the beans are tender and a thick red gravy has developed.
4. Check from time to time and add water so that the beans don't dry out.
5. Salt to taste.
6. Serve over steamed rice.

YIELD: 12 cups beans
FAT GRAMS IN ENTIRE RECIPE: 12

BTW: Serve this with crusty French bread and watch these beans disappear.

Notes:

THE ALASKAN THREE BEAN SOUP

This soup is unbelievably delicious and filling. If you are using canned beans you'll have some beans left to throw into a salad. This recipe makes a big pot, but don't let that scare you. It freezes beautifully for a quickie dinner with just a bit of time in the microwave. Have some crusty French bread or sourdough bread handy to eat with this soup. It's a peasant's delight.

Cooking utensils: An 8 quart non-stick pot, a non-stick skillet and a blender or food processor

---

1/2 cup white wine or defatted stock
3 cups onion, chopped
2 ribs celery, chopped
3 cloves garlic, minced
6 sprigs fresh parsley
1 1/2 tsp. dried thyme, crushed
2 bay leaves
6 cups defatted chicken stock
1/2 cup navy beans, cooked or canned
1/2 cup black beans, cooked or canned
1/2 cup red kidney beans, cooked or canned
1/2 cup barley
1 green bell pepper, chopped
1 red bell pepper, chopped
2 tsp. olive oil
1 1/2 tsp. liquid smoke
3 Tbs. sherry
Salt and pepper to taste

---

1. Place the onion, carrot, celery and garlic in a large pot with 1/2 cup wine or stock and cook over low heat until the vegetables are tender, about 20 minutes.
2. Add the parsley, thyme and the bay leaves, along with the stock,
3. Drain the beans and add along with the barley to the pot.
4. Bring to a boil; reduce the heat and simmer, partially covered, for 40 minutes.
5. Pour the soup through a strainer and reserve the stock.
6. Discard the bay leaves and parsley.
7. Remove about 25% of the bean and veggie mixture, along with 1 cup

stock and purée in a blender or food processor.

8. Return the purée to the reserved stock and add the extra chicken stock gradually, until it reaches the consistency you want.

9. Now return the rest of the beans and vegetables to the pot of soup.

10. Sauté the green and red bell peppers in the olive oil in a separate skillet, about 10 minutes; add to the soup with a slotted spoon.

11. Add the liquid smoke and the sherry; simmer for about 20 minutes.

YIELD: About 12 cups
FAT GRAMS IN ENTIRE RECIPE: 15

BTW: It is a labor-intensive soup but it can be prepared ahead of time for guests. You can leave the last 2 steps (steps 10 and 11) until the last minute and enjoy a glass of sherry with your guests while you're waiting for the last 20 minutes of cooking.

Notes:

LENTILS

1 cup dried makes 1 2/3 cups cooked.
1 cup cooked lentils will bring about 1 gram of fat to your table.

Lentils are available in red, yellow and the familiar brown. They are easy to prepare since they require no presoaking. Use them in soup, with rice, with noodles, and anytime with spinach.

LENTILS, SPINACH AND RICE

The magic combination: lentils and spinach, here with white rice. This recipe is not as complicated as it looks.

Cooking utensil: An 8 quart non-stick pot

1/4 cup white wine or defatted stock
1 large onion, chopped
1 rib celery, sliced diagonally
2 cloves garlic, minced
1/2 tsp. extra virgin olive oil
1 cup lentils, picked, rinsed, uncooked
4 cups defatted chicken stock, additional
1/2 cup white rice, uncooked
2 packages (10 oz. ea.) frozen spinach, thawed
1/2 cup defatted chicken stock, additional
Salt and pepper to taste

---

1. Sauté the onion, celery and garlic in the wine or 1/4 cup stock, to which the olive oil has been added, until translucent.
2. Add the lentils and stir the mixture to coat the vegetables with the olive oil mixture. Set aside.
3. Bring the 4 cups additional stock to a boil; add to the lentil-vegetable mixture; return to boiling.
4. Reduce the heat to low; simmer, covered, for 20 minutes or until the lentils are tender.
5. Add the rice; stir and bring back to a boil; reduce heat and simmer 15 minutes.

6. Add the spinach and the additional 1/2 cup stock.
7. Cover and cook until the rice is done.
8. Season with salt and pepper to taste.

YIELD: About 6 cups
FAT GRAMS IN ENTIRE RECIPE: 4

Notes:

_____

_____

_____

_____

_____

_____

_____

_____

_____

_____

_____

_____

_____

_____

_____

_____

LENTILS WITH RICE AND CILANTRO

This dish is Middle Eastern in flavor. Very simple to prepare, with a salad...it's dinner.

Cooking utensil: A 3 quart non-stick saucepan

---

1 cup lentils, picked, rinsed and uncooked
2 cups water
1/4 cup defatted chicken stock
2 large onions, chopped
4 large cloves garlic, minced
1 tsp. ground cumin
1 tsp. salt
1 1/2 cups long-grain white rice
Freshly ground pepper to taste
Cayenne pepper to taste
2 Tbs. fresh cilantro, chopped

---

1. Place lentils in water and bring to a boil; cover and cook over medium heat about 20 minutes or until lentils are tender.
2. Drain liquid and add enough additional water to make 3 cups. Set aside the lentils; set aside the water separately.
4. Combine the onion mixture with the lentils. Add the 3 cups liquid and bring to a boil.
3. Sauté the onion and garlic in the stock until tender; add the cumin and sauté 2 minutes.
5. Add the rice and salt; bring to a boil; cover, reduce the heat to low and cook for 20 minutes.
6. Remove cover, taste and adjust seasonings.
7. Toss with the cilantro and serve.

YIELD: About 5 cups
FAT GRAMS IN ENTIRE RECIPE: 2

Notes:

LENTILS WITH PIMIENTO AND SPINACH

An easy way to season a pot of ingredients is to add the spices in a pouch of cheesecloth, tied with a string. You can then remove the packet of herbs and spices and discard, leaving none of the bits and pieces of the seasonings in the pot. Instead, you're leaving only the flavor.

Cooking utensil: A 4 quart non-stick pot

---

4 cups water
1 small onion, chopped
1 rib celery, sliced
1/2 tsp. dried thyme leaves
1 bay leaf
1/2 tsp. whole black peppercorns
1 cup dried lentils, picked, rinsed, uncooked
3 Tbs. water, additional
3 Tbs. red wine vinegar
1/2 tsp. chicken bouillon granules
1 1/2 tsp. Dijon mustard
1 jar (4 oz.) diced pimiento, drained
1 pound fresh spinach leaves, cleaned and stemmed
1 Tbs. fresh parsley, chopped

---

1. Place the water, onion, celery and thyme in a large saucepan.
2. Place bay leaves and peppercorns in a piece of cheesecloth and tie with string; add to the saucepan.
3. Bring to a boil; reduce heat and simmer 20 minutes.
4. Add lentils; cover and cook 25 to 30 minutes, or until lentils are tender.
5. Remove and discard bay and pepper in its cheesecloth packet.
6. Stir together the additional water, vinegar, bouillon and mustard in a separate bowl.
7. Add the vinegar mixture to the lentils along with the pimiento, spinach and parsley.
4. Heat until the spinach is just wilted.

YIELD: About 6 cups
FAT GRAMS IN ENTIRE RECIPE: 3

BTW: This does well as a side dish with grilled seafood, but try it as a one-dish meal with brown rice or wide, eggless noodles, either one prepared with no oil or margarine.

GREEK LENTIL SOUP

This recipe is so easy to prepare, if you're not eating this as a one-meal dinner, you'll have time to throw some grilled chicken and Bari's Shake 'N Bake Potatoes together, and serve with some pita bread.

Cooking utensil: A 6 to 8 quart non-stick pot

2 cups lentils, picked, rinsed and uncooked
8 cups water
3/4 cup onion, chopped
1 clove garlic, minced
3/4 cup carrot, chopped
1 cup celery, chopped
1 cup potato, raw and chopped
2 bay leaves
1/2 tsp. ground cumin
Salt to taste
2 tsp. fresh lemon juice
Fat free sour cream, optional

1. Place all ingredients except the lemon juice and sour cream in a large pot; cook over medium heat until the lentils are tender, about 45 minutes.
2. Add the lemon juice and serve. A dollop of sour cream on top is the way you would do it in Greece.

YIELD: About 12 cups
FAT GRAMS IN ENTIRE RECIPE: 5

Notes:

PROGRESSO TO THE RESCUE LENTIL SOUP

Believe it or not, I'm going to tell you how to *really* make life simple. This is another one of those, "What to do, the refrigerator's empty!" recipes.

Cooking utensil: A 3 quart non-stick saucepan

---

1 can Progresso Healthy Classics Lentil Soup
1 box (10 oz.) frozen leaf spinach

---

1. Open the can of soup and pour into medium saucepan.
2. Place the frozen spinach in the microwave and cook on high for 4 minutes.
3. Add the spinach to the soup and cook on medium heat until the soup is bubbling.

YIELD: 3 cups
FAT GRAMS IN ENTIRE RECIPE: 2

BTW: Serve with heated pita bread. If you want to make this a meal, make a bed of steamed rice, cooked without any additional oil, and pour soup over the rice.

Notes:

Fish Stewed With Lentils, Peas and Beans

There are some combinations you never thought of and you just have to taste to believe. Here's one.

Cooking utensil: An 8 quart non-stick pot or non-stick wok

---

2 cups water
1/2 cup lentils, picked and rinsed
1/2 cup split peas, picked and rinsed
1 can (15 oz.) stewed tomatoes
1 small onion, minced
1/2 medium green bell pepper, minced
1 carrot, finely chopped
1 rib celery, minced
1 pound yellowfin tuna, cubed
1 can (16 oz.) great northern or navy beans with liquid
1 package (10 oz.) frozen corn kernels
Freshly ground pepper to taste

---

1. Place the water, lentils, split peas, tomatoes, onion, pepper, carrot and celery in a large pot and bring to a boil; lower heat and simmer for 25 minutes.
2. Add the fish, beans and corn; add water to cover, if necessary; cover and simmer for 15 minutes or until the lentils and peas are cooked through.
3. Season to taste with the pepper and serve.

YIELD: About 10 cups
FAT GRAMS IN ENTIRE RECIPE: 20

Notes:

LIMA BEANS

1 cup dried makes 2 cups cooked
1 cup cooked has about 1 fat gram.

Lima beans are available both fresh and dried. There are some really good frozen limas, too. This bean, with corn, was originally an American Indian dish called succotash. You've probably eaten this at one time or another and it's a perfect protein in a side dish. We'll look at that recipe first, and then go on to a more exotic lima bean dish.

SUCCOTASH

I don't know of any dish more American than succotash, even hot dogs. The Native American was preparing this dish before Columbus could spell "ocean."

Cooking utensil: A 2 quart non-stick saucepan

---

2 Tbs. prepared Butter Buds
1/3 cup onion, minced
1/3 cup celery, minced
1 package (10 oz.) frozen corn kernels
1/4 cup water
1 package (10 oz.) frozen lima beans, thawed
1 Tbs. fresh thyme or 1 tsp. dried
Salt and freshly ground pepper to taste
Pinch of cayenne pepper to taste, optional
1 Tbs. fresh parsley, minced

---

1. Heat the Butter Buds in a saucepan.
2. Add the onion and celery; sauté for about 5 minutes.
3. Add the corn and water, cover; bring to a boil.
4. Reduce heat to low and cook, stirring occasionally, until the corn is tender.
5. Add the beans, thyme, salt and peppers; cook on low until lima beans are cooked through.
6. Add the parsley and serve.

YIELD: 3 cups
FAT GRAMS IN ENTIRE RECIPE: 2

LIMA BEANS AND SMOKED TURKEY

Although usually prepared with ham, we think you'll find this a suitable, and delicious, substitute. You're saving about 5 grams of fat in the recipe.

Cooking utensils: A medium-sized non-stick skillet, a saucepan or microwave dish for cooking the frozen lima beans

1 package (10 oz.) baby lima beans, cooked
1/4 cup defatted chicken stock
1 large onion, sliced
2 cloves garlic, minced
1/4 cup fresh cilantro, chopped
1 small carrot, thinly sliced
3/4 cup defatted chicken or vegetable stock, additional
4 ounces smoked turkey, sliced
Salt and pepper to taste

1. Cook the lima beans according to package directions. Set aside.
2. Cut the onion in half and slice. Place with 1/4 cup stock and garlic in a medium saucepan and sauté until tender.
3. Add cilantro, carrot and 1/2 cup additional stock; bring to a boil; reduce heat, cover, and cook for about 8 minutes.
4. Add beans and turkey; heat through. Season to taste.

YIELD: 3 cups
FAT GRAMS IN ENTIRE RECIPE: 3

Notes:

BAKED LIMA BEANS

This fantastic recipe comes from the Cape May, New Jersey Lima Bean Festival with a bunch of conversion work to cut the fat.

Cooking utensils: A 3 quart saucepan, a large non-stick skillet and a shallow baking dish, 9 x 9 or 8 x 13

---

1 pound dried baby lima beans, presoaked overnight
6 cups water
2 bay leaves
6 slices turkey bacon, divided
1/4 cup wine
1 cup celery, chopped
2/3 cup onion, chopped
1/2 cup green bell pepper, chopped
2/3 cup fresh cilantro, minced
1 clove garlic, minced
1 cup ketchup
2/3 cup light molasses
1 tsp. dried mustard
1 tsp. chili powder
1 tsp. ground cumin
1 tsp. salt
Ground pepper to taste
1/8 tsp. cayenne pepper to taste

Preheat the oven to 325°

1. Drain the beans; transfer them to a heavy saucepan and add the 6 cups water and the bay leaves.
2. Bring to a boil; reduce heat to simmer; cook, uncovered, for 30 minutes or until the beans are tender. Skim off any foam that forms on top.
3. Brown 2 slices of the turkey bacon in the skillet over medium heat. When cooked, crumble and set aside.
4. Add the wine to the skillet along with the celery, onion, bell pepper, cilantro and garlic. Cook over medium heat, stirring often, until the veg etables are tender.
5. Drain all but 2 1/2 cups liquid from the beans. Toss out the bay leaves.

6. Gently stir in the crumbled bacon, onion mixture and add the ketchup, molasses, mustard, chili powder and other seasonings.
7. Place the bean mixture in the baking dish; place the remaining bacon slices on top and bake, uncovered, for 1 1/2 hours.
9. Remove from the oven. Wait about 15 minutes for the flavors to meld and serve.

YIELD: About 8 cups
FAT GRAMS IN ENTIRE RECIPE: 10

BTW: It's not the easiest recipe in this book, but it's one of those that is worth the time. A salad on the side and you'll be in heaven!

Notes:

Bean Casserole With Chicken Links

This recipe calls for sausage and we've found a really tasty chicken sausage made by Bilinski. They've got a few different flavors and we're using the Chicken & Sundried Tomato Sausage with Basil for this recipe to take the place of Italian sweet sausage. It does the trick.

Cooking utensils: A non-stick skillet and a 5 quart oven-proof casserole

---

4 links Bilinski's Chicken & Sundried Tomato Sausage with Basil
1 can (16 oz.) vegetarian baked beans, undrained
1/2 cup spicy barbecue sauce
1 can (16 oz.) red kidney beans, undrained
1 can (16 oz.) white kidney beans, drained
1 can (16 oz.) butter beans, drained
1 can (16 oz.) hot chili beans, undrained
1 can (16 oz.) lima beans, drained
1 can (10 3/4 oz.) condensed tomato soup, undiluted
3 oz. tomato paste
1/2 cup brown sugar or to taste

Preheat oven to 325°

1. Slice the sausage in 1/2 inch thick slices.
2. Brown in a skillet and drain.
3. Combine with all other ingredients in a 5-quart casserole or a small roasting pan.
4. Bake for 1 1/2 hours. Can be served hot or cold.

YIELD: About 16 cups
FAT GRAMS IN ENTIRE RECIPE: 30

BTW: If you have a problem finding these sausages, call Bilinski at 800-3-EATWELL (800-332-8935)

Notes:

NAVY BEANS

1 cup dried makes 2 2/3 cups cooked.
1 cup cooked beans gives you about 1 gram of fat.

Also known as Great Northern, these are medium-sized white beans and are great to have in the freezer for those quickie defrosts for soup or salad.

CROCK POT BAKED BEANS

We usually make a crock pot full of these beans and then eat on them for a week or so, with corn and salad, on rice, with grilled chicken or turkey sausage. I've even thrown them into a salad.

And they're great with a bagel at breakfast! The recipe is from Cynthia May. Thank you, Cynthia.

Cooking utensil: A crock pot

---

1 pound dried navy beans, presoaked
1 small onion, diced
2 cloves garlic, minced
1/2 cup molasses
1/3 cup ketchup
1/4 cup firmly packed brown sugar
3 Tbs. maple syrup
2 Tbs. dry mustard
1/4 cup Worcestershire sauce
1 tsp. paprika
1/2 tsp. ground cloves
1 Tbs. liquid smoke
1/8 tsp. ground red pepper
4 cups water
Salt to taste

---

1. Drain and rinse the beans and place them in a crock pot and cover with water to about 1/2 inch above the beans.

2. Add all the remaining ingredients and mix gently.
3. Put the crock pot on high for 2 hours.
4. Turn to medium and let the beans cook overnight, or while you're at work, all day.
5. Season to taste.

YIELD: About 8 cups
FAT GRAMS IN ENTIRE RECIPE: 8

Notes:

SALAD WITH BEANS

Preparation utensil: A large bowl

3 cups cooked beans (navy, kidney, cannellini, garbanzo, black)
1 purple onion or Vidalia onion, thinly sliced
1 green bell pepper, sliced
1 Tbs. fresh basil, chopped
1 Tbs. fresh rosemary or thyme, chopped
2 Tbs. fresh parsley, chopped
2 cups brown rice, cooked
1 clove garlic, mashed
3 Tbs. red wine vinegar
4 Roma tomatoes, quartered
6 cups, Romaine lettuce, cleaned and torn
1/2 cup fat free Italian dressing
1/2 cup fat free grated Parmesan

1. Toss all the ingredients together except the tomatoes and the lettuce.
2. Just before serving, toss in the tomatoes and lettuce or fill bowls with lettuce, place tossed ingredients in the bowls and top with the tomatoes.

YIELD: About 12 cups
FAT GRAMS IN ENTIRE RECIPE: 5

Notes:

NAVY BEAN SOUP

Thank goodness for soup on a cold winter's eve. Here's one we enjoy with a pita pocket of steamed veggies with shredded cheddar.

Cooking utensil: An 8 quart non-stick pot

---

2 cups presoaked navy beans
8 cups water
1/2 tsp. black pepper
1 bay leaf
1/2 tsp. salt
2 cups celery, chopped
1 cup carrots, chopped
1 cup onion, chopped
1/2 tsp. garlic powder
1/4 cup fresh parsley, chopped
1 can (8 oz.) tomato sauce
Dash ground cloves, optional

---

1. Add the water to the drained, rinsed beans, along with the pepper and bay leaf.
2. Bring to a boil; reduce to a simmer and cook for about 2 hours or until the beans are tender.
3. Add the salt and the rest of the ingredients; simmer for 1 hour.
4. Mash some of the beans to thicken the soup and simmer for 1 hour more.

YIELD: About 12 cups
FAT GRAMS IN ENTIRE RECIPE: 7

Notes:

Bean With Garlic Soup

When preparing these recipes or for that matter, most recipes, you can substitute dried herbs for fresh (in this recipe sub 2 tsp. dried basil, crushed, for the 2 Tbs. fresh), and white kidney for navy beans.

Cooking utensil: An 8 quart non-stick pot

1/4 cup white wine or defatted stock
1 onion, chopped
6 garlic cloves, minced
4 carrots, chopped
2 ribs celery, chopped
2 quarts water
1 can (15 or 16 oz.) stewed tomatoes
1/4 tsp. dried thyme leaves, crushed
3 cups navy beans, cooked or canned and drained
1 package (10 Oz.) frozen French-cut green beans, thawed
2 Tbs. fresh basil, minced
Granulated chicken bouillon to taste
Freshly ground pepper to taste

1. In a large pot sauté the onion, garlic, carrots and celery in the wine or stock until tender.
2. Add the water, tomatoes and thyme; bring liquid to a boil; reduce to simmer; cook for 30 minutes, uncovered.
3. Add the beans, basil, bouillon and pepper; for a thicker soup mash about 1 cup of the beans and return to the soup.

YIELD: 14 cups
FAT GRAMS IN ENTIRE RECIPE: 6

Notes:

_____

_____

_____

BEAN, BARLEY AND CARROT STEW

Navy beans and barley are a natural. Add carrots and the ease of throwing this stew together and you've got a winner.

Cooking utensil: An 8 quart non-stick pot

---

1 cup lentils, cooked
3 cups navy beans, cooked
2 cups onion, chopped
1 tsp. garlic, chopped
2 cups celery, chopped
5 cups carrots, in chunks
1/4 cup brown sugar
1 cup barley
2 bay leaves
1/2 cup dry red wine
1 quart V8 juice
2 cups water
2 tsp. freshly ground pepper or to taste
Louisiana hot sauce

---

1. Combine all ingredients in the pot; cook over medium heat for 2 hours.
2. Season to taste and serve.

YIELD: About 12 cups
FAT GRAMS IN ENTIRE RECIPE: 4

BTW: As so many other recipes for soup or stew, this can be prepared in the crock pot. Instead of 2 hours it cooks for 8 to 10 hours in the crock pot on medium or low heat, 5 to 5 hours on high. There's quite a bit of liquid with this stew so we like it with a base of brown rice in the bowl. The stew is sweet as a result of the brown sugar. If you prefer a spicier stew, omit the sugar and add 1/2 tsp. each, oregano leaf and thyme leaf.

Notes:

PINTO BEANS

1 cup dried makes 2 2/3 cups cooked.
1 cup pinto beans, cooked, delivers about 1 gram of fat.

The pinto bean got its name from the painted ponies which their markings resemble. A bit smaller than the kidney, this creamy-colored bean is the basic bean of Tex-Mex food.

JIM'S BEANS

I promised earlier in the book that you'd get a chance to see some of Jim's country cookin'. These beans are easy to make, freeze beautifully and you can't beat them with Red Rice and corn, either on-the-cob or kernels.

Cooking utensil: An 8 quart non-stick pot

---

8 cups pinto beans, presoaked and cooked, with liquid
1 large onion, chopped
1 green bell pepper, chopped
1/4 to 1/2 cup pickled jalapeño peppers, sliced, optional
1 can (14 1/2 oz.) whole or stewed tomatoes, with juice
1 Tbs. liquid smoke
Salt and pepper to taste
Louisiana hot sauce or salsa to taste

---

1. Place beans with the liquid in which they were cooked, along with all the other ingredients, in the pot.
2. Cook over medium-low heat for 1 1/2 hours.
3. Adjust seasonings to taste.

YIELD: About 12 cups
FAT GRAMS IN ENTIRE RECIPE: 4

BTW: These beans are great on brown rice, white rice or Red Rice. Try them in a pita pocket with some salsa.

Quick Chili Beans

I can't tell you how many times these beans have been prepared for workshops I've done, alongside the Red Rice, Chili Con Queso and Old El Paso Thick and Chunky Salsa, with Utz Baked Corn Chips. They're usually served buffet-style, and they usually disappear. No one can believe this Tex-Mex food is virtually fat free.

Cooking utensil: A 3 quart non-stick saucepan

---

2 cans (15 oz. ea.) Old El Paso Mexe-Beans
1 medium onion, in half and sliced
1 medium green bell pepper, in half and sliced
1/2 can (14 1/2 oz.) diced tomatoes

---

1. Combine all ingredients in the saucepan.
2. Cook until onion and green bell pepper are tender.

YIELD: About 4 cups
FAT GRAMS IN ENTIRE RECIPE: 4

BTW: These beans, like Jim's Beans, are really good stuffed in a pita pocket with some of the rice, grated fat free cheddar and salsa.

Notes:

_____

_____

_____

_____

_____

_____

_____

_____

REFRIED BEANS

This is a wonderful way to use up leftover Jim's Beans or Quick Chili Beans. In fact, they are so much a part of Tex-Mex fare that they are sometimes served for burrito stuffing when they're not even leftover.

Cooking utensil: A non-stick skillet

Olive Oil Pam
1 small onion, minced
1 tsp. garlic, minced
2 cups Jim's Beans or Quick Chili Beans, mashed

1. Spray Pam on the skillet, sparingly.
2. Sauté onion and garlic until soft.
3. Place beans in blender with the onion and garlic and purée.
4. Heat in a skillet or microwave.

YIELD: About 2 cups
FAT GRAMS IN ENTIRE RECIPE: 2

BTW: Serve these refried beans with any of your favorite Tex-Mex fixings.

Notes:

SPLIT PEAS

1 cup dried makes 1 1/2 cups cooked.
1 cup, cooked, is less than 1 gram of fat.

These peas are available in yellow or the familiar green. They are known for soup-making. They require no presoaking.

SPLIT PEA SOUP

You always thought a good pea soup had to have ham, or at least a ham bone, cooked in it for flavor. Wait till you taste this one, without the ham. You'll never miss it!

Cooking utensils: A 3 quart non-stick saucepan, a 6 or 8 quart non-stick pot and a blender or food processor

---

1 pound dry green split peas
5 cups water
4 bay leaves
1 cup onion, chopped
1/2 cup dry white wine
2 cloves garlic, minced
1 tsp. dried thyme, crushed
1/2 tsp. dried rosemary, crushed
1 cup carrots, chopped
1 cup celery, chopped
1 cup red bell pepper, chopped
1/2 cup vegetable stock or bouillon
1 Tbs. fresh basil, chopped or 1 tsp. dried, crushed
Salt and freshly ground black pepper to taste

---

1. Place the peas in the water with the bay leaves in the saucepan; cook until most of the water has been absorbed, about 45 minutes.
2. While that's cooking, in a large pot, sauté the onion in the wine along with the garlic, thyme, rosemary and some of the freshly ground pepper.
3. When the onion is tender, add the carrots and celery.
4. Continue to cook until all the vegetables are tender; add the red bell pep-

per and cook for 2 to 3 minutes. Turn off the heat and set aside.
5. When the peas are cooked, remove the bay leaves and run the peas through the blender or food processor.
6. Combine the peas with the other vegetables in the pot and stir; add the stock gradually, until you reach the consistency most pleasing to you. Some like a thicker soup than others.
7. Add the basil, then salt and pepper to taste.

YIELD: About 8 cups
FAT GRAMS IN ENTIRE RECIPE: 4

BTW: If the little chunks of ham are terribly important to you, chop some smoked turkey breast, at 1 gram for 4 ounces, and add it to the soup.

Notes:

_____

_____

_____

_____

_____

_____

_____

_____

_____

_____

_____

_____

_____

_____

GRAINS

Amber waves. Is there anything more American than a picture of our magnificent mid-west? The Great Plains, covered in gold. The breadbasket, we call it. And most of us, when we think of grains think first of wheat! Barley, oats, rye, buckwheat, corn, rice, quinoa, couscous...these are grains, too.

As you proceed into the land of low fat, the protein that you'll acquire in your daily mini-meals will come more from grains and beans than from the flesh foods with which you may have previously satisfied this need. There is nothing new in this. The human animal, in many parts of the world and in different eras throughout our time on earth, has turned to rice and beans or corn and beans to survive. Perhaps there is an important message here. There was a time when the more abundant physique was desirable since it indicated affluence. The poor could not afford to eat enough to become overweight. Nowadays the slim are the beautiful...that precious time that the poor can ill afford, today, is spent in a fitness or athletic club. And the tight, firm physiques have turned back to the grains and legumes to feed the body and the soul.

The grains that we'll be using in our recipes will include the more convenient to incorporate into meals, since we won't be getting into grinding and milling our own. That means the wonder of barley, corn, rice, couscous, pastas in some of their glorious incarnations will be at your fingertips in the next pages. We'll be using the prepared, packaged products since we won't be making our own pasta, or baking our own bread...not in this book, anyway. We'll save that for another time. But we will touch on some of the more interesting products.

BARLEY

1 cup dry makes about 3 to 3 1/4 cups cooked.
1 cup, cooked, is less than 1 gram of fat.

The kind of barley we're used to cooking with in this country is the pearled barley. Barley is chewy, has a nutty flavor and it's most common in soups, usually with mushrooms. It's a good source of protein.

BARLEY SOUP

Everyone has a recipe for barley soup. See how this one measures up.

Cooking utensil: A 3 quart non-stick saucepan

1/4 cup pearl barley
6 cups water
1 cup carrots, sliced
1/2 cup celery, diced
1/2 cup onions, chopped
2 cups canned tomatoes, chopped with juice
1 cup peas
Salt and freshly ground pepper to taste

---

1. Cook barley in water for 1 hour.
2. Add remaining ingredients; simmer about 30 to 45 minutes, until the vegetables are tender and the flavors have blended.

YIELD: 8 cups
FAT GRAMS IN ENTIRE RECIPE: 2

Notes:

MUSHROOM BARLEY CASSEROLE

This is a throw-together kind of dinner. Change the veggies to utilize whatever you have on hand or whatever your favorites are.

Cooking utensils: A non-stick skillet and a 1 1/2 quart oven-proof casserole

---

1 Tbs. Fleischmann's Fat Free Low Calorie squeeze margarine
2 cups mushrooms, thickly sliced
3/4 cup pearl barley, uncooked
1 small onion, chopped
2 Tbs. fresh parsley, chopped
1 medium zucchini, thinly sliced
1 small carrot, shredded
1 3/4 cup defatted chicken stock
Salt and pepper to taste

Preheat oven to 350°

1. Heat the margarine in a skillet; add the mushrooms, barley, onion and parsley; sauté until the barley is browning.
2. Place this mixture with the zucchini and carrot in a small casserole.
3. Boil the stock; add the stock to the casserole; mix gently; season to taste.
4. Bake for 45 minutes or until barley is tender and the liquid has been absorbed.

YIELD: 5 cups
FAT GRAMS IN ENTIRE RECIPE: 4

Notes:

BRAN

Everyone talks about the necessity of eating bran and there is the feeling that if it's bran, it's good for you. Prepared correctly, this is so. But what about the cereals that include bran along with a bunch of sugar, seeds and nuts, introducing the extra calories and fat we don't need? The bran is the part of the grain just under the outer hull. By consuming the bran along with the rest of the grain we are consuming all the nourishment the grain has to offer. Be wary, however of bran products baked in stores which offer nutritional labels, many of which are far from the truth. Because it has a label claiming to be low or no fat, doesn't necessarily mean the product really is. Carry your own bran muffins with you whenever possible and you avoid this problem.

RAISIN BRAN MUFFINS

Carrying your own bran muffins with you makes sense. The heartiness of this muffin is just like the muffins that have 10 to 25 grams of fat.

Baking utensil: Jumbo muffin tin (6 muffins), treated with spray-on oil

---

4 cups raisin bran or bran flakes
2 1/2 cups all purpose flour
1 1/2 cups sugar
1 tsp. salt
1/2 cup Egg Beaters
2 cups applesauce
1/2 cup liquid Butter Buds, prepared
1 cup raisins, optional addition if using raisin bran

Preheat the oven to 400°

1. Mix all dry ingredients in a large bowl.
2. Add the liquid ingredients and mix well; this may require your bare hands since you want to get all the dry ingredients blended with the liquid ingredients.
3. Place the batter into the muffin tins about 2/3 full; bake for about 20

minutes, testing with a toothpick, which should come out clean when inserted in the center of one of the muffins.

YIELD: 9 muffins
FAT GRAMS IN ENTIRE RECIPE: 3

BTW: These are my favorite bran muffins, but prepare to spend some time with your hands in the batter!

Notes:

BRAN MUFFINS WITH RAISINS AND DATES

You'll enjoy this muffin, too. A slightly different consistency and taste because of the cereal and molasses, yet both this muffin, and the muffin on the previous page, have the bran along with wonderful flavor.

Baking utensil: A jumbo muffin tin (6 muffins), treated with spray-on oil

---

1 cup all-purpose flour
2 cups Nabisco 100% All Bran
1/4 cup corn meal
1/2 tsp. salt
1/3 cup non-fat powdered milk
1 cup water
1 tsp. baking soda
1/4 cup Egg Beaters
1/2 cup molasses
2 Tbs. dates, chopped
2/3 cup raisins

Preheat oven to 325°

1. Combine all ingredients.
2. Spoon into the muffins tins; bake for about 25 to 35 minutes, or until a toothpick, inserted into the center of one of the muffins, comes out clean.

YIELD: 6 muffins
FAT GRAMS IN ENTIRE RECIPE: 5

BTW: For an interesting, tart flavor, add some dried cranberries!

Notes:

BUCKWHEAT GROATS

1 cup dried makes 2 cups cooked.
1 cup groats is about 1 gram of fat.

Also known as kasha, these kernels of wheat are an interesting change of pace. We have one recipe for you. See what you think of it.

KASHA WITH MUSHROOMS AND WATER CHESTNUTS

Kasha is a favorite dish in areas of eastern Europe. If you've never tried groats, here's an opportunity.

Cooking utensils: 2 non-stick skillets, large and small

---

1 1/2 buckwheat groats
1/4 cup Egg Beaters
3 cups boiling water
1/4 cup defatted chicken stock
1 small onion, chopped
1 clove garlic minced
6 mushrooms, sliced
1 Tbs. dry sherry
2 ribs celery, chopped
1/2 small can water chestnuts, drained
Salt and freshly ground pepper to taste

---

1. Mix the groats with the egg and stir together to coat.
2. Heat a heavy, dry non-stick skillet and add the groats mixture.
3. Stir over a medium heat until all the Egg Beater is absorbed and the groats are beginning to toast.
4. Add the boiling water; bring the mixture bake to a boil; reduce the heat, cover, and simmer 20 minutes or until all the liquid is absorbed.
5. In the meantime, sauté the onion and garlic in the stock until the onion softens.

6. Add the mushrooms and the sherry and sauté for 3 minutes.
7. Add the celery and water chestnuts and sauté for 2 minutes.
8. Add the kasha and cook another 3 minutes.
9. Season to taste with salt and pepper.

YIELD: 5 to 6 cups
FAT GRAMS IN ENTIRE RECIPE: 9

Notes:

Corn

We usually forget that corn is a grain because we have become so accustomed to eating this grain as a vegetable. We 're not going to talk much about corn-on-the-cob because whether you grill it, steam it, or boil it, when you want to put butter on it, use I Can't Believe It's Not Butter Spray, or Fleischmann's Fat Free Low Calorie squeeze margarine. It will give you just as much bang for the buck and save you a load of fat grams. Remember that butter (the real thing) is 11 grams of fat per tablespoon.

1 cup of corn kernels delivers 1 gram of fat.

Air popping pop corn is the way to go if you want that addictive nosh. It's so healthy when prepared properly with a few sprays of Weight Watchers Buttery Spray or add McCormick's Imitation butter flavor to water in your own spray bottle and have at it. No fat to speak of and more fiber than whole wheat!

Boiled Corn-On-The-Cob

Corn-on-the-cob is delicious when just-picked. This is a summertime favorite for just about everyone.

Cooking utensil: A 3 quart saucepan

---

4 ears of corn
Boiling water, lightly salted

Place the ears of corn in the boiling water; cook over high heat until the kernels are tender, about 10 minutes. The older the corn, the longer it takes.

YIELD: About 3 1/2 cups kernels, if stripped
FAT GRAMS IN ENTIRE RECIPE: 5

BTW: Remember to dress these ears of corn with Molly McButter or one of the fat free margarine or butter substitutes.

CORN AND CHILI PEPPER WITH TOMATO

Here's a keen twist to an old staple with a touch of the hot stuff.

Cooking utensil: A large non-stick skillet

---

1 large onion, chopped
1/4 cup prepared Butter Buds
1 can (4 oz.) green chilies, chopped, drained
1 can (15 oz.) stewed tomatoes
3 cups corn kernels
1/2 cup fat free cheddar, shredded

---

1. Sauté the onion in the Butter Buds until tender.
2. Add the chilies and tomatoes; cook on medium heat, uncovered, for about 15 minutes.
3. Add the corn; cook 10 minutes longer.
4. Add the cheese, stirring until it begins to melt.

YIELD: 6 cups
FAT GRAMS IN ENTIRE RECIPE: 4

Notes:

CORN AND ZUCCHINI

Not only does this combination taste good, but it's a pretty picture with the yellow, green and red.

Cooking utensil: A non-stick wok

1/2 cup defatted chicken stock
1 green bell pepper, chopped
1 red bell pepper, chopped
4 medium zucchini, chopped in 1/2 inch pieces
3 cups corn kernels
2 medium cloves garlic, minced
2 green onions, chopped
Salt and freshly ground pepper to taste
Cayenne pepper or chili powder to taste

---

1. Sauté the green and red bell peppers in the stock for about 5 minutes.
2. Add the zucchini, the corn and the garlic; stir and sauté for about 10 minutes or until the zucchini is crisp-tender.
3. Add the green onion; heat through and season to taste.

YIELD: About 8 cups
FAT GRAMS IN ENTIRE RECIPE: 4

Notes:

GRITS PLUS

Cooking utensil: A 3 quart non-stick saucepan

1 package (10 oz.) frozen black-eyed peas
1 can (14 1/2 oz.) stewed tomatoes, drained, chopped
8 oz. turkey ham, cubed
1/8 tsp. cayenne pepper
1 clove garlic, minced
1/2 cup quick-cooking grits, cooked
Salt and freshly ground pepper

1. Cook the black-eyed peas according to directions; drain and leave in the saucepan.
2. Add all ingredients, except the grits; cook, uncovered over medium-low heat until heated through.
3. Add the grits; season to taste; toss well and serve.

YIELD: 5 to 6 cups
FAT GRAMS IN ENTIRE RECIPE: 10

Notes:

NACHOS

One of the greatest gifts for the inveterate nosher is this gift from our Tex-Mex repertoire. And now we can have them (almost) fat free.

Baking utensil: A non-stick baking sheet

1/2 bag (4 oz.) Utz or Tostito Baked Corn Chips
1/2 cup Quickie Chili Beans
1/2 cup Chili Con Queso Dip

Preheat oven to 375°

1. Spread chips out on the baking sheet.
2. Evenly distribute the bean mixture and then the cheese mixture on the chips.
3. Bake until cheese melts, about 5 to 7 minutes.

YIELD: 1 tray of nachos
FAT GRAMS IN ENTIRE RECIPE: 6

BTW: They'll never realize it's low fat! Serve with fat free sour cream, salsa and sliced, pickled jalapeño peppers. For Super Nachos, dress the above recipe with chopped lettuce and tomato, the salsa and peppers.

Notes:

COUSCOUS

1 cup dry makes about 2 cups cooked.
Cooked couscous has less than 1/2 gram of fat per cup.

Couscous is made from semolina flour and is most commonly purchased already cooked. All that's needed is the addition of boiling water or defatted chicken stock and you're good to go.

COUSCOUS AND BULGUR PILAF WITH VEGETABLES

The saving grace of this recipe is the time saved since both the bulgur and couscous are not cooked, they merely soak. The couscous we know is available in your supermarket. You may need to order the medium bulgur in a Middle Eastern specialty shop. If you like tabbouleh, you'll enjoy this dish.

Cooking utensils: 2 bowls, a 3 or 4 quart non-stick saucepan and a non-stick skillet

---

3/4 cup medium bulgur
2 cups instant medium grain couscous
1 cups defatted chicken stock, boiling
3 cups defatted chicken stock, boiling, additional
1/4 cup prepared Butter Buds
1 Tbs. Fleischmann's Fat Free Low Calorie squeeze margarine
I Can't Believe It's Not Butter Spray
2 cups leeks, finely chopped (white part and 1 inch of green)
6 medium carrots, finely chopped
1 cup frozen peas, thawed
Salt and freshly ground pepper to taste
3 Tbs. chives, snipped

---

1. Place the bulgur in one bowl and the couscous in another, larger bowl.
2. Pour 1 cup of the boiling stock over the bulgur; let stand for about 15 minutes or until the stock is absorbed; fluff with a fork.
3. In the meantime, add the Butter Buds and Fleischmann's to the 3 cups of

stock and bring back to a boil. Pour into the couscous; let stand 10 minutes or until the stock is absorbed; fluff with a fork.

4. Combine the bulgur with the couscous and fluff again; set aside.
5. Spray a large skillet with I Can't Believe It's Not Butter; add the leeks and carrots and sauté over medium heat until the leeks are wilted.
6. Add to the bulgur-couscous mixture along with the rest of the ingredients and toss lightly to keep the grains fluffy. Serve hot.

YIELD: About 8 cups
FAT GRAMS IN ENTIRE RECIPE: 4

Notes:

Couscous And Spinach

This is the kind of dinner you can change according to the veggies you have available in the fridge.

Cooking utensils: A bowl and a non-stick skillet

---

2 cups couscous
3 cups defatted chicken stock, boiling
1/4 cup defatted chicken stock, additional
1 medium onion, in half and then sliced
1 medium green bell pepper, in half and then sliced
1 clove garlic, minced
2 1/2 pounds fresh spinach

---

1. Add the 3 cups boiling stock to the couscous in a large bowl; let stand about 10 minutes or until the liquid is absorbed.
2. In the meantime, sauté the onion, bell pepper and garlic in the additional stock until translucent.
3. Add the spinach and cook only until wilted.
4. Toss the vegetables with the couscous and serve.

YIELD: 7 to 8 cups
FAT GRAMS IN ENTIRE RECIPE: 3

BTW: The more you use this grain, the more you'll get the hang of the fixin's you like with it.

Notes:

Couscous With Mixed Veggies

When you want a change from the rice and pasta you can throw this together in no time for a satisfying one-dish meal.

Cooking utensils: A 2 quart non-stick saucepan and a large non-stick skillet or non-stick wok

---

1 1/2 cups water
1/2 tsp. salt
1 cup couscous, uncooked
1/2 cup defatted stock
10 ounces fresh asparagus spears, cleaned, cut in 1 inch pieces
1 cup mushrooms, thickly sliced
1/2 cup green onions, finely chopped
1/2 red bell pepper, chopped
2 Tbs. fresh parsley, chopped
2 Tbs. dry white wine
1/2 tsp. dried basil, crushed
1 clove garlic, minced
1/3 to 1/2 cup fat free grated Parmesan

---

1. Boil the water with the salt added; remove the saucepan from the heat; add the couscous; let stand 5 minutes or until tender.
2. In the meantime, heat the stock in a large skillet; sauté the asparagus and all other ingredients, except the grated Parmesan, in the stock; sauté until the vegetables are crispy-tender.
3. Fluff the couscous with a fork; add the skillet mixture and grated Parmesan.
4. Toss gently and serve.

YIELD: 5 to 6 cups
FAT GRAMS IN ENTIRE RECIPE: 7

Notes:

PASTA

2 ounces dry pasta makes 1 loosely packed cup cooked.
That 1 cup of cooked pasta delivers 1 gram of fat.

Most often we think of pasta as being produced from semolina wheat but there are a variety of pastas from whole wheat to spinach and tomato based. You'll find some favorites in the boutique of pastas. The recipes here are based primarily on those that are easy to find in a local supermarket.

There are all shapes and sizes. You'll find cappellini, very thin pasta also called angel hair and linguine, a rather flat spaghetti, bowties and rigatoni, the twisted macaroni. Check the shelves at the market, pick and choose the kinds that turn you on. Most of the dry pasta runs 1 fat gram in 2 ounces which swells up to a loose cup after being cooked. When you arrive at the refrigerated section of your market, check the fat grams on the fresh pastas. They're usually much higher in fat, cook a shorter time (check the instructions) and I don't know if the taste warrants the extra fat grams. Here again, a decision for you to make. When the difference is not earth-shattering, and I can enjoy a similar flavor without the high fat, I go with a lower fat or fat free version.

Pasta should be prepared *al dente* (to the tooth), not tough but not too mushy, either. When you break the pasta to test for doneness, you should not see a white uncooked heart. We've tried the old wives' tale...throwing at the wall and if it sticks, it's ready...but it stuck even though it was hard inside. You'll soon learn how you like it. And that's the way to make it!

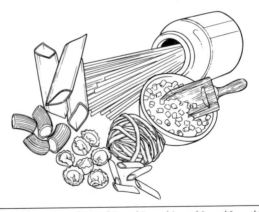

How To Cook Pasta

Cooking utensil: An 8 quart non-stick pot

1 pound pasta
4 quarts water
2 tsp. salt

1. When the water is boiling hard, place the pasta in the water. If it's a macaroni, the bubbling water will keep it separate and a stir with a spoon will be all you need. If it's spaghetti, twist it (don't break it!) as you put it in the water so the noodles separate. Although many people believe that a splash of olive oil is necessary to keep the pasta from sticking, the olive oil is definitely not needed.
2. Stir the pasta, to keep it moving, until the water is at a good rolling boil; now it won't stick together.
3. If it's thin spaghetti it will cook faster than thick noodles, so check the time recommended on the package and start checking about 2 minutes before the recommended time, to be on the safe side. 8 to 10 minutes is the norm for most pasta.
4. Have a colander in the sink, waiting for the pasta. When it's ready you want to get it out of the water, so it won't continue cooking.
5. Dump the pasta into the colander and run hot water over the pasta so the noodles won't stick together.
6. Use tongs or a pasta spoon and dish out the pasta into a bowl or onto a platter and cover with the sauce of your choice.

YIELD: About 8 cups
FAT GRAMS IN ENTIRE RECIPE: 8

Notes:

THE MARINARA SAUCE

Have you always wanted to make a "drop-dead" pasta sauce? There is no way that I can talk about pasta, or write a book with recipes in it, without including my famous marinara sauce. It has become so much a part of my own signature that friends call to tell me they found some new way of using *the marinara sauce*. I present it to you, here, and follow it with a group of modifications. You'll see it in this section of the book, in this recipe and that. It works when you're looking for a pasta sauce, a lasagna sauce or a pizza sauce. It works with chicken, seafood and vegetables. It's even a good dip for oven-baked zucchini!

Don't let the fact that it appears to have a load of ingredients scare you. It's a 15 minute preparation. The cook time is long, but we've been known to leave it on the stove on a low heat, go shopping and return to give it a stir.

Cooking utensil: An 8 quart non-stick pot

1/2 cup dry wine (red or white) or defatted stock
1 large onion, chopped
1 Tbs. garlic, minced
2 Tbs. mixed dry Italian seasonings
1 Tbs. oregano leaves, crushed
2 tsp. thyme leaves, crushed
2 Tbs. chicken bouillon granules
2 tsp. crushed red pepper flakes, optional
3 cans (16 oz. ea.) Italian plum tomatoes, broken up, with juice
2 bay leaves
2 cans (6 oz. ea.) tomato paste
1 cup water
2 cans (15 oz. ea.) tomato sauce or purée
1 to 2 tsp. sugar (white or brown)

---

1. Sauté the onion and garlic in the wine or stock with the seasonings and bouillon until the onions are tender.
2. Add the tomatoes and the bay leaves; cook on medium heat, uncovered for 20 minutes.
3. Add the tomato paste and the rest of the ingredients; simmer on low, partially covered, for 3 to 4 hours.

5. For a thicker sauce, use the purée. Add more water if you like a lighter sauce. Allow your individual taste to prevail.
6. Allow the sauce to cool, then refrigerate it overnight to give the flavors time to marry and for the sauce to thicken.

YIELD: 10 to 12 cups
FAT GRAMS IN ENTIRE RECIPE: About 4 to 5 (sauce, only)

BTW: This sauce freezes extremely well. It can freeze in heavy-duty freezer bags, Seal-A-Meal bags or Pyrex glassware. Once frozen, if it's in a plastic bag, run hot water over the bag and the sauce will pull away from the sides of the bag and remain in a large, frozen block to easily transfer to a bowl for defrosting in the microwave or a pot to heat, stove-top. We freeze it in meal-sized packages and always have some marinara, to which we can add either veggies or other goodies, for a fantastic meal in minutes.

Notes:

CHICKEN-SGHETTI

This dish is good enough for company, anytime, but it's a great low-cost meal for the family that takes no appreciable prepare-time and is almost all cook-time.

Cooking utensil: You are adding this chicken to The Marinara Sauce in its own pot

---

1 to 2 pounds chicken breasts, bone-in
The Marina Sauce, Steps 1 and 2
Fat free grated Parmesan

---

1. Remove the skin from the chicken breasts; leave in the ribs; set aside.
2. Begin preparation of The Marinara Sauce. During Step 3, after adding the tomato sauce and paste, add the chicken breasts. Then, continue with the cooking for about 2 1/2 hours.
3. Check the chicken in the sauce. If it's falling off the bone at the touch of a fork, it's ready.
4. Cool and remove the bones, especially if serving to little ones.
5. After cooling, refrigerate the sauce, with the chicken in it, and the next day, either reheat for serving, or freeze, as described in the instructions for the sauce. The sauce can be frozen with the chicken in it for a future dinner.
6. Serve with fat free grated Parmesan.

YIELD: 12 to 14 cups
FAT GRAMS IN ENTIRE RECIPE: 16 grams for each pound of skin-
     less breasts plus 4 to 5 for the sauce

BTW: When defrosting, this dish will take a bit longer to thaw because of the density of the chicken.

Notes:

SHRIMP MARINARA

You have The Marina Sauce in the freezer and unexpected company arrives! No problem! Thaw out the sauce in the microwave, and then...

Cooking utensil: A 3 quart non-stick saucepan

---

6 cups of The Marinara Sauce
1 pound large or jumbo raw shrimp, peeled and deveined
Fat free grated Parmesan

---

1. Place The Marinara Sauce in a large pot; heat on high until the sauce is rolling.
2. Add the cleaned shrimp; lower heat to medium.
3. Cook until the shrimp turn pink and start to curl. Do not overcook or the shrimp will become rubbery.
4. Serve on pasta, cooked without oil, with fat free grated Parmesan.

YIELD: 12 to 14 cups
FAT GRAMS IN ENTIRE RECIPE: 7 (excluding pasta)

BTW: If you have only 1/2 of The Marinara Sauce, use about 1/2 pound shrimp. Judge the amount of shrimp according to the quantity of sauce. I recommend freezing the sauce and adding shrimp after the sauce is thawed. If you freeze the shrimp after cooking, reheating will make the shrimp rubbery. If you're intending to use the Shrimp Marinara, always cook the shrimp in the sauce and then serve immediately.

Notes:

CLAMS IN RED SAUCE

The Marinara Sauce needs just a slight adjustment to prepare it for the clams. This is a nifty change of pace.

Cooking utensil: A 3 quart non-stick saucepan

---

6 cups of The Marinara Sauce
1 Tbs. garlic powder
2 cans (10 oz. ea.) baby clams with broth, or 4 cans (6 1/2 oz. ea.)
   chopped clams with broth
Fat free grated Parmesan

---

1. Place The Marinara Sauce in a pot and add the garlic powder; heat on medium, partially covered.
2. Separate the clams from the broth; set the broth aside.
3. Add the clams when the sauce is hot; add the broth to taste; cook to heat through.
4. Serve on pasta, cooked without oil, with fat free grated Parmesan.

YIELD: About 6 to 7 cups
FAT GRAMS IN ENTIRE RECIPE: About 5 (excluding pasta)

BTW: Now you're getting the hang of it. Almost anything goes with The Marinara Sauce. Mussels and clams in the shell (well scrubbed) are great, too. Just throw them in and when the shells open, they're ready. Discard any shells that don't open. For a Fra Diavalo (hot and spicy) sauce, add a can or two of Rotel (tomatoes with green chili peppers) to taste.

Notes:

Pasta Primavera With Sugar Snap Peas

Now here is a dandy vegetarian pasta sauce that does all you ever wanted to fill the need for hearty eating with nary a fat gram.

Cooking utensil: A non-stick wok

1/2 package Birds Eye Sugar Snap Stir-fry
1/2 cup defatted chicken broth
1/2 pound (about 8 cups) fresh spinach leaves, cleaned and stemmed
1 to 2 tsp. garlic powder to taste
1 to 2 cups of The Marinara Sauce
6 to 8 cups cooked pasta, no oil added
Fat free grated Parmesan

---

1. Place the frozen vegetables in a colander and thaw by placing under cold running water; drain; set aside.
2. Heat the stock; add the spinach; sprinkle with the garlic powder.
3. Wilt the spinach leaves (about 1 to 2 minutes) stirring the garlic through the leaves.
4. Add the drained vegetables; toss with the spinach; add The Marinara Sauce to the consistency you prefer; heat through.
5. Add the cooked pasta to the sauce and toss to cover the pasta and heat through; sprinkle with fat free grated Parmesan.

YIELD: 11 to 14 cups
FAT GRAMS IN ENTIRE RECIPE: 9 to 12 (including the pasta)

BTW: There are a few recipes that are my super-duper favorites that I must have from time to time or I miss them. This is one of those.

Notes:

LINGUINE PRIMAVERA

Here's another classic vegetable pasta dish. You'll find a number of them in these pages.

Cooking utensil: A non-stick wok

1/4 cup dry white wine
2 cans (15 oz. ea.) chopped tomatoes, with juice
4 cloves garlic, minced
1 large onion, in half and sliced
1 large green or red bell pepper (or 1/2 ea.)
2 tsp. chicken bouillon granules
2 cups mushrooms, thickly sliced
1/4 cup fresh basil, chopped
1/2 cup fresh parsley, chopped
1/2 tsp. dried thyme leaves, crushed
1/2 pound linguine, cooked (4 cups), prepared without oil
Fat free grated Parmesan

1. Place wine in the wok; drain the juice from the tomatoes and add the juice to the wine; set aside the tomatoes.
2. Heat the wine and tomato juice; add the garlic, onion, bell pepper and bouillon; sauté until crisp-tender.
3. Add the mushrooms, tomatoes and seasonings; cook on medium heat until the mushrooms are tender.
4. Serve hot on cooked linguine. Sprinkle with fat free grated Parmesan.

YIELD: 8 to 10 cups
FAT GRAMS IN ENTIRE RECIPE: 6

Notes:

_____

_____

_____

CREAMY CILANTRO AND BOW TIES

Cooking utensil: A 6 quart pot, a blender or food processor and a non-stick skillet

---

Boiling water (about 2 quarts)
1/4 pound bowtie pasta
1/4 cup fat free ricotta cheese
2 Tbs. nonfat sour cream
1/4 tsp. salt
Olive Oil Pam
2 cloves garlic, minced
Pinch crushed red pepper flakes
1 1/2 Tbs. fat free grated Parmesan

---

1. Add the bowties to the boiling water to which the salt has been added; cook until al dente; drain and set aside.
2. Combine ricotta cheese, sour cream, cilantro and salt in a blender or food processor and blend for about 30 seconds; set aside.
3. Spray Olive Oil Pam in a skillet or wok; sauté the garlic for about 1 minute; add the red pepper; add the cheese and the sour cream mixture.
4. Toss with the bowties and sprinkle with grated Parmesan.

YIELD: About 2 cups
FAT GRAMS IN ENTIRE RECIPE: 4

Notes:

WHITE CLAM SAUCE WITH SHRIMP

For years the white clam sauce was off-limits because of the huge amount of olive oil necessary to fix it. Try this recipe and see if we didn't capture the mouthfeel and the gusto. The shrimp help to buoy up the flavor.

Cooking utensil: A non-stick wok, treated with spray-on oil

1/2 pound shrimp, cleaned and deveined
Olive Oil Pam
1 tsp. garlic powder
1/2 cup defatted chicken stock
2 Tbs. fresh garlic, minced
1 can (10 oz.) whole baby clams with broth
    or 2 cans (6 1/2 oz. ea.) chopped calms with broth
1/2 cup fresh parsley, minced
2 Tbs. Fleischmann's Fat Free Low Calorie squeeze margarine
3 Tbs. fat free grated Parmesan
3 slices fat free Swiss cheese
Fat free grated Parmesan, additional

---

1. Pat the shrimp dry; place in a large non-stick pan or wok that has been sprayed with Olive Oil Pam; sprinkle with the garlic powder.
2. Sauté on high heat until the shrimp are pink on one side; flip them over and when they are pink and curling, remove the shrimp from the pan; set aside.
3. Add the stock to the pot in which the shrimp were sautéed; add the minced garlic; sauté about 2 minutes.
4. Add the clams and broth, the parsley and the margarine; simmer for about 2 to 3 minutes.
5. Add the cheeses and simmer until the cheese melts and the sauce looks somewhat creamy.
6. Serve on pasta, cooked without added oil, with fat free grated Parmesan.

YIELD: About 4 cups
**FAT GRAMS IN ENTIRE RECIPE: 6 to 8 (excluding pasta), depend-
    ing on the amount of Pam used**

BTW: As you see there are a number of ways to approximate the flavors and consistencies of a full fat dish...without the full fat!

MUSHROOM MARINARA SAUCE

Cooking utensil: A 3 quart non-stick saucepan

---

4 cups of The Marinara Sauce
1 pound (about 6 cups) thickly sliced button mushrooms
Fat free grated Parmesan

---

1. Heat The Marinara Sauce in a large saucepan on medium.
2. Add the mushrooms and cook until the mushrooms are soft.
3. Serve on cooked pasta with fat free grated Parmesan.

YIELD: About 5 cups
FAT GRAMS IN ENTIRE RECIPE: 2 (sauce, only)

BTW: Was there any other add-on you'd like to try out with your marinara sauce?

Notes:

_____

_____

_____

_____

_____

_____

_____

_____

_____

_____

Pasta In Broth

Cooking utensil: A non-stick wok

---

1 Tbs. Fleischmann's Fat Free Low Calorie squeeze margarine
1/2 pound fresh button mushrooms, thickly sliced
1/2 cup dry white wine
1 onion, thinly sliced
1 green bell pepper, thinly sliced
1 tsp. garlic, minced
1 tsp. dried oregano, crushed
2 Tbs. fresh parsley, chopped
1/2 cup defatted chicken stock
2 to 3 cups vermicelli, cooked without oil
Fat free grated Parmesan

---

1. Sauté the mushrooms in the margarine in the wok; remove the mushrooms and set aside.
2. Place all remaining ingredients, except the pasta, into the wok and cook until the liquid has reduced by 1/3.
3. Add the mushrooms and vermicelli to the wok and toss; heat through.
4. Serve with fat free grated Parmesan.

YIELD: About 5 cups
FAT GRAMS IN ENTIRE RECIPE: 5 to 6

Notes:

BARI'S TURKEY TETRAZZINI

This was an impossible recipe before Campbell's Healthy Request lowered the fat count for Cream of Mushroom soup. The best part of this soup is that it has a more mushroomy taste than the original, adding to the flavor rather than detracting from it.

Cooking utensil: A large non-stick skillet

---

2 Tbs. white wine
1/2 onion, minced
4 oz. button mushrooms, sliced
1 cup defatted chicken stock
1 can (10 3/4 oz.) Healthy Request Cream of Mushroom Soup, undiluted
1/4 cup dry vermouth
Salt and pepper to taste
6 Tbs. fat free grated Parmesan
2 cups cooked turkey breast, diced
2 cups cooked thin spaghetti, prepared without oil

---

1. Sauté the onion and mushrooms in the wine until soft.
2. Combine all other ingredients, except the turkey and the pasta; stir well; cook, uncovered, until hot, about 4 or 5 minutes.
3. Add the turkey and the pasta; toss lightly; simmer, covered, until piping hot, about 6 to 8 minutes.

YIELD: About 4 cups
FAT GRAMS IN ENTIRE RECIPE: 14

BTW: We've heard raves on this dish that Bari threw together one evening using leftovers. Your refrigerator is a treasure trove of goodies with some canned soups to enhance the stuff you find in there.

Notes:

THE FAR EAST INFLUENCES SHRIMP AND CILANTRO

There's a Burmese restaurant in Washington D.C., where we've enjoyed some absolutely marvelous food. This next recipe is a modified version of a dish we've fallen in love with there.

Cooking utensil: A non-stick wok treated with spray-on oil

1/4 pound medium shrimp, peeled and deveined
1 tsp. garlic powder
1/2 cup defatted chicken stock
1/2 cup fresh cilantro, chopped
4 cups cooked thin spaghetti, prepared without oil
1/2 tsp. sesame oil

---

1. Clean the shrimp; mince very fine; sprinkle with the garlic powder and sauté, quickly, in a wok that's been sprayed with the Pam or Mazola on a high heat; set the shrimp aside.
2. In the wok that still has the shrimp residue, add the stock; cook down by 1/3.
3. Add the cilantro and the spaghetti; toss and heat through.
4. Add the oil, toss; add the sautéed shrimp, toss and serve.

YIELD: 4 cups
FAT GRAMS IN ENTIRE RECIPE: 10

Notes:

_____

_____

_____

_____

_____

CANNELLINI AND SPINACH ON PASTA

Every now and then, you find that throwing a bit of this and that together, turns out to be a simple favorite. That's what this one turned out to be!

Cooking utensil: A non-stick wok

1/2 cup defatted chicken stock
1 large onion, cut in half, thinly sliced
2 cups cannellini, cooked or canned
2 pounds fresh spinach (about 16 cups), cleaned and stemmed
2 tsp. garlic powder
1/4 tsp. crushed red pepper flakes, optional

---

1. Heat the stock in the wok; add the onion and cook until crisp-tender.
3. Add the red pepper, toss again.
4. Serve on pasta, cooked with no oil.

YIELD: About 5 cups
FAT GRAMS IN ENTIRE RECIPE: 3 (excluding pasta)

Notes:

QUINOA

One of the three basic foods, along with corn and potatoes, of the Inca civilization, this grain is exceptionally high in protein. There is a naturally occurring bitter coating on this grain which is removed, in most instances, prior to sale. The residues, or powder, from this coating may remain and, therefore, the quinoa must be rinsed thoroughly in a strainer and then drained, before use in any recipe.

One of the most difficult features of this grain is the pronunciation, so many people say it incorrectly. It's pronounced *keen-wah*. It is easy enough to prepare and gives you another grain, a light and delicious one, to add variety to your life.

1/4 cup dry quinoa makes 3/4 cup, cooked.
1 cup cooked quinoa delivers about 3 grams of fat.

PREPARING BASIC QUINOA

Be sure to properly rinse this grain before cooking.

Cooking utensil: A 2 quart non-stick saucepan

---

2 cups water
1 cup Quinoa

---

1. Place the Quinoa in the saucepan with the water; bring to a boil; lower the heat, cover, and simmer for about 15 minutes.
2. The quinoa is done when the water has been absorbed and the grains have turned from opaque to transparent and the spiral germ has separated.
3. Let it stand for 5 minutes or so and you're good to go.

YIELD: 3 cups
FAT GRAMS IN ENTIRE RECIPE: 8

Notes:

Quinoa Vegetable Soup

Try this one on for size and let's see what you think of this as it compares to your usual barley based veggie soup. Remember to rinse the quinoa before cooking.

Cooking utensil: An 8 quart non-stick pot

1/4 cup quinoa, rinsed and well-drained
1 tsp. canola or olive oil
1/4 cup defatted chicken stock
1/2 cup carrots, chopped
1/4 cup celery, chopped
1/2 cup onion, chopped
1/2 cup green bell pepper, chopped
2 cloves garlic, chopped
4 cups defatted chicken stock, additional
1 cup tomatoes, chopped
1 cup cabbage, shredded
1/2 cup fresh parsley, chopped
Freshly ground pepper and salt to taste

---

1. Brown the quinoa in the oil until golden.
2. Place 1/4 cup stock in the pot and add the carrots, celery, onion, bell pepper and garlic; sauté until these vegetables are tender.
3. Add the remaining ingredients and simmer, uncovered, until the veggies are tender and the flavors have blended.

YIELD: About 8 cups
FAT GRAMS IN ENTIRE RECIPE: 8

Notes:

RICE

This grain is a staple food for more than half of the earth's population. Ana Martinez, a beautiful, dear friend, asked me for my marinara recipe when she was planning a dinner for some guests. The day after the dinner I, of course, asked her how the sauce turned out and were her guests pleased. She said, in her melodic, Peruvian accent, "Oh, Tree, they loved it. And, you know, I eat rice at every meal. I don't consider a meal complete without rice. So, I ate the sauce on my rice. My sister did, too. It was wonderful!"

As the years have rolled by since I started eating more of a vegetarian diet, I have become tremendously attached to rice. Yes, Annie, you're right. Sometimes a day doesn't seem complete unless I've had my rice ration.

In Burma, 500 pounds of rice is consumed per person each year; and in China, the word for rice is the same as the word for food.

Although we don't depend on rice as the basis of our diet here in the United States, rice consumption has doubled in the last ten years. There are a number of different kinds of rice available to us, and we'll talk about a few of the varieties that we'll use in these recipes.

The rices we'll be using in recipes in this book can be found in our supermarkets: Basmati rice, brown rice, long-grain white rice, Arborio rice and Converted rice. While I refer to these rices as "steamed" when the recipe calls for serving on the rice, I intend for the rice to be prepared in the following manner or prepared in a rice-steamer. Either manner of preparation is just fine. We've had steamers and find it's easier to use the old-fashioned method. We *never use oil or butter* when steaming rice. If it is used, and we've made the taste test, you cannot tell the difference. Why ingest 14 grams of fat per tablespoon of oil when you receive no benefit?

1 cup of raw rice will yield about 3 1/2 cups, cooked.
1 cup of cooked rice will deliver less than 1 gram of fat. Check the nutritional label of the rice you're preparing for an exact count.

FREEZING: Any of these rices can freeze for future use. Whenever we make rice we make lots of it, sometimes 24 cups at a time! The logic is it takes just as much time to cook 8 cups as 1, so why not? When reheated in the microwave, it tastes just as good as just-made. Place in freezer-proof gallon-sized plastic bags. Squeeze out the air and lay flat on the counter. Press the rice flat, no more than about 1/2 inch thick. Freeze it flat on a shelf, one layer on top of another.

THAWING AND HEATING: When you want to eat the rice you've frozen, remove the flat bag from the freezer. Hit the bag gently, on the edge of the counter. The rice will break up into smaller pieces so that you can remove the amount you want. Place in a microwave-proof bowl, cover with plastic and heat on high for about 3 to 4 minutes, depending on the power of your microwave. Fluff with a fork and set it for another 2 to 3 minutes. There is no need to add any water. The water already stored in the frozen rice is sufficient to re-steam the rice. If you don't tell them...they'll think you just cooked it up!

ARBORIO

Arborio rice is very different from the others in texture, mouthfeel and cooking method. The texture is softer. The only way I've seen this rice prepared is as risotto. The mouthfeel is creamy rather than starchy. The recommended cooking method is time-consuming and labor-intensive. Some people love it and a restaurant isn't "with it" unless it's on the menu. I must admit that the difference in consistency from the other types of rice did not make the lengthy preparation seem worth it. If you have followed a recipe for risotto you're smiling because you know whereof I speak. For those of you unacquainted with this endeavor, allow me to expand. The rice is sautéed with the vegetables that will be part of the dish. Warm stock is added, 1 cup at a time. After each addition of stock the rice is stirred, constantly, until that cup of stock is absorbed. The procedure continues until the full compliment of stock has been absorbed and the dish is ready to serve. This may take as long as 40 minutes! After this I would expect no less than heaven.

Since our first experience with risotto, we've been trying to come up with an answer to the amount of work necessary to arrive at the finished product. The solution we've devised is simple and close enough to the original to suffice.

Vegetable Risotto With Mushrooms

The exciting thing about this recipe is the lack of work entailed. This is risotto, for goodness sakes!

Cooking utensils: A non-stick skillet and a 2 quart baking dish with lid, both treated with Olive Oil Pam

---

1 Tbs. Fleischmann's Fat Free Low Calorie squeeze margarine
1 medium onion, thinly sliced
1/2 green bell pepper, thinly sliced
1/2 carrot, chopped
1 cup mushrooms, thinly sliced
1 cup Arborio rice, uncooked
4 cups defatted stock, heated
Salt and freshly ground pepper to taste
3 Tbs. fat free grated Parmesan

Preheat the oven to 350°

1. Sauté the vegetables and rice in the margarine in the treated skillet over high heat until well-coated.
2. Place the mixture in the baking dish with the stock and cover; bake for 30 minutes; if all the liquid is not absorbed, continue to bake, checking every 5 minutes or so.
3. Add the salt and pepper to taste.
4. Sprinkle with Parmesan and serve.

YIELD: 6 CUPS
FAT GRAMS IN ENTIRE RECIPE: 5

BTW: I have found the method outlined in this recipe can be applied to almost any of the risotto recipes you'll find. If the addition of vegetables is called for at different times of the cooking, add those vegetables to the rice mixture at the appropriate time and return to the oven to continue the cooking.

Notes:

BASMATI

1 cup raw makes 3 cups cooked.

COOKING BASMATI RICE

Cooking utensil: A 2 quart non-stick saucepan

---

1 cup Basmati rice
1 1/2 cups cold water
1 tsp. salt

---

1. Place the rice in a saucepan; add water in the amount that measures 1 1/2 times the amount of rice and cook on high heat, uncovered, until the water is disappearing in craters formed by the rice.
2. Cover the pot, reduce the heat to very low, and allow to cook for 15 minutes.
3. Turn off the heat. Allow the rice to steam for about 5 minutes.
4. Remove the cover; fluff the rice with a fork.

YIELD: 3 cups
FAT GRAMS IN ENTIRE RECIPE: 3

BTW: Basmati is an aromatic rice that elongates when it's cooked rather than expanding in width as most other rices do. Before cooking, it's hard to tell Basmati from other long grain rice. It not only looks different after cooking, the fragrance sets it apart from other rices.

Notes:

LENTILS WITH BASMATI RICE AND MACARONI

This is another one of the rather long recipes that in all likelihood will turn into a weekend cookery that you enjoy eating during the week, or that you prepare specifically intending to freeze for your own frozen dinners.

Cooking utensils: A 3 quart non-stick saucepan, a large non-stick skillet and a small non-stick skillet

---

4 cups lentils, cooked
6 cups Basmati rice, cooked
4 cups elbow macaroni, cooked
1/4 cup white wine
1 medium onion, finely diced
1/2 green bell pepper, finely diced
2 cloves garlic, minced
1 can (28 oz.) plum tomatoes, chopped, with juice
1 Tbs. fresh parsley, chopped
1/2 tsp. dried oregano, crushed
1/2 tsp. dried thyme leaves, crushed
1 bay leaf
1 tsp. salt
Freshly ground pepper to taste
Pam or Mazola spray-on oil
4 fresh red chili peppers, seeded and deveined, minced
1 cup water
4 Tbs. vinegar
Pam or Mazola spray-on oil, additional
2 large onions, coarsely chopped

---

1. Combine the lentils, rice and macaroni; set aside and keep warm.
2. Sauté the finely diced onion, the bell pepper and the garlic in the wine, in a large saucepan, until tender.
3. Add the tomatoes, juice, parsley, oregano, thyme and bay leaves; season to taste and set aside.
4. In a large skillet, spray the oil; when hot, add the red chili pepper and stir for about 2 minutes. If necessary hit with another blast of oil to avoid sticking.
5. Add the tomato sauce that had been set aside, with the 1/2 cup water and the vinegar; lower heat and simmer gently, stirring frequently for 5 minutes.

6. Meanwhile, sauté the chopped onion in a skillet sprayed with the additional Pam or Mazola, until limp and brown.
7. Transfer the lentil, rice mixture to a large platter, top with the sautéed onion and pour the tomato sauce over the whole thing and serve.

YIELD: About 14 cups of lentil, rice, macaroni mixture and about 4 cups of sauce
FAT GRAMS IN ENTIRE RECIPE: 18

BTW: We prepare the entire recipe at one time. We freeze the different components, leaving the sautéing of the coarsely chopped onion to be prepared at the time the meal will be served. By separately freezing the different parts of this recipe to make 4 meals, we need only pull the different parts of the dinner from the freezer, defrost, sauté the onion and we're in business. Another way to handle this is make the sauce, add the chili pepper, freeze it in meal sizes and prepare the rice, lentil, macaroni mixture fresh each time. Either way you should try this at least once.

Notes:

BROWN RICE

1 cup raw makes 3 cups, cooked.
1 cup cooked is 1 gram of fat.

COOKING BROWN RICE

Cooking utensil: A 2 quart non-stick saucepan

---

1 cup brown rice
2 1/2 cups cold water
1 tsp. salt

---

1. Place rice in a saucepan; add the water; cook on a very high heat until the water boils; continue to boil for 5 minutes, uncovered.
2. Cover the pot; reduce the temperature to very low heat; cook for 35 minutes.
3. Turn off the heat; allow the rice to steam for about five minutes.
4. Remove the cover; fluff the rice with a fork.

YIELD: 3 cups
FAT GRAMS IN ENTIRE RECIPE: 3

BTW: Brown rice, the hull of which has been removed but which retains the bran layers that are still on the grain, is a very popular rice with vegetarians. The taste is nuttier than white, and there is five times the vitamin E, three times the magnesium, and twice the fiber in the brown rice. It has a chewier texture than the white, and if you overcook it you can use it as a substitute for oatmeal.

In any recipe where you've used white rice, or which calls for white rice, you may use brown rice, instead. Find out which recipes you prefer with each of the rices.

Notes:

CURRIED RICE

This dish is a great rice base for a mixture of steamed vegetables. It's an exciting alternative to a simple steamed brown rice or white rice.

Cooking utensil: A 3 quart non-stick saucepan

---

1 medium onion, chopped
1 clove garlic, minced
1/2 medium green bell pepper, chopped
1/4 cup white wine or defatted chicken stock
1/2 cup raisins
1/4 to 3/4 tsp. curry powder, to taste
1 cup water
3 cups brown rice, cooked

---

1. Sauté the onion, garlic and bell pepper in the wine or stock until tender.
2. Add the raisins, curry powder and the water; simmer 10 minutes.
3. Combine with rice and cook for 15 minutes.

YIELD: About 5 cups
FAT GRAMS IN ENTIRE RECIPE: 3

Notes:

BROWN RICE AND LENTILS

This is as basic as you can get, when it comes to healthy food. A complete protein, the lentils and the rice take about the same amount of time to cook. You can use this rice as a substitute in almost any recipe that calls for "steamed rice" for a healthier, higher fiber dish than the white rice offers.

Cooking utensil: A 3 quart non-stick saucepan

---

1 onion, chopped
1 cup green bell pepper, chopped
3 cloves garlic, minced
1 cup brown rice, uncooked
1 cup dried lentils, picked and rinsed
1 bay leaf
4 cups water
Salt and freshly ground pepper to taste

---

1. Place all ingredients in a large saucepan; bring to a boil.
2. Cover; reduce to a low heat; cook 40 minutes.
3. Uncover and cook on low an additional 10 to 15 minutes, or until the water has been thoroughly absorbed.
4. Season to taste and serve.

YIELD: 6 cups
FAT GRAMS IN ENTIRE RECIPE: 4

Btw: This can be frozen in meal-sized containers and can turn any soup, canned or home-made into a bonanza of good health.

Notes:

Long Grain White Rice

1 cup, raw, makes 3 cups, cooked.
1 cup, cooked, is about 1 gram of fat.

Long-grain rice is a snap to fix and is extremely inexpensive. We buy it in 25 pound bags from the discount clubs. It freezes like a dream and reheats like just cooked. 90% of all American rice is enriched with thiamin, niacin and iron. Check the label, it may be enriched with riboflavin, vitamin D and calcium, too. It depends on the brand.

Cooking White Rice

Cooking utensil: A 3 quart non-stick saucepan

---

1 cup rice
1 1/2 cups water
1 tsp. salt

---

1. Place the rice and the water in a saucepan; bring the water to a boil and watch for craters to form as the rice begins to absorb some of the water.
2. Cover the pot; reduce the heat to low; cook for 20 minutes.
3. Turn off the heat; allow 5 minutes for the rice to steam.
4. Remove cover and fluff with a fork.

YIELD: 3 cups
FAT GRAMS IN ENTIRE RECIPE: 3

BTW: This recipe gives you rice that sticks together a bit. It's perfect for Oriental food and beans on rice.

Notes:

GREEN RICE

A lovely, delicately seasoned rice dish to serve alongside any entrée such as seafood or poultry.

Cooking utensil: A 3 quart non-stick saucepan

---

1 cup white rice, uncooked
1/2 small onion, chopped
1 tsp. dried basil, crushed
1 1/2 tsp. chicken or vegetable bouillon granules
1 1/2 cups water

---

1. Combine all ingredients; bring to a boil.
2. Cover and reduce heat to low; cook for 20 minutes.
3. Remove cover and fluff with a fork.

YIELD: 3 cups
FAT GRAMS IN ENTIRE RECIPE: 3

BTW: Try this recipe using different herbs, fresh and dried.

Notes:

CONVERTED RICE

This rice is also know as parboiled rice. The most popular brand we know of is Uncle Ben's. Take a look at the package if you'd never noticed the word "converted" before. When I was a young cook, I thought the only "good" rice was Uncle Ben's! There are still many recipes that demand a converted rice and you'll see that brand name in the recipes. It just makes it easier to recognize. Each kernel of rice remains individual. There is no stickiness with converted rice, making it ideal when you're cooking with other ingredients, such as soups and sauces.

COOKING CONVERTED RICE

Cooking utensil: A 3 quart non-stick saucepan

---

1 cup converted rice
2 cups boiling water
1 tsp. salt

---

1. Add the rice to the boiling water and add the salt.
2. As soon as the water returns to a boil, lower the heat and cover.
3. Cook for 20 minutes; remove from heat.
4. Uncover and fluff with a fork.

YIELD: 3 cups
FAT GRAMS IN ENTIRE RECIPE: 3

BTW: These rices can all substitute for one another in the event you need to make an unexpected substitution.

Notes:

_____

_____

_____

RED RICE

This rice is mentioned numerous times in other recipes, especially the bean recipes, because it's such a winner. If you like rice at all, you must prepare this one recipe and see what you think. The greatest compliment I ever received for any of my rice dishes came from a young woman of Mexican descent. She was at a workshop and tasted the rice and was amazed because it has no oil in it. She said it tasted better than her family's recipe that was loaded with oil. I figure if it can compare with Mexican red rice we're doing well.

Cooking utensil: An 8 quart non-stick pot

---

1 large can (15 oz.) tomato sauce
1 can (16 oz.) Choice Cut tomatoes with juice Boiling water
4 cups Uncle Ben's Converted Rice, uncooked
1 large onion chopped
1 medium green bell pepper, chopped
2 Tbs. chicken bouillon granules

---

1. Combine the tomato sauce and tomatoes with juice in a large measuring cup; add enough boiling water to measure 8 cups.
2. Place in large pot with the rest of the ingredients; return to a boil.
3. Cover and reduce heat to low; cook for 20 minutes or until all liquid is absorbed.
4. Uncover and fluff with a fork.

YIELD: 12 cups
FAT GRAMS IN ENTIRE RECIPE: 8

Notes:

Faux Fried Rice

You love fried rice, but you know that the way it gets to taste so good is that taboo method of cooking...frying! Well, here's a way to get all the flavor and none of the fat from doing it fried.

Cooking utensil: A 3 quart non-stick saucepan

---

2 cups Uncle Ben's Converted Rice, uncooked
4 cups boiling water
1 rib celery, thinly sliced
1 medium onion, thinly sliced
1/2 cup mushrooms, sliced
1/2 cup fresh or canned bean sprouts, optional
1/2 cup frozen peas
1/2 cup water chestnuts, sliced
1 1/2 Tbs. chicken bouillon granules
Soy sauce or Tamari to taste
1/4 cup Egg Beaters

---

1. Combine all the ingredients, except the Egg Beaters.
2. Bring water back up to a boil; cover and reduce heat to low; cook for 20 minutes.
3. In the meantime, scramble the Egg Beaters and cook in the microwave or in a non-stick skillet; set aside until the rice is done.
4. Remove the rice from the pot and put in a bowl; slice the egg and arrange as a garnish on top.

YIELD: 8 cups
FAT GRAMS IN ENTIRE RECIPE: 3

BTW: Throw some stir-fried veggies on top of this rice and see what happens to your Oriental dinner!

Notes:

PAELLA

The classic peasant dish of Spain, the dish has become an elegant entree in the finest restaurants all over the world. Paella means "pan" and refers to using the large skillet for preparation. This recipe is one of thousands for paella since paella changes according to the ingredients the kitchen happens to offer. The *must have* ingredient in this dish is the saffron that gives it the gorgeous yellow hue and adds an aromatic nuance that cannot be imitated. You can't go wrong with whatever you add. Many of the recipes call for sausages, along with other meats, poultry and seafood.

Cooking utensil: A very large skillet or (don't tell anyone!) the wok, treated with spray-on oil

---

1 cup onion, chopped
1/2 cup green bell pepper, chopped
1/2 cup red bell pepper, chopped
4 cloves garlic, minced
1 package (10 oz.) frozen artichoke hearts, thawed
3 cups fresh spinach, cleaned and trimmed, tightly packed, torn
6 cups plus 1 Tbs. defatted chicken stock
2 1/2 cups Uncle Ben's Converted Rice, uncooked
1/2 tsp. Hungarian sweet paprika
1/2 tsp. saffron threads
1 cup frozen lima beans, thawed
2/3 cup frozen peas, thawed
1 pound medium shrimp, peeled and deveined, optional

---

1. Place the treated skillet or wok over medium-high heat until heated.
2. Add the onion, bell peppers and garlic; sauté for 3 minutes.
3. Add the artichoke hearts; sauté 2 minutes .
4. Add the broth; bring to a boil; stir in the spinach, rice, paprika and saffron; cover, reduce heat; simmer for 15 minutes.
5. Add lima beans, peas and shrimp; toss gently; cover, continue simmer for additional 10 minutes or until the liquid is absorbed and the shrimp are cooked through; remove from heat.
6. Let stand for 5 minutes, covered; then serve.

YIELD: About 15 cups
FAT GRAMS IN ENTIRE RECIPE: 6

BTW: The shrimp, which are optional, may be added at your discretion, as well as muscles and clams (in the shell, well-scrubbed), firm fish (mahi mahi or cod), and of course, skinless chicken breasts. Let your imagination be your guide. If you're using shellfish in the shell, discard any shells that have not opened after cooking,

Notes:

Broccoli And Rice Casserole

This is one of my family's favorites. It reminds my kids of when they were young and this was a standard way of getting them to eat their broccoli. Whenever we get together for Thanksgiving, this one dish is just about as important as the turkey.

Cooking utensils: A 3 quart non-stick saucepan, a dish for the microwave for steaming and a 3 to 5 quart casserole or baking dish, treated with spray-on oil

2 cups Uncle Ben's Converted Rice, uncooked
1 large onion, cut in half and sliced
2 cans Healthy Request Cream of Mushroom soup, undiluted
4 cups boiling water
3 Tbs. chicken or vegetable bouillon granules
2 Tbs. Worcestershire sauce
6 cups fresh broccoli flowerets
9 oz. Healthy Choice loaf cheese

Preheat the oven to 350°

1. Combine the rice, onion, soup and water with the bouillon and Worcestershire sauce in a saucepan; return to a boil.
2. Cover and reduce heat to low; cook for 20 minutes.
3. In the meantime, steam the broccoli until bright green, but still crispy; set aside.
4. Layer the casserole with 1/2 the rice mixture, then 1/2 the broccoli, then dot on 3 ounces of the cheese; repeat this once more and then finish up with the cheese.
5. Cover with aluminum foil and bake for 30 minutes.

YIELD: 10 cups
FAT GRAMS IN ENTIRE RECIPE: 15

BTW: When steaming the broccoli, the microwave will do it in a minute or two. Place the broccoli in a dish with about 2 Tbs. water; cover and steam on high until bright green. If you have any leftover cooked chicken or turkey, sprinkle it on one layer after the rice.

RICE AND VEGETABLE SALAD

We don't usually think of rice as a base for a salad, but there are a few I've found that make the grade. It's a definite change of pace from the tired, head lettuce and tomato mix you find so often. Salads can be fun and interesting if you use a little ingenuity. To defrost the peas, merely place them in a strainer or colander and place under cold, running water.

Preparation utensil: A large bowl

---

2 cups Uncle Ben's Converted Rice, cooked without oil
1/2 cup broccoli flowerets
1/2 cup frozen peas, thawed
1 medium carrot, sliced
2 ribs celery, diagonally sliced
6 cherry tomatoes, cut in quarters
1/2 cup raisins
Fat free Caesar salad dressing, to taste
Freshly ground black pepper

---

1. Toss all ingredients in a large bowl.
2. Add the salad dressing; toss again
3. Chill for about 1 to 2 hours and serve.

YIELD: About 6 cups
FAT GRAMS IN ENTIRE RECIPE: 4

BTW: If you've got some leftover seafood or poultry, add that to this salad, too. Just add the appropriate fat grams, unless you know you've got plenty of room for the day. Just throw the extras in and sit back and enjoy.

Notes:

CHICKEN AND RICE BAKE

This was another big favorite when the kids were small. Fixing these one-dish meals made them happy and I didn't end up with a bunch of pots to clean! Talk about win, win! And I still love one-dish meals.

Baking utensil: A shallow baking dish 8 x 8 or 7 x 10, treated with spray-on oil

---

1 can (10 3/4 oz.) Healthy Request Cream of Mushroom soup, undiluted
1 1/2 cups water
3/4 cup Uncle Ben's Converted Rice
2 tsp. chicken bouillon granules
2 ribs celery, diagonally sliced
1/2 cup frozen peas, thawed
1 cup button mushrooms, sliced
2 chicken breasts (4 oz., ea.) skinless and boneless, sliced in 1/2 inch
   strips
1/2 cup fat free shredded cheddar cheese

Preheat the oven to 350°

1. Combine all ingredients, except the cheese, in the baking dish.
2. Bake for 45 minutes.
3. Sprinkle with the cheese; bake 10 minutes more or until cheese melts.

YIELD: About 8 cups
FAT GRAMS IN ENTIRE RECIPE: 20

BTW: You may find yourself using this recipe for a number of casseroles, with different vegetables and seafood, too, to change the presentation.

Notes:

VEGETABLES

Do you remember hearing your mother say, "First you have to finish your vegetables." That was either prior to leaving the table, before enjoying the reward of dessert, or perhaps, for the right of growing up to be a big boy or girl. Whatever the reason behind the statement, it's obvious that first the vegetables had to be eaten and the reward was not the vegetables! Well, that was then!

We have available to us, today, the most exciting variety of veggies from all over the world. And these vegetables are with us, at our fingertips, in the supermarket, at ethnic specialty shops and sometimes by order from firms that specialize in the exotic! There is no reason that in today's small world we cannot find an array of vegetables that will make us sing...even though years ago eating them was only the means to an end.

In the following pages we will prepare delicious, mouthwatering vegetables from Artichokes to Zucchini. There should be a number of these dishes that will turn you on, even if you've always fought to have that part of your plate filled with more meat. For our friends like Tony Pryor, who has finally begun to swallow the asparagus, instead of just toying with it...grab a fork, sugar-puddin'!

ARTICHOKES

The whole artichoke is a fascinating looking vegetable. Its preparation is simple and eating it is an art in itself. It's not difficult to steam the whole artichoke, after snipping the sticky ends of the leaves, and it's relaxing to leisurely suck the bottoms of the leaves that have been dipped in a creamy, fat free sauce, while anticipating getting to the luscious heart and bottom. Here's a quickie dip to use for the artichoke leaves to keep you away from a Hollandaise made with butter.

1 cup of artichoke heart is less than 1/2 gram of fat.

DIP FOR NIBBLING ARTICHOKE LEAVES

Preparation utensil: A small bowl

1/2 cup Smart Beat Fat Free Mayonnaise
2 Tbs. Dijon mustard
1/4 tsp. cayenne pepper
1/4 tsp. garlic powder
1 tsp. fresh lemon juice or more to taste

---

1. Combine all ingredients; mix well.

YIELD: 3/4 cup
FAT GRAMS IN ENTIRE RECIPE: 0

Notes:

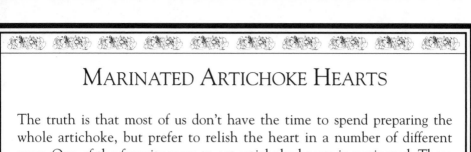

MARINATED ARTICHOKE HEARTS

The truth is that most of us don't have the time to spend preparing the whole artichoke, but prefer to relish the heart in a number of different ways. One of the favorite ways to eat artichoke hearts is marinated. There are a few brands available offering fat grams in the olive oil marinade. This can be prepared fat free.

Preparation utensil: A sealable glass bowl

---

1 cup artichoke hearts, canned in water, drained
1/4 cup fat free Italian salad dressing
1/2 tsp. mixed Italian seasonings

---

1. Toss all ingredients; place in the covered dish or jar; refrigerate overnight.

YIELD: About 12 artichoke hearts
FAT GRAMS IN ENTIRE RECIPE: 0

BTW: These hearts can be served with toothpicks as a nibble or throw some into your next salad. Compare these marinated artichoke hearts to Cara Mia brand, the same number of hearts, 12 fat grams. Not a bad reduction.

Notes:

_____

_____

_____

_____

_____

_____

_____

Artichoke Heart Spread

We're always looking for new and exciting appetizers or hors d'oeuvres to serve to guests. I like them easy to prepare so I have time to enjoy the people. This spread fills the bill.

Baking utensil: An oven-proof bowl or dish

---

2 cups water-packed artichoke hearts, drained, chopped
2/3 cup fat free mayonnaise
2 tsp. lemon juice
1/2 tsp. garlic powder
2 tsp. mixed Italian seasonings, crushed
1/4 cup fat free grated Parmesan
4 slices fat free Swiss cheese, divided

Preheat oven to 375°

1. Toss all ingredients together, except the cheese; break up the cheese into small pieces and add 2 slices to the mixture.
2. Place in the oven-proof dish and bake for about 10 minutes or until warmed through.
3. Top with the remaining Swiss cheese and bake again until the cheese is melted.
4. Serve warm or at room temperature.

YIELD: 3 cups
FAT GRAMS IN ENTIRE RECIPE: Traces

BTW: You'll be amazed at how tasty this spread is. Serve with baked pita triangles or melba toast.

Notes:

_____

_____

_____

ASPARAGUS

About 14 asparagus spears, 9 to 10 inches long, 1/2 inch, or so, thick will amount to about 1 pound. A very delicate vegetable, the asparagus is all too often smothered in Hollandaise sauce when its natural flavor is so special.

Asparagus is delicious tossed with other veggies, with pasta or rice, and it's wonderful steamed, chilled and used cold, in salad.

1 cup of cooked asparagus is less than 1/2 gram of fat.

STEAMED ASPARAGUS

I've read about quite a few ways to steam this delicate aristocratic vegetable. There are three ways that I feel are the easiest.

POT STEAMING

1. Peel the hard stalks with a potato peeler; cut off the ends (about 1/2 inch).
2. Take the bunch together and cover the tops with a piece of aluminum foil about half-way down the stalks; place standing up in a saucepan filled with water.
3. Bring the water to a boil and cook for about 4 minutes; test the stalk with a sharp knife; if the knife pierces the stalk, it's done.
4. The asparagus should be crisp and bright green. If it's soft or yellowish, it's over-cooked.

BAMBO STEAMER

1. Cut the stalks midway to the tops; put the stalks in the bottom tray of the bamboo steamer; put the tops in the top tray.
2. Place steamer, stacked, on boiling water in a wok; cook for about 3 minutes; test as shown for pot steaming.

MICROWAVE STEAMING

1. 1 pound peeled asparagus placed in a covered dish with 1/4 cup water; cook on high for approximately 3 to 5 minutes. You'll retain more nutrients with microwave steaming than any other method.

Asparagus With Shrimp

Asparagus is a natural with another delicately flavored food, shrimp, and the touch of dill adds a lift.

Cooking utensils: 2 small (2 quart) non-stick saucepans

1/2 cup dry white wine
1/2 cup bottled clam juice plus 2 Tbs. water
1 tsp. dried dill to taste
1/4 pound small or medium shrimp, peeled and deveined
2 Tbs. Fleischmann's Fat Free Low Calorie squeeze margarine
1 Tbs. flour
Salt and freshly ground pepper to taste
1/3 cup nonfat sour cream
1 1/2 Tbs. fresh dill, chopped
1 1/2 pounds asparagus, peeled and steamed

---

1. Place wine, broth and dried dill in a small saucepan; bring to a boil.
2. Add the shrimp; cover and cook for about 3 minutes, until barely is tender; remove from heat and spoon out the shrimp; set aside.
3. Heat the margarine in another small saucepan; add the flour, slowly, stirring, to avoid lumping.
4. When the flour has dissolved, add the salt and pepper and gradually add the wine mixture, stirring to avoid lumping.
5. Simmer uncovered for about 2 minutes, stirring occasionally.
6. Place sour cream in a bowl and add about 1/3 of the sauce; stir and then gently add this sour cream mixture back to the sauce; add the shrimp and the chopped fresh dill and simmer until heated through, about 3 to 5 minutes.
7. Place asparagus in a platter and cover with the sauce.

YIELD: About 20 asparagus spears with about 2 cups of sauce
FAT GRAMS IN ENTIRE RECIPE: 3

BTW: While this makes a lovely presentation, it will serve about 4 appetizers.

ASPARAGUS AND ANGEL HAIR PASTA

Cooking utensils: Steaming apparatus for asparagus and a non-stick wok

1/2 cup white wine or defatted chicken stock
4 ripe Roma (plum) tomatoes, chopped
1/2 tsp. dried thyme leaves, crushed
2 Tbs. fresh parsley, chopped
2 slices fat free Swiss cheese
Salt and freshly ground pepper
1/2 pound asparagus, steamed crisp-tender
1/2 pound angel hair pasta, cooked and drained
Fat free Parmesan cheese

1. Heat wine or stock in the wok; add the tomatoes, thyme and parsley; stir-fry rapidly on high heat; lower heat.
2. Add the Swiss cheese; when the cheese is melted and the mixture is somewhat creamy, add the asparagus and simmer until just heated through.
3. Season with salt and pepper; add pasta and toss.
4. Serve with grated Parmesan.

YIELD: 6 cups
FAT GRAMS IN ENTIRE RECIPE: 5

Notes:

BEETS

Most of the beets that I see are in the supermarket, since we don't grow our own. They're the big guys, 2 to 2 1/2 inches in size. About a tablespoon, grated, is wonderful on a salad and you should try them pickled. Take a look at the Beets with Sour Cream. You peel them with a potato peeler.

1 pound makes about 2 1/2 cups, cooked.
1 cup of cooked beets is less than 1/2 gram of fat.

PICKLED BEETS

Preparation utensils: A large bowl, a 2 quart non-stick saucepan and a tight-lidded jar

---

4 cups beets, cooked, peeled and sliced
1 medium onion (Vidalia, if possible), chopped or thinly sliced
1 cup cider vinegar
1 cup beet juice or water
1/4 cup sugar

---

1. Combine the beets and onion; place in a bowl; set aside.
2. Heat the vinegar and water; add the sugar.
3. As soon as the sugar dissolves, pour the mixture over the beets and onions.
4. Cool at room temperature and then refrigerate in the jar.

YIELD: 4 cups
FAT GRAMS IN ENTIRE RECIPE: Less than 1

Notes:

Sweet And Sour Beets With Cabbage

Serve this tangy dish as a hot veggie with boiled potatoes (a perfect compliment), or try it cold with other assorted salads.

Cooking utensil: An 8 quart non-stick pot

---

2 beets, thinly sliced
1/2 large onion, in half and sliced
1 carrot, thinly sliced
1/2 cup dry red wine
1/4 medium head cabbage, thinly sliced
1 1/2 Tbs. chicken bouillon granules
1/2 cup water
1 1/2 Tbs. wine vinegar
1 1/2 tsp. sugar
1 tsp. fresh lemon juice
Orange marmalade to taste

---

1. Place the beets, onion, carrot and wine in the pot; cook on medium heat until tender.
2. Add the cabbage; cook until tender.
3. Add the remaining ingredients except the marmalade; adjust the sugar and lemon juice to taste.
4. Add the marmalade to taste.

YIELD: About 4 cups
FAT GRAMS IN ENTIRE RECIPE: Traces

Notes:

BEETS WITH SOUR CREAM

You can see how a buffet of beautiful cold salads and relishes is possible with the added color of these beet dishes.

Preparation utensil: A plate

---

1 pound beets, cooked, peeled and sliced
1 medium onion (Vidalia, if possible), diced
3/4 cup fat free sour cream
Salt to taste
3/4 tsp. freshly ground pepper
2 tsp. grated horseradish

---

1. Place the beets on a plate; top with the onion.
2. Mix the sour cream seasonings and horseradish; spread on the beets.
3. Refrigerate for about 3 to 4 hours.

YIELD: 4 cups beets, almost 3/4 cup sauce
FAT GRAMS IN ENTIRE RECIPE: Less than 1

Notes:

BROCCOLI AND CAULIFLOWER

These two vegetables are so similar in makeup and so often prepared together, that it seems natural to put them together here, in this chapter.

BROCCOLI

It could be that you can spot the children that will grow up to be vegetarians. I remember when I was a little girl and I'd ask my mother when she was going to make those little trees I loved so much. It could be because they were so pretty, that I looked forward to having them on the plate. To this day this vegetable is one of my favorites. Unfortunately, it does get overcooked a lot. Please prepare broccoli so that it is bright green, firm and crispy. It was meant to be eaten that way...not yellow and mushy.

1 1/2 pounds raw will give you about 4 cups, cooked.
1 cup of cooked chopped broccoli (or flowerets) is less than 1 gram of fat.

Peel the stems and slice, instead of tossing them out. They are loaded with fiber. When choosing broccoli at the supermarket, choose the green buds, not the yellow or flowering broccoli. The flowering broccoli was not picked early enough and has turned bitter.

CAULIFLOWER

The magic of cauliflower is its tendency to give extra chew to a dish without changing the flavor very much. As with the other vegetables we're talking about, overcooking is a good way to kill whatever good the vegetable had in store for you, in nutrients and in flavor.

A 1 1/2 pound head, after trimming should yield about 6 1/2 cups.
1 cup, cooked, is less than 1/2 gram of fat.

Cooking doesn't change the cauliflower in size very much. Buy the white, creamy heads. If brown or yellow on the crown, the cauliflower is aging. A touch of tan spotting can be removed, if it happens after you've left it too long in the refrigerator, but don't buy them that way.

STEAMED BROCCOLI AND CAULIFLOWER

The easiest ways to steam broccoli or cauliflower are in the bamboo steamer or the microwave. In the microwave it takes no more than just a few minutes to steam either vegetable (time varies, according to your own microwave). Too long, and the broccoli will lose color, texture and flavor. The beauty of steaming for 2 to 3 minutes is that the broccoli, then chilled, is fantastic in salads. If using in a salad, run cold water on the vegetable, immediately after steaming, to stop the cooking from continuing. Steamed, both vegetables are perfect for adding to an Oriental mix for a quick toss and then onto the rice.

STIR-FRIED BROCCOLI AND CAULIFLOWER

You can decide whether you want to keep the cauliflower as part of this stir-fry or whether you prefer the broccoli alone.

Cooking utensil: A non-stick wok

---

1 cup defatted stock
4 tsp. heavy soy sauce
2 tsp. light soy sauce
1 Tbs. sugar
2 tsp. fresh ginger
3 Tbs. cornstarch
1/4 cup rice wine vinegar
1/4 cup white wine or defatted stock, additional
2 cloves garlic, minced
1 large onion, cut in eighths
2 cups broccoli flowerets, barely steamed
2 cups cauliflower flowerets, barely steamed

---

1. Prepare the sauce (the first eight ingredients) by combining 1 cup stock, soy sauces, sugar, ginger, vinegar, sherry and cornstarch; set aside.
2. Heat your wok and add 1/4 cup wine or stock; add the onion and stir-fry for about 4 minutes, until the onion pieces are translucent.
4. Add the broccoli and cauliflower and stir-fry until heated through,

about 2 to 3 minutes; add the sauce and stir fry an additional 2
minutes or so or until the sauce thickens.
5. Serve on steamed white rice.

YIELD: About 6 cups
FAT GRAMS IN ENTIRE RECIPE: 5

BTW: The addition of any other vegetables that turn you on in a stir-fry can
only enhance this recipe!

Notes:

Broccoli, Red Onion And Red Pepper Stir-Fry

The onion and bell pepper really sweeten up the taste of this stir-fry. Barely steaming the broccoli before using in these recipes makes them much easier to prepare.

Cooking utensil: A non-stick wok

---

3 Tbs. Fleischmann's Fat Free Low Calorie margarine
1/4 cup defatted chicken stock
1 head broccoli, cut into flowerets, the stems diagonally sliced and barely steamed
1/2 red onion, thinly sliced
1 red bell pepper, sliced
2 Tbs. fresh basil, chopped
1 Tbs. fresh oregano

---

1. In the wok or a large skillet place the margarine and the broccoli; toss to coat the broccoli and cook to heat through.
2. Add the onion and cook with the broccoli until the onion is translucent, about 5 minutes; add the red bell pepper; continue cooking until the pepper is crispy-tender.
3. Toss with the basil and oregano and serve.

YIELD: About 6 cups
FAT GRAMS IN ENTIRE RECIPE: 5

BTW: Of course, stir-fry means you can put this over rice. It's also an easy and fine-tasting topping for a baked potato.

Notes:

MIXED STIR-FRY

If you like to play with herbs and spices you'll love this recipe. You may want to vary the vegetables that are in the stir-fry reflecting the season or your own favorites. A few hours before preparing this recipe, mix the first 3 ingredients and marinate the broccoli, the mushrooms and the bell pepper in that mixture.

Cooking utensil: A non-stick wok

1 tsp. garlic, minced
1 tsp. grated ginger root
1/4 cup dry sherry
1/2 cup broccoli flowerets, broken into small pieces
1/2 cup cauliflower flowerets, broken into small pieces
1/2 cup mushrooms, sliced
1/2 cup red bell pepper, thinly sliced
1 cup onion, thinly sliced
1/4 defatted chicken stock
1 cup fresh bean sprouts
1/2 tsp. Chinese five spice powder
1 Tbs. tamari or low-sodium soy sauce to taste
1 Tbs. cornstarch

1. Mix together the first 3 ingredients for marinating the broccoli, mushrooms and bell pepper. If you don't have sufficient time to marinate. continue with this recipe as if you had. The flavor is not quite as intense, but still good. Set aside the broccoli, mushrooms and bell pepper.
2. Heat the wok and add the garlic, ginger root and sherry; add the onion and stir-fry until crisp-tender.
3. Add the other vegetables and stir-fry for about 5 minutes, until crisp-tender; add the bean sprouts and cook 1 more minute.
4. In a small bowl, combine the Chinese five spice, tamari and cornstarch, blend well; make a well in the center of the vegetables and add the corn starch in the well; cook while stirring, adding the vegetables into the well as the liquid thickens, about 1 minute.
5. Serve on steamed white rice prepared with no oil or margarine.

YIELD: About 4 to 5 cups
FAT GRAMS IN ENTIRE RECIPE: 2

BTW: The five spice powder can be purchased in Oriental specialty markets or in the Foreign Foods area of most supermarkets.

Notes:

BROCCOLI CASSEROLE

Here's a quickie dish that you'll enjoy on the run or as a leftover.

Cooking utensils: A 2 quart saucepan and a 2 or 3 quart casserole, treated with spray-on oil

---

6 oz. Healthy Choice loaf cheese
1 cup white rice, cooked
1/2 cup mushrooms, sliced
1/2 cup onion, diced
1/4 cup skim milk
1 Tbs. plus 1 tsp. Fleischmann's Fat Free Low Calorie margarine
1/4 tsp. salt
2 packages (10 oz. ea.) frozen chopped broccoli, thawed

Preheat oven to 350°

1. Combine all ingredients, except the broccoli, and place in a medium-sized saucepan; cook over low heat until the cheese melts, stirring constantly.
2. Add the broccoli and cook 2 minutes or until the broccoli is thoroughly heated.
3. Spoon the mixture into the casserole and bake for 30 minutes.

YIELD: 5 cups
FAT GRAMS IN ENTIRE RECIPE: 6

Notes:

MUSTARD, BROCCOLI AND CAULIFLOWER PASTA

With a name like that it had better be good.

Cooking utensils: A 2 quart non-stick saucepan and an 8 quart pot of boiling water

---

1/4 cup white wine or defatted stock
1/3 cup shallots, minced
2 cloves garlic, minced
3/4 cup fresh tomato, chopped
2 Tbs. fresh parsley, chopped
2 Tbs. Dijon mustard
1 Tbs. balsamic vinegar
1/4 tsp. freshly ground pepper
1/2 pound linguine, uncooked
2 cups small cauliflower flowerets, uncooked
2 cups small broccoli flowerets, uncooked
1/4 cup fat free grated Parmesan

---

1. Sauté the shallots and garlic in the wine or stock for about 2 minutes.
2. Add the tomato, parsley, mustard, vinegar and pepper; cook for 3 minutes or until thoroughly heated; set aside and keep warm.
4. Place the linguine in boiling water; cook for 5 minutes; add the broccoli and cauliflower; cook an additional 3 minutes or until the linguine and the vegetables are tender; drain well.
5. Combine the pasta, vegetables and the tomato mixture; toss well.
6. Place in a pretty bowl, sprinkle the cheese over it and serve.

YIELD: 8 cups
FAT GRAMS IN ENTIRE RECIPE: 6

Notes:

TURKEY BROCCOLI MELT

A meal in a sandwich. That's always neat. You can do this one with steamed asparagus, too.

Cooking utensil: A non-stick baking sheet

---

1 large package (16 oz.) frozen broccoli spears
4 Tbs. prepared mustard
4 slices fat free bread
4 slices deli turkey breast
4 slices fat free sharp cheddar

Preheat the oven to 450° or broil

1. Thaw the broccoli and set aside.
2. Spread the mustard on the bread.
3. Top the bread with the turkey; follow with 3 broccoli spears; follow with the cheese.

YIELD: 4 open-faced sandwiches
FAT GRAMS IN ENTIRE RECIPE: 6

BTW: A slice of tomato between the turkey and the broccoli would enhance the sandwich. If you happen to see the mustard brand Batempte, which you should find in the deli section of your supermarket, it is an exceptionally good deli mustard reminiscent of New York delicatessens.

Notes:

_____

_____

_____

_____

_____

PASTA WITH BROCCOLI AND SNOW PEAS

This one-pot technique saves clean-up time. Always a help!

Cooking utensils: A small non-stick skillet and an 8 quart pot

---

3 shallots, minced
1/4 cup white wine or defatted stock
2 quarts water
1 bunch broccoli cut up
1/2 pound fresh snow peas
1 pound dried fusilli pasta
1 cup fat free grated Parmesan
1/2 tsp. hot pepper flakes

---

1. In a small skillet, sauté the shallots until tender; set aside.
2. In a large pot, boil the water; when boiling, put in the broccoli; cook until bright green, about 3 to 4 minutes; remove with a slotted spoon; set aside.
3. Blanch the snow peas in the same boiling water until bright green, about 30 seconds; remove with a slotted spoon; set aside with the broccoli.
4. Bring water back to a boil and add pasta. Cook until al dente, about 10 to 12 minutes; drain.
5. Combine all ingredients with 1/2 cup of the cheese in a serving bowl; toss.
6. Sprinkle the rest of the cheese on top and serve.

YIELD: About 12 cups
FAT GRAMS IN ENTIRE RECIPE: About 13

BTW: Feel free to change the pasta style and the veggies on this one.

Notes:

BROCCOLI AND CAULIFLOWER PASTA SALAD

You always wanted an easy way to put pasta salad together. Try the plastic bag method. You'll end up using this method with other salads, too, I'll bet.

Preparation utensil: A sealable, gallon-sized plastic bag

---

1 cup broccoli flowerets, blanched
1 cup cauliflower flowerets, blanched
1 cup fresh mushrooms, sliced
1/2 cup scallions, chopped
1/2 cup red bell peppers, sliced
1/2 cup green bell peppers, sliced
2 Tbs. fresh cilantro, chopped
1/2 cup fresh snow peas, cut diagonally
1 cup red kidney beans, cooked or canned and rinsed
1 cup garbanzo beans, cooked or canned and rinsed
1 cup corn kernels, cooked or canned and drained
4 cups rotini or other macaroni, cooked firm
1/3 cup fat free Italian salad dressing or to taste
Salt and freshly ground pepper to taste

---

1. Combine all ingredients in the bag, except the dressing; massage the bag to mix the ingredients.
2. Add the amount of dressing that pleases you; start with 1/3 cup and add appropriately.
3. Season to taste and serve.

YIELD: 12 cups
FAT GRAMS IN ENTIRE RECIPE: 8

BTW: This is one of those recipes that must be a reflection of your own tastes. If you like Creamy Italian, so be it. If Ranch is your favorite, do it. Change the seasonings and, in fact, the recipes, to suit yourself. And when you're invited to a "bring a dish" picnic...bag it!

Notes:

CURRIED VEGETABLE STEW

Curries are a matter of individual taste. In India the curry is made of the combination of the spices shown here. There is no pre-mixed "curry powder."

Cooking utensil: A large non-stick skillet

---

3 zucchini, cut into 2 inch pieces
2 Japanese eggplant in 1/2 inch rounds
1 red bell pepper, cut in 2 inch pieces
1 pound cauliflower, flowerets, stems in 1/2 inch rounds
1 pound broccoli, flowerets, stems in 1/2 inch rounds
2 carrots, cut in 1 inch rounds
1 tsp. coriander seed, cracked
1/2 cup defatted chicken stock
2 onions, chopped
2 cloves garlic, minced
1 1/2 Tbs. fresh ginger, minced
1/2 tsp. cayenne pepper
2 tsp. ground cumin
1 tsp. ground turmeric
1/2 tsp. salt
2 cups defatted chicken stock, additional
4 or 5 fresh cilantro sprigs for garnish

---

1. Prepare the vegetables and set aside, in different containers.
2. Heat the 1/2 cup stock in the shallow skillet; add onion, garlic and ginger; cook over medium heat for about 10 minutes or until onions are translucent.
3. Add the coriander, cayenne, cumin, turmeric and salt; stir to mix well and cook for 5 minutes; add additional chicken stock and mix again.
4. Add the eggplant and carrots; cover and cook 15 minutes.
5. Add the cauliflower, broccoli and bell pepper; stir to mix well; cover and cook for 15 minutes more.
6. Add the zucchini and cook, uncovered, for 5 minutes.
7. Serve and garnish with cilantro sprigs.

YIELD: 15 to 18 cups
FAT GRAMS IN ENTIRE RECIPE: 10

Btw: If you don't have the individual spices listed, and would like to try the recipe before you purchase this array of goodies, try this recipe with a substitution of 4 Tbs. curry powder for all the spices in the recipe. If you do have the individual spices and want to play with this recipe, adjust the different spices to your own tastes.

Notes:

CAULIFLOWER KIDNEY BEAN CASSEROLE

This recipe is a no-brainer and is made even easier if you have a couple or more cups of cauliflower, already steamed, looking for a dish to call home.

Baking utensil: A 3 quart non-stick casserole with cover or aluminum foil for covering tightly

---

1 can (15 oz.) red kidney beans, drained
1 can (8 oz.) tomato sauce
1/4 tsp. dried basil, crushed
1/4 tsp. dried oregano leaves, crushed
1 cup rice (brown or white), cooked
2 cups cauliflower, steamed or 2 packages frozen (10 oz. ea.), cooked
2 to 4 oz. fat free shredded cheddar

Preheat oven to 350°

1. Mix together the kidney beans, tomato sauce, basil and oregano; set aside.
2. In a casserole dish layer half of each: rice first, kidney bean mixture, cauliflower and then, cheese; repeat the scenario, ending with the cauliflower; cover and bake for 30 to 40 minutes.
3. Remove cover; sprinkle the remaining cheese; cover until it melts.

YIELD: About 6 cups
FAT GRAMS IN ENTIRE RECIPE: About 4

Notes:

_____

_____

_____

_____

_____

LEMON PEPPER VEGETABLES

For those times when you're looking for a side dish that's fast and a little different.

Cooking utensil: A 3 quart non-stick saucepan

---

2 cups broccoli flowerets
2 cups cauliflower flowerets
1 cup carrots, thinly sliced
2 Tbs. Fleischmann's Fat Free Low Calorie squeeze margarine
1 Tbs. lemon pepper
1/2 tsp. garlic powder

---

1. Steam the broccoli, cauliflower and the carrots; set aside, keep warm.
2. Heat together the margarine, lemon pepper and garlic; combine with the vegetables; toss well and serve.

YIELD: 5 cups
FAT GRAMS IN ENTIRE RECIPE: 4

Notes:

BRUSSELS SPROUTS

These little cabbages are unique in flavor and are not as popular as one might expect. Perhaps the reason for that is the flavor, which is quite a bit stronger than cabbage's, makes a definite statement.

1 pound of trimmed sprouts is about equivalent to 4 cups.
1 cup cooked Brussels sprouts has less than 1/2 gram of fat.

Steam Brussels sprouts for the best results. The age and size of the heads will determine the amount of time necessary. You don't want to overcook these gems because they lose the edge of good flavor if they're overcooked. Cook until bright green and still crunchy, but tender. If you intend to steam or boil them to use later, cool them immediately under cold water to stop the cooking. They're great precooked, chilled, and cut up in salads.

STEAMED BRUSSELS SPROUTS

Cooking utensil: A bamboo steamer or covered dish for microwaving

---

1 pound Brussels sprouts
Appropriate water for steaming
Salt to taste

---

1. Cut the end of the stem off the sprouts; cut each stem end with a cross about 1/8 inch deep.
2. Cook for about 5 to 7 minutes in the steamer or 2 to 4 minutes in the microwave; remove one with a slotted spoon and pierce the base with a very sharp knife. If there's some resistance but the base is not hard, you're on the mark.

YIELD: About 4 cups
FAT GRAMS IN ENTIRE RECIPE: 4

BTW: Frozen Brussels sprouts are easy to prepare and offer one advantage: the heads are uniform in size and help to make the cooking more fool-proof.

BRUSSELS SPROUTS AND MUSHROOMS

This simple sauce can be prepared for many of the different vegetables when you're looking for a side dish for an entree or serving a variety of veggies on a platter for dinner.

Cooking utensil: A 2 quart non-stick saucepan

---

2 Tbs. Fleischmann's Fat Free Low Calorie squeeze margarine
1 medium onion, minced
1/2 pound mushrooms, thickly sliced
Salt and freshly ground pepper to taste
1 tsp. sweet paprika
2 tsp. all-purpose flour
1 cup defatted chicken stock
Cayenne pepper to taste
1 pound Brussels sprouts, steamed

---

1. Sauté the onion and mushrooms with the salt and pepper until just tender.
2. While the onion and mushroom are sautéing, mix together the paprika, flour and stock; gradually add this mixture to the sauté; cook over medium-low heat until thickened.
3. Add the cayenne pepper to taste.
4. Serve, poured over the Brussels sprouts.

YIELD: 5 to 6 cups
FAT GRAMS IN ENTIRE RECIPE: 5

Notes:

_____

_____

_____

_____

_____

SPROUTS WITH LEMON-MUSTARD SAUCE

Here's another easy sauce to prepare for this interesting vegetable.

Cooking utensil: A 2 quart non-stick saucepan

---

4 Tbs. prepared Butter Buds
Juice of 1/2 lemon
1 1/2 tsp. Dijon mustard
1 pound Brussels sprouts, steamed

---

1. Heat the Butter Buds in the saucepan; add the lemon juice and mustard; blend well.
2. Add the sprouts; toss and serve.

YIELD: 4 cups
FAT GRAMS IN ENTIRE RECIPE: 4

Notes:

CABBAGE

There are so many things a cook can do with cabbage to make a meal. Whether it's combining cabbage and potatoes, a dish that kept Russians and Irish alive for centuries, or dressing it up into slaw, a favorite on salad buffets all over America, there's much to be said for this hearty vegetable that is always available and inexpensive.

A 2 pound head, trimmed (outer leaves and core removed), weighs in at about 1 1/2 pounds. That equals just about 9 to 10 cups, sliced or shredded, 5 to 6 cups, cooked.

1 cup cooked cabbage has about 1/2 gram of fat.

Look for cabbage heads that are firm and heavy, with green outer leaves and no black spots. If there are a few on the outer leaves, remove them and check to see good color and a spot-free inside head. There is no need to cook cabbage ahead of time and in the dishes that follow you'll see some nifty ways of preparing it.

There's no question that the cabbage is no longer a vegetable to think of "with potatoes." It can be cooked in the microwave (3 cups take about 6 minutes, depending on the power of your oven) for a delicate side-dish with a touch of non-fat butter substitute and a sprinkle of salt and pepper.

You can certainly add shredded cabbage to your stir-fry or a canned soup to bring up a more "home-cooked" flavor. Just shredded and added, raw, to salads gives a fresh extra crunch, whether it's red or white cabbage.

CABBAGE AND REDSKIN POTATOES

Cabbage and potatoes are as natural a duo as mushrooms and onions. This dish is an easy one to prepare but you may want to make just enough for one dinner. Sometimes the leftovers are hard to sell, since the flavors are best when the ingredients are just-cooked.

Cooking utensil: An 8 quart non-stick pot

---

1 pound redskin potatoes, scrubbed and quartered
2 quarts water, lightly salted
2 large onions, in half and then quartered
4 Tbs. chicken bouillon granules
1 Tbs. garlic powder
1 head cabbage, heart removed, cut in wedges or large pieces
Molly McButter to taste
Salt and pepper to taste

---

1. Place potatoes in the pot in cold salted water to cover; bring to a boil; cook about 5 minutes.
2. Remove most of the water, leaving about 1/2 to 3/4 cup liquid in the pot; add the remaining ingredients; cook on a medium heat until the potatoes are easily pierced with a fork and the onions are cooked through.
3. Sprinkle Molly McButter and toss if you like this dish with a buttery flavor. Season with salt and pepper.

YIELD: About 12 cups
FAT GRAMS IN ENTIRE RECIPE: 2

Notes:

CABBAGE AND TOMATOES WITH POTATOES

Some turkey sausage or Bilinski's chicken sausage is a natural partner for this cabbage dish.

Cooking utensil: An 8 quart non-stick pot

---

4 or 5 small redskin potatoes, cut in eighths
1/2 head cabbage, cut in large pieces
1 large onion, thickly sliced
1/2 cup defatted chicken stock
1 can (15 oz.) white northern beans or white kidney
1 can (16 oz.) stewed tomatoes
1/4 tsp. sugar
Salt and pepper to taste

---

1. Parboil the potatoes for 5 minutes in a large saucepan or pot; drain.
2. Add all other ingredients; simmer, covered, until the onion is cooked through, about 10 minutes.

YIELD: About 8 to 10 cups
FAT GRAMS IN ENTIRE RECIPE: 3

Notes:

CABBAGE AND RICE WITH TOMATOES

The raisins in this recipe cut the acidity of the tomatoes and are a foil for the spices.

Cooking utensil: An 8 quart non-stick pot

1/2 cup defatted chicken stock
2 large onions, sliced
1 head cabbage, shredded
4 cloves garlic, minced
2 tsp. ground cumin
1/2 tsp. turmeric
2 cups long-grain white rice, uncooked
4 cups defatted chicken stock, additional
1 can (16 oz.) stewed tomatoes
1/2 tsp. salt
1/2 cup raisins
Salt, additional to taste
Freshly ground pepper to taste

---

1. Sauté the onion in the 1/2 cup stock, in the large pot, until soft; add the cabbage; cover; cook over low heat, stirring frequently, until the cabbage wilts, about 5 minutes.
2. Add the garlic, cumin, turmeric and rice; mix and cook for 2 minutes.
3. Add the rest of the ingredients and cover; cook for about 20 minutes or until the rice is cooked.
4. Add additional salt and freshly ground pepper to taste.

YIELD: About 10 cups
FAT GRAMS IN ENTIRE RECIPE: 3

BTW: If you purchase the bagged, shredded cabbage, this recipe should take only 10 minutes preparation-time. Brown rice is good with this, too, but you must adjust your cook-time.

Notes:

SWEET AND SOUR CABBAGE

A touch of Oriental sweet-sour for an interesting deviation.

Cooking utensil: A non-stick wok

1/4 cup defatted chicken stock
1 large onion, sliced
2 carrots, diagonally sliced
1/2 large head cabbage, sliced
1/2 cup fresh bean sprouts
2 Tbs. water
2 tomatoes, sliced
1/4 cup honey
1/4 cup wine or cider vinegar
2 tsp. cornstarch
Tamari or soy sauce to taste

---

1. Sauté the onion in the stock, in your wok, until tender; add the carrots and stir-fry for about 3 minutes.
2. Add the cabbage and bean sprouts and stir-fry for an additional 2 to 3 minutes; add the tomatoes and water; toss.
3. Cover; cook on medium heat for 10 minutes.
4. In the meantime, combine the honey and vinegar and stir well; stir in the cornstarch and dissolve.
5. Add the sauce to the vegetables and stir until the sauce thickens and the vegetables look glazed.

YIELD: 6 cups
FAT GRAMS IN ENTIRE RECIPE: 2

BTW: I like this served on white or brown rice.

Notes:

Cabbage Slaw I

It's nice to know there are special foods in the refrigerator to help enhance a salad. We love slaw and you'll find three of them here. Different strokes for different folks. Surely one of these slaws will turn you on.

Preparation utensil: A large bowl with a cover

2 Tbs. sugar
2/3 cup boiling water
1/3 cup white vinegar
1/2 tsp. salt
1/2 tsp. celery seeds
8 cups cabbage, shredded
1/2 red bell pepper, chopped
1/2 green bell pepper, chopped
1 large carrot, grated
Freshly ground pepper to taste

1. Stir the sugar in the water; add the vinegar, salt, celery seeds; stir together.
2. Place cabbage and other vegetables in a large bowl; pour dressing over the vegetables and toss.
3. Refrigerate for 2 to 3 hours before serving.

YIELD: About 6 cups
FAT GRAMS IN ENTIRE RECIPE: 2

Notes:

CABBAGE SLAW II

This slaw may be more like the kind you're used to because of the creamy dressing.

Preparation utensil: A large bowl with a cover

---

8 cups cabbage, shredded
1 large carrot, grated
1/2 medium green bell pepper, minced
1/2 cup Smart Beat Fat Free Mayonnaise
1/8 tsp. Dijon mustard
1/2 tsp. sugar
1 Tbs. white vinegar
1 Tbs. skim milk
3/4 tsp. salt
Freshly ground pepper to taste

---

1. Place shredded cabbage in a large bowl with the carrot and bell pepper; set aside.
2. Mix together all remaining ingredients; pour on cabbage mixture and toss.
3. Refrigerate for about 2 to 3 hours before serving.

YIELD: About 6 cups
FAT GRAMS IN ENTIRE RECIPE: 2

Notes:

_____

_____

_____

_____

_____

_____

COLE SLAW III

We like this slaw because it adds a little Italian flavoring to the dressing that picks up the flavor a bit, for a nifty switch.

Preparation utensil: A large bowl with a cover

---

1 cup Smart Beat Fat Free Mayonnaise
1/2 cup white wine vinegar
1 package Good Seasons Italian Dressing dry ingredients
1/2 tsp. sugar
Freshly ground black pepper
10 to 12 cups cabbage, shredded
2 carrots, grated
1/2 green bell pepper, minced
1/2 red bell pepper, minced

---

1. Stir the mayonnaise as you add the vinegar; when smooth, add the dry ingredients (regular, not the fat free) Good Seasons Italian Dressing, the sugar and the pepper; mix to blend; set aside.
2. Place the vegetables in a large bowl; add the dressing mix; toss to cover.
3. Refrigerate for at least 2 to 3 hours before serving.

YIELD: About 10 cups
FAT GRAMS IN ENTIRE RECIPE: 4

Notes:

CARROTS

Talk about a fantastic vegetable for good health and satisfaction. The mere act of chewing a carrot is probably as good for us as 10 minutes of meditation! This colorful root can be used in a number of recipes to add a touch of sweetness. Just grate and add to the recipe for sweetening.

Can there be a salad worth its salt without carrot? For a new look, after peeling, slide the potato peeler down the carrot and use the curls you get in the next salad you make. If you have a Salad Shooter it will grate the carrot fine enough for the cole slaws listed in the cabbage recipes.

They can be boiled, of course, but the full flavor of carrots is enhanced by braising in just a bit of defatted stock. You can peel them with a potato peeler or scrub them with a vegetable brush and a mild soap (be sure to rinse thoroughly).

1 pound of carrots will give you about 3 to 3 1/2 cups grated or sliced.
1 cup of carrots, cooked, has about 1/4 gram of fat.

BRAISED CARROTS

Cooking utensil: A 3 quart non-stick saucepan

---

1 pound carrots, cut into 2 inch pieces
1 cup defatted chicken broth

---

1. Place the carrots in the pot with the stock and simmer until the carrots can be pierced with a small sharp knife.

YIELD: About 4 cups
FAT GRAMS IN ENTIRE RECIPE: 1

Notes:

JEWISH PENICILLIN

This marvelous chicken soup. The kind my mother used to make when any one of us caught a cold, is known to have healing powers but the doctors still don't know whether there is some reaction of the ingredients that simulate a drug, whether it's the heat of the vapors, entering the nostrils, that clears the air passages and make the patient feel better, or if it's just the love with which the soup was made that has its very own healing powers.

Cooking utensil: An 8 quart non-stick pot

---

1 whole stewing chicken, skinned
6 ribs celery with tops, cut in large pieces
4 carrots, cut in large pieces
2 large onions, cut in large pieces
1 parsnip, cut in large pieces
1 Tbs. whole black peppercorns
6 sprigs fresh parsley
1 large piece cheesecloth
Salt and pepper to taste
Dill weed, fresh or dried to taste

---

1. Clean the poultry and place the whole bird, including the neck and giblets, in a large pot in water to cover.
2. Place all remaining ingredients, except the salt, pepper and dill weed for seasoning, in the cheese cloth and tie off with a piece of string; place this bundle in the pot with the chicken.
3. Add 1 Tbs. salt to the water and boil, uncovered; reduce to a simmer; cook, uncovered, until the meat falls off the bone when touched with a fork, about 1 1/2 hours.
4. Remove the bundle of vegetables and open; return the carrots to the soup; discard the rest of the bundle.
5. Season with the salt, pepper and dill; continue to cook the soup, uncovered, so that it cooks down by about 25%. To taste the soup during this time, take the spoon and stir until the fat on the top dissipates, so you can get a spoonful of broth to taste.
6. When the taste of the soup meets your expectations, remove the chicken; cool the soup; refrigerate.
7. The chicken meat can be used for sandwiches or chicken salad; discard

the neck and giblets.

8. After cooling, remove the fat that has congealed on the top of the soup, and you have defatted stock or chicken soup to heal your loved ones.

YIELD: 6 to 8 cups

FAT GRAMS IN ENTIRE RECIPE: The broth: 1 to 2 grams if defatted properly. The meat varies: Dark meat: 2 1/2 grams per ounce White meat: 1 gram per ounce

BTW: If you have no cheesecloth, prepare the soup and use a strainer to remove the unwanted, overcooked vegetables that were used solely for seasoning the broth. Add cooked rice or noodles to the broth for variety.

Notes:

SCOTCH BROTH

Another nifty soup for you to use to warm up on a cold winter's eve. Carrots give the sweet, round flavor to so many soups and stews.

Cooking utensil: An 8 quart non-stick pot

---

2 large carrots, cut into 1 inch pieces
4 cups cabbage, shredded
2 white turnips, peeled and cut into 1 inch chunks
1 Tbs. sugar
4 cloves garlic, minced
3/4 cup pearled barley
2 quarts defatted chicken stock
1 package (10 oz.) frozen peas
1 pound turkey breast, cooked and skinned, cut into 1 inch cubes
Freshly ground pepper and dill weed to taste

---

1. Place the first 6 ingredients in a large pot with the chicken stock; bring to a boil; reduce to simmer.
2. Cover; cook gently for about 1 1/2 hours; retain liquid at the same level by adding water from time to time.
3. Add peas and turkey; simmer 10 minutes.
4. Add pepper and dill weed; serve

YIELD: About 12 cups
FAT GRAMS IN ENTIRE RECIPE: 6

BTW: Soups are great as one-dish meals and this one is truly satisfying with a hunk of fat free rye or sourdough.

Notes:

_____

_____

_____

Vegetable Soup With Basil

More soup to quell that need for warm fuzzies we all have. There's nothing like a bowl of home-made soup to bring it all together.

Cooking utensil: An 8 quart non-stick pot

1/2 cup white wine or defatted stock
1 medium onion, chopped
2 ribs celery, coarsely chopped
1 medium carrot, sliced
1 large russet potato, peeled, cut in 1 inch slices
1 can (14 1/2 oz.) diced tomatoes with juice
6 cups defatted chicken stock, additional
2 Tbs. fresh basil, chopped or 1 tsp. dried, crushed
1/2 small head cauliflower, flowerets
1/4 pound green beans, cut in 2 inch pieces
2 small zucchini, sliced
1 package (10 oz.) frozen peas
1 cup cabbage, shredded
Salt and freshly ground pepper to taste

---

1. Place the wine or stock in the pot; sauté the onion, celery and carrot until tender.
2. Add the potato, tomatoes, the additional stock and basil; bring to a boil; reduce heat; simmer for 20 minutes.
3. Add the cauliflower and green beans; simmer 10 minutes.
4. Add the peas and cabbage; simmer another 5 minutes or until all vegetables are tender.
5. Season with salt and pepper and serve.

YIELD: 12 cups
FAT GRAMS IN ENTIRE RECIPE: 4

Notes:

CARROT AND CABBAGE STIR-FRY

Clean out the refrigerator on this one, if you like. Always start with the first 5 ingredients, then add whatever other additions turn you on.

Cooking utensil: A non-stick wok

---

1 large or 2 medium carrots, sliced into match-sticks
2 to 4 cups cabbage, shredded
1 to 2 onions, thinly sliced
1 Tbs. garlic, minced
1/2 cup defatted chicken stock
1 green bell pepper, sliced or 1/2 green, 1/2 red
2 Tbs. soy sauce or tamari
1 Tbs. sugar
1 Tbs. rice wine vinegar
1/4 cup defatted chicken broth, additional
2 Tbs. cornstarch

---

1. Add the 4 ingredients to the wok with the defatted 1/2 cup chicken stock; stir-fry for 2 minutes; add the bell pepper; stir-fry an additional 2 minutes; take the wok off the heat source.
2. Mix together the rest of the ingredients, dissolving the cornstarch in the liquid; replace wok to medium heat; add the cornstarch mixture, slowly adding it as you stir.
3. When the vegetables are crisp-tender and the sauce has thickened, serve on steamed rice.

YIELD: Varies depending on vegetables and quantities used
FAT GRAMS IN ENTIRE RECIPE: With this mix and 4 cups cabbage, 4

BTW: During the vegetable addition stage, you may want to add zucchini, asparagus, green beans, snow peas, bean sprouts, water chestnuts...it's all yours.

Notes:

Carrot And Raisin Salad

This gives you some fruit along with your carrots. A grand idea, and sweet, too.

Preparation utensils: A large bowl and a small bowl

---

2 cups grated carrots
1/2 cup raisins
1/4 cup canned pineapple chunks, drained
1/2 cup fat free mayonnaise
3/4 tsp. salt
1/2 tsp. sugar, optional
1 Tbs. fresh lemon juice or vinegar
Freshly ground pepper to taste

---

1. Place the carrots, raisins and pineapple in the bowl; set aside.
2. Combine the mayonnaise, salt, sugar (if desired), lemon juice and pepper in a separate bowl.
3. Add the mayonnaise mixture to the carrot mix; toss to cover the carrot mix evenly with the mayonnaise mixture.
4. Refrigerate for at least 3 to 4 hours before serving.

YIELD: 3 cups
FAT GRAMS IN ENTIRE RECIPE: Less than 1

BTW: This is a great nibble at the office.

Notes:

MARVELOUS CARROT MUFFINS

I found this muffin recipe years ago, made the appropriate conversion, and loved it. You've really got to love a heavy muffin to appreciate it. Light and fluffy is not this muffin...but it's so good.

Baking utensil: Jumbo muffin tin (6 muffin cups), treated with spray-on oil

---

2 cups whole wheat flour
1 cup sugar
1 tsp. baking powder
1 tsp. baking soda
2 tsp. ground cinnamon
1/2 tsp. salt
6 egg whites, at room temperature
2 cups carrots, shredded
1 can (8 oz.) crushed pineapple with juices
1/3 cup raisins

Preheat the oven to 350°

1. In a large bowl, mix all dry ingredients with a fork; set aside.
2. Beat the egg whites until frothy; combine the egg whites with the carrots and the pineapple, with the juice; add to the dry ingredients; mix until thoroughly blended.
4. Add the raisins and stir again.
5. Bake for 35 to 45 minutes, or until a toothpick, inserted in the center of one of the muffins, comes out clean.

YIELD: 6 muffins
FAT GRAMS IN ENTIRE RECIPE: 6

BTW: Add an extra touch to these muffins: cream cheese with which a spoon of orange marmalade has been blended.

Notes:

CELERY

Years ago I was told that celery was the dieter's best food because you expend more energy chewing it than the celery adds calories. It was, therefore, a negative calorie vegetable. Whether that's true or not doesn't really matter...we know it's virtually fat free. It brightens up the taste of so many dishes, and lasts for weeks in a plastic bag in the crisper drawer of the refrigerator.

1 pound of celery stalks becomes 4 cups chopped or sliced. 4 cups raw cooks down to about 3 cups, cooked.
1 cup chopped celery has less than 1/2 gram of fat.

THE CELERY STIR-FRY

Instead of using bok choy or carrots, cabbage and onions as the base of the vegetable stir-fry, use the outer ribs of the celery.

Cooking utensil: A non-stick wok

1/4 cup defatted chicken stock
2 Tbs. soy sauce
1/2 tsp. ginger
2 Tbs. sugar
1 Tbs. rice wine vinegar
2 Tbs. cornstarch
1/2 cup defatted chicken stock, additional
1 Tbs. garlic, minced
4 ribs celery, diagonally sliced
1 large onion, in half and sliced
1 cup mushrooms, thickly sliced
1/2 green bell pepper, thinly sliced
1/2 red pepper, thinly sliced

---

1. Mix first 5 ingredients; add the cornstarch and dissolve; set aside.
2. Heat the additional stock; add the garlic and stir-fry for about 1 minute.
3. Add the celery and onion; stir-fry about 2 minutes; add the other vegeta-

bles; stir-fry 2 minutes.

4. Add the sauce and stir-fry on medium heat until the sauce thickens and the vegetables are shiny.

5. Serve on steamed white or brown rice, prepared with no oil or margarine.

YIELD: 2 to 3 cups
FAT GRAMS IN ENTIRE RECIPE: 1

BTW: Just this simple and just this fast, if you take 10 minutes to slice and 10 minutes to stir-fry, you have a dinner to remember. If you happen to have some leftover cooked turkey or chicken, or the spirit moves you, stir in some shrimp, for a meal fit for people who like heavier fare.

Notes:

Tuna Salad

Yes, I know this is elementary. But that's the name of this book. And many people have a particular love for tuna salad but don't make it low fat. This one is.

Preparation utensil: A small bowl

---

1 can (6 1/2 oz.) tuna, packed in water, drained
1 Tbs. Smart Beat Fat Free Mayonnaise
1/8 tsp. Dijon mustard
1/2 tsp. fresh lemon juice
1/4 tsp. pickle relish, optional

---

1. Place the tuna in a bowl; add the rest of the ingredients; toss.
2. Serve in salad, on a salad tray, in a sandwich.

YIELD: 3/4 cup
FAT GRAMS IN ENTIRE RECIPE: About 3 depending on the packager

BTW: The relish is optional because some purists prefer their tuna salad with just the celery, mayo and lemon juice. Others like a touch of raw, minced onion in it, too. Do your thing!

Notes:

_____

_____

_____

_____

_____

_____

_____

CELERY WITH DILL

Now this is an unusual side veggie...really good with an assortment of other vegetables on a dinner platter.

Cooking utensil: A 2 quart non-stick saucepan

---

3 cups celery, chopped
1 tsp. water
1/2 tsp. dill seed
1 Tbs. Fleischmann's Fat Free Low Calorie squeeze margarine
   or 1 Tbs. prepared Butter Buds
Salt and freshly ground pepper to taste

---

1. Place the celery, in the saucepan with the water; cover and cook on medium-high heat for one minute.
2. Reduce the heat and cook on low for about 10 minutes; add the remaining ingredients.
3. Toss and serve.

YIELD: About 2 cups
FAT GRAMS IN ENTIRE RECIPE: Less than 1

Notes:

CELERY AND TOMATO STEW WITH BEANS

It doesn't sound like much but it tastes good and, my goodness, it's easy to make.

Cooking utensil: An 8 quart non-stick pot

---

4 cups celery, diagonally sliced
1 large onion, sliced
1 red bell pepper
1/4 cup white wine or defatted chicken stock
2 cloves garlic, minced
1 can (14 1/2 oz.) diced tomatoes, with juice
1/2 tsp. celery salt
1/2 cup fresh dill, chopped or 3 Tbs. dried dill weed
1/2 cup defatted chicken stock, additional
2 cups white kidney beans, cooked or canned, drained
Salt and freshly ground pepper to taste

---

1. Sauté the celery, onion and bell pepper in the 1/4 wine or stock until crisp-tender; add the garlic and cook about 1 minute.
2. Add the remaining ingredients; cook on medium-low for about 20 minutes.
3. Season to taste with salt and pepper and serve.

YIELD: 8 cups
FAT GRAMS IN ENTIRE RECIPE: 4

BTW: Some brown rice served with this stew is just right. Be sure to prepare it without any oil or margarine.

Notes:

CUCUMBERS

Cucumbers are pretty. They are also mostly water. There is about 1/2 gram of fat in a pound of unpeeled cucumbers. They are an important component of a well-rounded salad and their claim to fame is the crunchy version of this vegetable when they're pickled.

1 pound of cucumber, with skins on will give you about 4 cups. Seed, skin and slice the cucumbers and you end up with about 2 cups.
1 cup cucumbers has less than 1/4 gram of fat.

CUCUMBER SALAD

Preparation utensil: A bowl with a tight cover

---

1 cup Smart Beat Fat Free Mayonnaise
4 1/2 cups red wine vinegar
1 packet Good Seasons Italian Dressing (the envelope of dry ingredients)
6 cucumbers, peeled and sliced
3 large onions, sliced in rings
Freshly ground pepper to taste

---

1. Gradually add the vinegar to the mayonnaise in a small bowl; when it's thoroughly mixed, add the dry mix of Italian Dressing and combine; set aside.
2. In a large bowl, place the cucumbers and onions; add the dressing mix and toss.
3. Season to taste with the pepper; refrigerate for about 2 hours and serve.

YIELD: About 15 cups
FAT GRAMS IN ENTIRE RECIPE: 3

BTW: This is a big recipe. If you just want to make enough for 2 to 4 people, make the dressing using only 1 cup of mayo and 1/2 cup of vinegar with the packet of Good Seasons; use half the dressing with an additional cup of vinegar and 1/3 of the rest of the ingredients. That will give you a yield of 4 to 5 cups. Use the rest of the dressing on salads or cole slaw.

KIM'S CUCUMBER WHEELS

Our daughter, Kim, has a way of taking the ordinary and making it extraordinary. This little goody for serving before a summertime dinner is light and tasty.

Preparation utensil: A bowl and a plate

3 oz. fat free cream cheese
1 Tbs. chopped chives
1 Tbs. fresh parsley, snipped
1 tsp. fat free mayonnaise
1/4 tsp. paprika
1/2 tsp. fresh lemon juice
1 medium cucumber, peeled

1. Combine all ingredients except the cucumber.
2. Remove one end of the cucumber and seed it using an apple corer; fill the hollow cucumber with the creamy mixture; refrigerate.
3. Just before serving, slice into 1/4 inch thick rounds.

YIELD: One stuffed cucumber
FAT GRAMS IN ENTIRE RECIPE: 0

Notes:

EGGPLANT

This gorgeous purple vegetable is popular, not only in Mediterranean cuisine, but in Chinese and Japanese, as well. The taste varies depending on the maturity of the eggplant, when picked and its age, when prepared. Eggplant is exceedingly porous and is therefore not a good candidate for frying. It absorbs much more oil per ounce than any other vegetable (including French fried potatoes), making it a higher fat gram candidate, when fried for parmigiana recipes, than veal. There are other methods of preparing this vegetable that will please you so much that you can forget about frying. To give you an example, 8 ounces of eggplant, boiled and drained is about 1/2 fat gram. Celantano's Eggplant Parmigiana, 8 ounces (including cheese and sauce, of course), is 15 grams of fat.

A 1 pound eggplant is approximately 4 cups cubed. Cooked, it shrinks down by half.
1 cup of cooked eggplant is worth less than 1/4 gram of fat.

If you are baking the whole eggplant in the oven, or cooking it in the microwave, be sure to prick the skin with a fork. Otherwise it will blow up. When you're buying eggplant, choose heavy eggplants that are smaller in size. The skin should be shiny and firm, and should bounce back when finger-pressed. If the indentation remains, the eggplant is too ripe.

Many cooks salt and drain the eggplant for 30 minutes or so, before cooking, to eliminate some of the water natural to this vegetable.

Pre-Recipe Microwave

When you see a recipe that calls for cooked eggplant as one of the ingredients, or you are instructed to bake or broil the eggplant prior to preparation of the dish, microwaving will save you some time.

1 medium eggplant (about 1 1/2 pounds), whole

1. Pierce the eggplant with a long-pronged fork.
2. If you have a rack, set the eggplant on the rack; cook on high for 5 minutes.

3. Turn the eggplant over and cook 3 to 5 minutes more or until it feels slightly soft to the touch.
4. Set the eggplant aside until it's cool enough to handle; continue with the recipe.

YIELD: 1 cooked eggplant, good to go
FAT GRAMS IN ENTIRE RECIPE: Less than 1 gram

BTW: At this point it's easy enough to prepare any of the ratatouilles or stew that call for broiling or baking.

Notes:

_____

_____

_____

_____

_____

_____

_____

_____

_____

_____

_____

_____

_____

_____

BROILED EGGPLANT SLICES

You can broil slices of eggplant, and use in any recipe that calls for fried eggplant slices, when you're working on a conversion.

Cooking utensil: A non-stick baking sheet

---

1 eggplant (about 1 pound), in 1/4 inch thick slices
Olive Oil Pam
Salt and freshly ground pepper

---

1. Place eggplant on a foil-lined baking sheet; spray quickly with Olive Oil Pam, sprinkle with salt and pepper.
2. Broil for 8 minutes on one side; turn over and broil on the other side for about 7 minutes.

YIELD: About 18 to 20 slices
FAT GRAMS IN ENTIRE RECIPE: Less than 2 for the eggplant;
    about 1 gram for each 2 1/2 second spray of Pam

Btw: These slices can be sprinkled with garlic before broiling and can be used in a number of different recipes.

Notes:

_____

_____

_____

_____

_____

_____

_____

_____

BROILED EGGPLANT ITAIANO

This is simple to prepare and the consumers of this delicacy will think you worked very hard. The perfect recipe.

Cooking utensils: A non-stick baking sheet and a 9 x 9 non-stick baking dish

---

1 medium eggplant, sliced crosswise in 3/4 inch slices
1 bottle fat free Italian dressing
1/2 tsp. dried oregano leaves, crushed
1/2 tsp. dried rosemary, crushed
1 cup of The Marinara Sauce
6 Tbs. fat free breadcrumbs
Fat free grated Parmesan

---

1. Marinate the eggplant in the dressing with the seasonings.
2. Broil the eggplant slices on each side until lightly browned.
3. Spoon The Marinara Sauce on the bottom of a 9 inch x 9 inch baking dish to cover; alternate eggplant slices and marinara finishing with the marinara.
4. Place on lower shelf of the oven and broil until bubbly.
5. Sprinkle with fat free Parmesan and serve.

YIELD: 1 pan 9 inches x 9 inches
FAT GRAMS IN ENTIRE RECIPE: About 1

BTW: This is a good way to get to know eggplant if you've not cooked it before. Some crusty French bread and a salad makes this a delightful dinner.

Notes:

EGGPLANT CASSEROLE WITH WINE

This dish is a favorite of David's. He always made a face when I said, "Eggplant!" Now he cooks this one, himself. It gets a bit runny so don't be surprised by the liquid. You can cut down on the stock if you find that offensive.

Cooking utensils: A baking sheet treated with spray-on oil, a large, non-stick skillet and a large oven-proof casserole

---

1 large eggplant, cut in half, length-wise
Olive Oil Pam
1 medium onion, chopped
4 cloves garlic, minced
1/4 cup defatted chicken stock
2 cups mushrooms, halved
1 cup canned tomatoes, coarsely chopped, drained
1/2 tsp. dried thyme, crushed
1 cup dry white wine
1/2 cup defatted chicken stock, additional
1 pound redskin potatoes, scrubbed, diced
Salt and pepper to taste
1/4 cup fresh parsley, chopped
2 Tbs. fat free grated Parmesan

Preheat oven to 500°

1. Score the skin of the eggplant and place flat side down on the baking sheet; bake at 500° for 10 to 15 minutes.
2. Remove the eggplant; reduce heat in oven to 350°; set aside to cool.
3. In a large saucepan or skillet, soften the onion and half the garlic in the 1/4 cup stock; add the mushrooms, tomatoes, thyme, wine, additional stock, potatoes, the remaining garlic and a pinch of salt; simmer for 5 minutes.
4. Without peeling, dice the eggplant; add the eggplant to the rest of the ingredients with half of the parsley; cook, stirring for 10 minutes.
5. Move the entire pot full to an oven-proof dish or a large casserole dish; cover and bake for 30 to 40 minutes, or until the vegetables are tender.

6. Season with salt and pepper to taste; sprinkle the remaining parsley and Parmesan on top and serve.

YIELD: 8 to 10 cups
FAT GRAMS IN ENTIRE RECIPE: 4 to 5

Notes:

_____

_____

_____

_____

_____

_____

_____

_____

_____

_____

_____

_____

_____

_____

_____

_____

_____

EGGPLANT AND CHICKPEA CURRY

There are some recipes that combine food from different cultures and turn out to be perfectly seasoned. You, hopefully, will feel that way about this dish.

Cooking utensil: An 8 quart non-stick pot

1/2 cup defatted chicken stock
1 large onion, chopped
4 large cloves garlic, minced
1 fresh jalapeño pepper, seeded and minced, more to taste
4 Tbs. curry powder
1 eggplant (about 1 pound) unpeeled, cut in 3/4 inch cubes
Salt to taste
1 can (28 oz.) plum tomatoes, coarsely chopped, drained
1 Tbs. tomato paste
1/2 cup water
2 cups garbanzo beans, cooked or canned and drained
Cayenne pepper to taste

---

1. Sauté the onion in the large pot; cook on low heat until soft.
2. Add the garlic, jalapeño pepper and curry powder; cook for 1 minute.
3. Add the eggplant and salt; mix well to coat eggplant with spices.
4. Add the tomatoes and bring to a boil.
6. Mix together the tomato paste and water until smooth; stir into the mixture; reduce heat and simmer for 20 minutes, stirring frequently.
7. Add garbanzo beans and simmer 10 to 20 minutes more or until the eggplant is very tender and the mixture has thickened.
8. Adjust seasoning and serve.

YIELD: About 7 to 8 cups
FAT GRAMS IN ENTIRE RECIPE: 7

BTW: Couscous or brown rice with this casserole makes one heck of a meal! Prepare either one with no oil or margarine

CAPONATA

Hors d'oeuvres are usually loaded with fat until you do some whittling. We've done some here and we think you'll be happy with the results.

Cooking utensil: A large non-fat skillet treated with Olive Oil Pam

---

1 eggplant (about 1 1/2 pounds), unpeeled, cut in 1/2 inch cubes
Olive Oil Pam
1 medium onion, chopped
1 rib celery, chopped
2 cloves garlic, minced
1 green bell pepper, chopped
1/4 cup defatted chicken stock
1 can (28 oz.) plum tomatoes, finely chopped and drained
4 oz. pimiento-stuffed green olives, sliced
3 oz. bottled capers, with liquid
2 Tbs. sugar
Salt and pepper to taste

---

1. Soak the eggplant in salted water for about 30 minutes; drain; sauté in a spray of the Olive Oil Pam.
2. Add the onion, celery, garlic and bell pepper; sauté in the Olive Oil Pam until soft; add a bit of the stock to the mixture if it's too dry.
3. Add the tomatoes, the olives, the capers and the sugar; cover; simmer for about 10 minutes, stirring often, until the eggplant is tender.
4. Season; serve at room temperature.

YIELD: About 6 cups
FAT GRAMS IN ENTIRE RECIPE: 8

BTW: Serve this spread with pita triangles: split a number of pita breads the round way into two halves; cut each half into fourths; bake at about 375° until crisp.

Notes:

Eggplant Appetizer

Following the Italian appetizer what could be better than going around the Mediterranean to bring you this spread that would be a neat go-along with the Hummus.

Preparation utensil: A large bowl

---

2 eggplants (about 1 pound each)
2 garlic cloves, minced
1/2 cup Smart Beat Fat Free Mayonnaise
1/8 tsp. Dijon mustard
1 to 3 Tbs. fresh lemon juice to taste
Salt and freshly ground pepper to taste
Cayenne pepper or hot sauce to taste
2 Tbs. fresh parsley, chopped

Preheat oven to 400°

1. Prick the eggplant a number of times to avoid a blow-up; bake for about 1 hour.
2. When you take out the eggplant, remove the skin and the stem, squeeze out any liquid from inside; chop the eggplant meat very fine.
3. Combine the meat of the eggplant with the garlic, the mayonnaise and the mustard; mix very well; add the lemon juice to taste.
4. Season well; top with parsley and serve with pita bread.

YIELD: About 4 cups
FAT GRAMS IN ENTIRE RECIPE: 2

Notes:

RATATOUILLE

In other words, eggplant stew. This ratatouille is easier to prepare than the one following, but since the flavor is different, as well, only you can decide which one is better for you.

Cooking utensil: An 8 quart non-stick pot

1 eggplant (1 1/2 pounds) peeled and cubed
3 medium onions, chopped
2 ribs celery, thinly sliced
1 clove garlic, minced
1 green bell pepper
1/2 cup defatted stock
2 small zucchini, cut in 1/2 inch cubes
3 large Roma tomatoes. chopped
1/4 cup fresh parsley, minced
Salt and freshly ground pepper to taste

1. Sauté the eggplant, onions, celery, garlic and bell pepper in the stock for about 5 minutes; cover; simmer for about 15 minutes until the eggplant is tender.
2. Add the zucchini and the tomatoes; simmer, uncovered until the zucchini is tender.
3. Season with salt and pepper and serve.

YIELD: 10 to 12 cups
FAT GRAMS IN ENTIRE RECIPE: 4

BTW: You can serve this as is or on rice or couscous.

Notes:

Roasted Ratatouille

The preparation of this stew is a bit different from the previous ratatouille because of the roasting. The only way you'll be sure which one you prefer is to try them both.

Cooking utensils: A baking sheet treated with Olive Oil Pam and a large non-stick skillet

---

1 eggplant (1 pound) unpeeled, sliced crosswise in 3/4 inch slices
Olive Oil Pam
3 medium zucchini, cut crosswise i 3/4 inch slices
1/4 cup defatted chicken stock
1 1/2 cup onion, in half, sliced
2 cloves garlic, minced
1 large red bell pepper, cut in 1/2 inch squares
1 large green bell pepper. cut in 1/2 inch squares
2 cups tomato, seeded, unpeeled, chopped
2 Tbs. fresh parsley, chopped
1/2 tsp. dried thyme leaves, crushed
Salt and pepper to taste

---

1. Cut the eggplant slices in 4 wedges each; place in a single layer on a baking sheet sprayed with the Pam; spray the wedges; broil 5 1/2 inches from the heat for 14 minutes or until browned; place in bowl; set aside.
2. Place the zucchini on the baking sheet sprayed with Pam; spray the zucchini; broil as you did the eggplant for about 7 minutes; add to the eggplant.
3. Place the stock in a large skillet and sauté the onion, the garlic and bell peppers for about 10 minutes or until tender.
4. Add the tomato; sauté 5 minutes more.
5. Add the eggplant and the remaining ingredients; cover; reduce heat and simmer for 15 minutes.
6. Season to taste and serve.

YIELD: 6 cups
FAT GRAMS IN ENTIRE RECIPE: 10 to 12 grams

GREEN BEANS

When I was a kid I thought green beans were only available in a can. You know the beans I'm talking about...from that big green guy. The color gray comes to mind, instead of green. Now there's almost nothing finer than fresh green beans, steamed, with Fleischmann's Fat Free Low Calorie squeeze margarine or Molly McButter. Choose beans that are similar in size for more even cooking. The pods should be young so that the beans are not mature, they should be barely visible. The pod should snap when broken, If the pods are too limp to snap they're not fresh.

1 cup of green beans, cooked, is less than 1/2 gram of fat.

STEAMED GREEN BEANS

Either use the bamboo steamer, following the directions as you would for asparagus or use a pot with a steamer or strainer. 1 pound, untrimmed makes about 4 cups, cooked.

Cooking utensil: A steamer pot or microwave dish

Steamer pot: Place 1 to 2 inches water to boil in a pot with a steamer attachment, or place a metal colander in the pot; place the beans in the strainer or colander and cover; cook until crisp-tender, about 3 to 5 minutes, depending on the thickness of the green beans.

Microwave: Place the beans in the dish; cook on high until bright green; time varies according to the power of your own microwave oven.

YIELD: 4 cups
FAT GRAMS IN ENTIRE RECIPE: Less than 1

Notes:

_____

_____

Green Beans With Mushrooms

This dish makes a dinner with a baked potato, and it's become a regular on our Thanksgiving dinner table.

Cooking utensil: A non-stick wok

1/4 cup white wine or defatted stock
1 medium onion, thinly sliced
1 clove garlic, minced
1 pound green beans
1/2 pound mushrooms, thickly sliced
Salt and fresh ground pepper to taste

---

1. Sauté the onion and the garlic in the wine or stock until crisp-tender.
2. Add the green beans; cook on medium heat for 3 to 5 minutes.
3. Add the mushrooms and continue to cook on medium until the mushrooms are tender. Add more stock, if necessary, to avoid sticking.
4. Season to taste.

YIELD: 5 cups
FAT GRAMS IN ENTIRE RECIPE: 3

BTW: It's not difficult to overcook this vegetable and end up losing most of the flavor.

Notes:

SEASONED GREEN BEANS WITH TOMATOES

It's not easy to find favorites among green bean dishes. The recipe preceding with the mushrooms and then this dish rank among our all-time best string bean meals.

Cooking utensil: An 8 quart non-stick pot or a non-stick wok

1/4 cup white wine or defatted stock
1 onion, thinly sliced
3 cloves garlic, minced
1 1/2 pounds firm ripe tomatoes, peeled, seeded and chopped
1 bay leaf
1/2 tsp. thyme leaves, crushed
2 Tbs. fresh parsley, chopped
1 tsp. vegetable or chicken bouillon granules
1/2 cup water
3 pounds tender green beans, steamed crispy
1/2 tsp. dried basil, crushed
1/2 tsp. dried oregano, crushed
2 Tbs. dry white wine, additional
Salt and freshly ground pepper to taste

1. Heat the wine or stock in a large, heavy pot; add the onion and garlic and sauté until tender.
2. Add the tomatoes, bay, parsley, thyme, bouillon and water; cover and simmer 15 minutes.
3. Remove the bay leaf; add the green beans; cover; simmer 5 minutes.
4. Add the basil, oregano and wine; uncover, raise the heat and cook over high heat until the mixture thickens.
5. Season with salt and pepper.

YIELD: About 12 to 14 cups
FAT GRAMS IN ENTIRE RECIPE: 6

BTW: Try serving this with some redskin potatoes, boiled and massaged in a plastic bag with I Can't Believe It's Not Butter spray to coat.

ZESTY GREEN BEANS

Now the beans get a kick-start with a different flavor.

Cooking utensil: A large non-stick skillet

---

2 Tbs. Fleischmann's Fat Free Low Calorie margarine
1 clove garlic, minced
1 pound green beans, trimmed and cut diagonally in 1 inch lengths
1/2 small red bell pepper, 1/2 inch strips
5 Tbs. water
2 tsp. red wine vinegar

---

1. Melt the margarine in the skillet over a medium-high heat; add the garlic and sauté for about 30 seconds.
2. Add the beans, bell pepper and water; cover; cook until crisp-tender.
3. Remove the cover; add the vinegar; increase the heat to high and cook until most of the liquid cooks away, about 1 to 2 minutes.

YIELD: About 4 cups
FAT GRAMS IN ENTIRE RECIPE: 2

Notes:

Marinated Mixed Beans

Try to find a Vidalia onion, if possible. The sweetness of the Vidalia or Texas-sweet onion makes all the difference. It takes away the bite.

Preparation utensil: A large bowl with a lid and/or a large tight-lidded jar

---

1 can green beans or 1 box frozen
1 can wax beans
1 can garbanzo beans, drained and rinsed
1 can red beans, drained and rinsed
1 large onion, very thinly sliced
4 to 6 Tbs. fat free Italian salad dressing
1 tsp. white wine vinegar

---

1. Combine all ingredients; refrigerate for at least 24 hours before serving.

YIELD: 7 to 8 cups
FAT GRAMS IN ENTIRE RECIPE: 4

BTW: These are great any old time in a salad or when you want a refreshing side dish.

Notes:

STIR-FRIED CHICKEN AND GREEN BEANS

It takes just minutes to cut the chicken into strips and get the beans and mushrooms ready and then you've got a chewy, crunchy Oriental dinner. Be sure to have some steamed rice handy, either freshly made or straight from the freezer to the microwave.

Cooking utensil: A non-stick wok

---

2 chicken breasts, boneless and skinless (about 4 oz. ea.)
1 tsp. cornstarch
1/2 cup defatted chicken stock
1 Tbs. soy sauce
1/2 tsp. sesame oil
3 Tbs. white wine or defatted stock, additional
1/2 pound green beans, snipped
1/4 pound mushrooms, sliced
1 can (8 oz.) bamboo shoots
1 can water chestnuts, rinsed and sliced
Freshly ground black pepper

---

1. Flatten the chicken until about 1/4 inch thick (this can be done with a flat plate, a meat mallet or a rolling pin); cut into 1/4 inch strips; set aside.
2. Mix together the 1/2 cup defatted chicken stock, the soy sauce and the sesame oil with the cornstarch; set aside.
3. Place the wok over high heat and add the 3 Tbs. wine or stock; add the green beans and stir-fry for about 3 to 4 minutes; add the mushrooms and stir-fry for an additional 1 to 2 minutes, until both green beans and mushrooms are crisp-tender; set aside and keep warm.
4. Place the chicken strips in the wok and stir-fry until the chicken is firm and white through the center; add the sauce and the bean/mushroom mixture and stir-fry until the sauce thickens, about 2 minutes.
5. Season with pepper and serve on steamed rice with additional soy sauce on the side.

YIELD: About 6 cups
FAT GRAMS IN ENTIRE RECIPE: 12

GREENS

There are so many different types of greens, from lettuces to the kinds we cook, such as mustard and collard, kale and spinach. Since we are aiming toward simplification I will include the basic greens which have the same purpose, whether it be salad greens or the kind you cook.

MUSTARD, TURNIP, COLLARD AND BEET GREENS

The weights on these greens before trimming are very different from what you end up with after trimming. Generally, 1 pound of leaves and stems will net you about half that amount, trimmed. You end up with about 14 cups to a pound, stemmed, which, when cooked, reduces down to about 3 to 4 cups. Mustard greens appear to have more weight in stems: a pound will net you about 9 cups, leaves, about 3 cups, cooked. 1 package, frozen, will give you about 1 1/3 cups, cooked.

1 cup of cooked greens varies, depending on the type of green, from 1/2 gram to 1 gram of fat.

Clean the leaves by rinsing under cold running water, removing any sand or soil and (ugh!) little bugs, if any. This can be accomplished by swishing in a sink full of cold water, then repeating the procedure with fresh water 3 or 4 times. The grit and sand will fall to the bottom of the sink. Tear off any wilted or brown parts to the leaves. The reason I stress cleaning is that the little bit of sand that may be clinging to the greens will simply ruin a dinner.

Bok choy is a little different from the other greens because the stem is an important part of the prepared dish. You can find bok choy in most larger supermarkets and, certainly, in Oriental markets. Unfortunately, most of the restaurants that serve Chinese food leave the leaves out of most of the dishes that include bok choy and serve the crisp stems or ribs, alone. When cooking at home, I always use both.

BOILED GREENS

When boiling greens you will normally add some seasonings. There are the milder greens, such as kale (we have a separate listing for kale and spinach) and collards. The beet, turnip and mustard greens have a stronger flavor.

Cooking utensil: A 3 quart non-stick saucepan

Boiling water
1 pound trimmed greens
Salt to taste

---

1. When the water is rolling, add the greens with the salt; cook on high until the greens wilt.
2. Pour into a colander, strain or remove with slotted spoon.

YIELD: About 3 to 4 cups
FAT GRAMS IN ENTIRE RECIPE: The average is about 1 to 4 grams of fat depending on the particular greens

BTW: Most of the time we add the greens, raw, directly to the recipe.

Notes:

_____

_____

_____

_____

_____

_____

_____

_____

_____

BOILED GREENS SOUTHERN STYLE

We've taken the liberty of making this dish without the pork-back or ham bone. While old southern cooks are aghast, we're healthier for it.

Cooking utensil: A 3 quart non-stick saucepan

---

1 pound trimmed greens, raw
2 cups defatted chicken stock
1 smoked turkey leg, skinless
Salt and pepper to taste
Hot sauce to taste

---

1. Place greens in the stock with the turkey leg; bring to a boil; lower heat and simmer, uncovered, until the greens are tender.
2. Season to taste and serve.

YIELD: About 6 cups
FAT GRAMS IN ENTIRE RECIPE: 1 gram per ounce turkey leg meat
      1 to 4 grams for greens

BTW: If you are into a smokier flavor, add some liquid smoke to taste.

Notes:

Lentil Soup With Collard Greens

Lentil soups are always better with greens and in this case we're using collards instead of spinach.

Cooking utensils: An 8 quart non-stick pot and a non-stick skillet

---

2 cans (10 3/4 Oz.) Campbell's Beef Bouillon, defatted and undiluted
5 1/2 cups water
2 cups lentils, picked and rinsed
2 leeks ribs, chopped
1 small carrot, chopped
1 smoked turkey leg, skinless
1 Tbs. Fleischmann's Fat Free Low Calorie margarine
1 small onion, chopped
2 ribs celery, chopped
4 cloves garlic, minced
8 cups fresh collard greens, cut in 1/2 inch strips
1 tsp. cider vinegar
Salt and freshly ground pepper

---

1. Boil the bouillon and water together in a large pot; place the lentils in the liquid with the leeks, carrot and turkey; simmer, partially covered, for 30 minutes.
2. In the meantime, sauté the onion, celery and garlic until just wilted; set aside until the lentils have cooked for the 30 minutes.
3. Add the onion mixture to the lentil pot with the greens and the vinegar; simmer, partially covered, until the lentils are tender, about 20 to 30 minutes more.
4. Remove the turkey leg; trim the meat off the bone; return the meat to the soup; season to taste and serve.

YIELD: 14 cups
FAT GRAMS IN ENTIRE RECIPE: 6 for the soup
    1 gram per ounce of turkey leg meat

BTW: For a change of taste and added gusto, add more smoke flavor with some liquid smoke. Spicy turkey sausage is another neat addition. Change the fat grams, accordingly.

BOK CHOY STIR-FRY

This is one of my favorite quick put-togethers. I can never finish my dinner in a Chinese restaurant and I like to take home my leftover Broccoli in Hot Garlic Sauce and add the leftovers to this dish for a more robust taste. It makes my guilts about not cleaning my plate (a hangover from childhood) non-existent.

Cooking utensil: A non-stick wok

---

1 onion, in half and thickly sliced
1/2 cup defatted chicken stock
4 or 5 bok choy ribs with leaves, cut in 2 inch pieces, the ribs diagonally
  cut
1 tsp. garlic powder
Soy sauce or tamari to taste

---

1. Stir-fry the onion in the stock until barely translucent; add the bok choy; turn the heat very high and wilt the bok choy while sprinkling with the garlic powder, constantly stirring.
2. Add soy sauce to taste and serve on steamed rice which has been prepared without oil or margarine. If you like a thicker sauce, add a dilution of 2 to 3 Tbs. cornstarch with 1 to 2 Tbs. water; stir to remove lumps; add slowly, stirring, while the sauce thickens.

YIELD: About 4 cups
FAT GRAMS IN ENTIRE RECIPE: 1

BTW: Add other Oriental vegetables such as bean sprouts, water chestnuts, bamboo shoots.

Notes:

BOK CHOY WITH BROCCOLI

The natural place for bok choy is in a stir-fry and what better stir-fry is there but bok choy with broccoli? Once you've got the veggies cut up, the rest of this recipe is a snap.

Cooking utensil: A non-stick wok

---

1 tsp. five spice powder
2 Tbs. soy sauce or tamari
2 Tbs. cornstarch
1 medium onion, thinly sliced
2 tsp. garlic, minced
1 tsp. grated ginger root
1/4 cup dry sherry
1 cup bok choy, diagonally sliced
1 cup broccoli fowerets
1 cup mushrooms, quartered
1/2 cup red bell pepper, thinly sliced
1/4 cup defatted chicken stock
1 cup mung bean sprouts

---

1. Combine soy sauce, five spice and cornstarch; set aside.
2. Stir-fry the onion, garlic and ginger root in the sherry in your wok for about 5 minutes.
3. Add the bok choy, broccoli, mushrooms, bell pepper and broth; cover; cook on medium-high heat until crisp-tender, about 3 to 5 minutes.
4. Add the bean sprouts; gradually stir in the soy sauce mixture; stir-fry until thickened.
5. Serve over steamed rice, prepared with no oil or margarine.

YIELD: About 4 cups
FAT GRAMS IN ENTIRE RECIPE: 2

BTW: This is another dish wherein the sky's the limit as far as the veggies you can throw in. Don't hesitate to use canned straw or dried, soaked shiitake mushrooms when the spirit moves you, or some baby corn or snow peas.

KALE

The reason for listing this particular green independently from the others, is my special love for this vegetable. Since it's my book, I figured I could choose which special veggies get star billing! Kale is that deep-green, curly-leafed stuff that is used so often as a decoration between the platters on restaurant buffet tables. Until a few years ago I didn't know that the leaves I was looking at have so much personality. Then David fixed up a pot of Portuguese Kale Soup and I was hooked! You'll find that recipe later on in this section.

1 pound of kale is 14 cups, loosely packed. The 14 cups cook down to 4 cups. 1 cup cooked kale has about 1 gram of fat.

Although Leo Capps eats the stems and all, the stems are extremely tough so I recommend that you strip the leaves from the stems.

GREENS WITH BEANS SOUP

There is no doubt in my mind you'll love this soup as we do.

Cooking utensil: An 8 quart non-stick pot

1/2 cup dry white wine
1 large onion, chopped
2 large carrots, chopped
1 clove garlic, minced
4 cups water
1 can (15 oz.) pinto beans, rinsed and drained
1/4 cup fresh parsley, chopped
1 tsp. chicken bouillon granules
1/2 tsp. dried thyme leaves, crushed
1/4 tsp. cayenne pepper
1 bay leaf
3 cups kale, coarsely chopped
1 tsp. liquid smoke
Salt and freshly ground pepper to taste
Louisiana hot sauce to taste

---

1. Sauté the onion and garlic in the wine on high heat, until crisp-tender.
2. Add all ingredients except the kale and liquid smoke; bring to a boil; cover; reduce heat and simmer 10 minutes.
3. Add the kale and liquid smoke; cook an additional 5 minutes.
4. Remove the bay leaf; season to taste and serve.

YIELD: 6 cups
FAT GRAMS IN ENTIRE RECIPE: 2

Notes:

Portuguese Kale Soup

There is something grand about kale and beans, or tomatoes, kale and beans. See if you don't agree after you try out this soup.

Cooking utensil: An 8 quart non-stick pot

1/4 cup white wine or defatted chicken stock
1 medium onion, chopped
1/2 cup carrots, chopped
2 tsp. garlic, minced
1 pound potatoes, peeled and cubed
2 quarts defatted chicken stock, additional
3 pound tomatoes, seeded, peeled and chopped
1 1/2 cups kidney beans, cooked or canned and drained
8 cups kale, trimmed, roughly chopped and uncooked
1/2 tsp. liquid smoke

---

1. Sauté the onion, carrots and garlic in the wine or 1/4 cup stock until tender.
2. Add the potatoes and additional stock; cook until the potatoes can be pierced with a fork, about 15 to 20 minutes; mash the potatoes against the side of the pot.
3. Add the tomatoes and the beans; simmer with the potato mixture for another 10 minutes.
4. Add the kale and the liquid smoke and simmer for an additional 10 minutes.

YIELD: About 16 cups
FAT GRAMS IN ENTIRE RECIPE: 6

BTW: Spicy turkey or chicken sausage can add some guts to this already hearty soup. Omit the liquid smoke if you add the sausage.

Notes:

Minestrone With Kale

Whenever we talk about foods that give us the warm fuzzies, I always mention this recipe. It's a direct takeoff on the Portuguese Kale Soup and takes only about 10 minutes to prepare and 10 minutes to cook. While it's cooking you've got just enough time to heat up some bread and set the table.

Cooking utensil: A 3 quart non-stick saucepan

---

4 to 6 cups kale, trimmed and uncooked
2 cans (16 oz. ea.) Progresso Healthy Classics Minestrone
1 can (15 1/5 oz.) red kidney beans
1 can (15 1/2 oz.) white kidney or great northern beans
1/2 cup defatted chicken stock
Hot pepper sauce
Steamed rice, cooked with no oil or margarine

---

1. Cut the kale in 2 inch pieces; place in a large pot along with the rest of the ingredients, except the rice and hot sauce; cook, covered, on medium heat until the kale is tender.
2. Place a small amount of rice in each bowl; add the soup and season with the hot pepper sauce to taste.

YIELD: About 7 to 8 cups
FAT GRAMS IN ENTIRE RECIPE: 12

BTW: Choose any kind of low fat vegetable soup to use as a base for this recipe. If you like more of a stew, simply add more rice. Frozen kale will work in this recipe, too.

Notes:

LEEKS

Leeks deliver a delicate onion flavor. The part of the leeks used are the white bulb end and just the beginning (about 1 inch) of the green. Discard the very green parts, they're too fibrous to eat.

1 pound of trimmed leeks will make about 4 cups, chopped, which will cook down to about 2 cups.
1 cup cooked leeks will add less than 1/2 gram of fat to your day.

When cleaning leeks it's necessary to carefully separate the leaves or ribs to get any grit from between the leaves. It may be necessary to soak the leeks in cold water for a few minutes and swish them around to dislodge any clinging soil. Discard the root end.

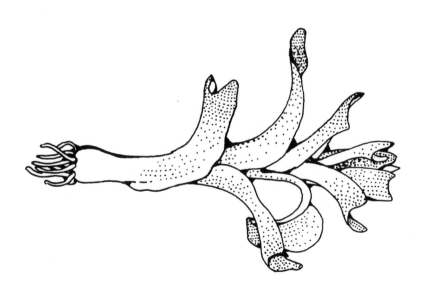

LEEKS AND SHRIMP

Since both the leeks and the shrimp are subtly flavored the overall feel of this dish is very delicate. If you're looking for an innovative appetizer, serve this without the rice.

Cooking utensil: A non-stick wok treated with spray-on oil

---

1 1/2 Tbs. light soy sauce
1 Tbs. dry sherry
1/4 tsp. sugar
1 Tbs. cornstarch
Pam or Mazola spray-on oil
1 pound medium shrimp, peeled and deveined
1/4 cup defatted chicken stock
1/2 pound leeks, trimmed, sliced in 2 inch rounds
1 tsp. fresh ginger, minced
1 clove garlic, minced
Soy sauce or tamari to taste
Steamed rice, cooked without oil or margarine

---

1. Combine soy sauce, sherry and sugar with cornstarch; set aside.
2. Spray the wok with Pam or Mazola; add the shrimp; sauté on high heat until the shrimp begin to turn white; remove the shrimp; set aside.
3. Add the stock to the same wok and add the leeks; sauté the leeks for 2 minutes and add the ginger and garlic; sauté for 2 minutes.
4. Add the shrimp; reduce the heat; gradually add the soy sauce mixture and simmer until the sauce thickens and becomes shiny.
5. Add additional soy sauce to taste; serve on steamed rice.

YIELD: About 4 cups
FAT GRAMS IN ENTIRE RECIPE: 6

Notes:

Potato, Fennel And Leek Soup

You will love this soup. The fennel adds a mellow, soft flavor that is reminiscent of anise.

Cooking utensil: An 8 quart non-stick pot

---

2 leeks, white and light green parts only
1 Tbs. prepared Butter Buds
1 tsp. olive oil
Defatted chicken stock, if necessary
1 carrot, chopped
1/2 bulb fennel, trimmed and chopped (3/4 cup)
3 baking potatoes, peeled and cut in chunks
1/2 tsp. dried thyme, crushed
2 Tbs. fresh parsley, chopped
1 small bay leaf
4 1/2 cups defatted chicken stock
Salt and pepper to taste

---

1. Place the leeks in a large pot with the Butter Buds and oil; cook slowly for 5 minutes; if too dry, add the stock to avoid sticking.
2. Add the carrot and fennel; cook 5 minutes more.
3. Add the other ingredients and bring to a boil; cover; simmer for 25 to 30 minutes or until the potato is tender.
4. Remove the bay leaf; mash 1/3 of the vegetables in the soup against the side of the pot and stir to mix through.
5. Season to taste and serve.

YIELD: 8 cups
FAT GRAMS IN ENTIRE RECIPE: 6

BTW: This is a lovely soup served as an appetizer in a cup before a seafood dinner.

Notes:

MUSHROOMS

Mushrooms are among the favorite foods of most of the people I know who enjoy the low fat lifestyle. It seems that the mushrooms round out the flavor and introduce a mouthfeel, when consumed with other vegetables, that satisfies the needs we low fat lifers have. I was talking to Jane Greenwell, who told me about one of my recipes that she prepared, and she "added some mushrooms..." The sign of a good cook, one who is comfortable in a kitchen, is the variations on the original recipe that are made. I'm overjoyed when folks doctor my ingredients, as long as the fat grams are not increased.

There are, as you know, a great variety of mushrooms. Different appearances, different tastes and different textures, some dried, some canned and some ready to cook. The most common mushrooms, those that are most often found in the supermarket, are the kinds of mushrooms we'll cook with in these recipes. Some day, perhaps we'll concentrate on some more of the gourmet foods and then we'll try a number of more exotic members of the mushroom family.

The domestic or button mushroom is extremely dependable for uniform taste and cooking characteristics. The most important features to be aware of is that the cap of the mushroom should enclose the stem, there should definitely not be an open gill and brown spots show age and the beginnings of spoilage. They are wonderful for stewing, in soups, in mixed vegetable dishes and sautéed as a stand-alone vegetable. When preparing this mushroom, both the stems and caps are edible.

The shiitake mushroom, originally from Japan, is usually available dried, although I have seen it in my supermarket, fresh. It has a musky, or smoky, flavor and is chewy or meaty. The stems are usually too fibrous to consume. Since most of the time, this mushroom is available dried, remember that reconstituting it is necessary before cooking. This is easily accomplished with a bit of hot water, allowing the mushrooms to soak for about 20 to 30 minutes, and then following the instructions in the recipe.

Cremini mushrooms are very much like the button mushroom. The shape is the same, sizes are similar, but the Cremini has a medium to deep brown

color, a heartier consistency and a slightly wilder taste. You will have to determine, for yourself, if these characteristics make the higher cost of the Cremini worth using instead of the button mushroom. They are interchangeable in recipes in my opinion.

The straw mushroom is a smaller mushroom, which I have seen available only in cans. It's a natural in Oriental dishes, primarily because of its attractiveness since it has very little definitive flavor.

Portobello mushrooms have taken our restaurants and supermarkets by storm in the last few years. The meaty texture and flavor have excited vegetarians and low fat lovers alike, since some portobello mushroom makes up for the lack of meat with the addition of less than 1 gram of fat for 8 ounces of mushroom.

All the mushrooms we include in the recipes in this book are at less than 1 gram of fat for 1 to 2 cups.

That's a fat gram count low enough to enjoy to your heart's content. It's not necessary to cook mushrooms before adding them to any pot of food. In fact, raw, sliced button mushrooms are popular on salad bars and do well in a salad, especially when topped with a fat free Dijon honey ranch dressing.

SAUTÉED MUSHROOMS

You can do so much with this dish. You can place it on a vegetable plate to round out the flavors. It's super on a baked potato. Add it to any frozen vegetable, after cooking, to add some personality.

Cooking utensil: A small non-stick skillet

---

8 oz. button mushrooms or Cremini, sliced
1/2 onion, in half and thinly sliced
I Can't Believe It's Not Butter spray
1/2 tsp. garlic powder

---

1. Place the mushrooms and onion in a skillet; spray about 10 sprays of the margarine; sprinkle with the garlic powder; sauté on high heat until the mushrooms and onion become tender.

YIELD: 1 1/2 cups
FAT GRAMS IN ENTIRE RECIPE: 1

Notes:

MUSHROOM GRAVY

A gravy that's virtually fat free is a joy that most people think they'll have to live without in this lifestyle. You'll love the simplicity of this one.

Cooking utensil: A non-stick skillet

---

10 to 12 sprays of I Can't Believe It's Not Butter spray
8 oz. mushrooms, sliced
1/2 onion, in half and thinly sliced
1/2 tsp. garlic powder
1/2 cup defatted chicken or beef stock
4 Tbs. cornstarch
2 Tbs. water
Salt and pepper to taste

---

1. Spray the skillet with the margarine; sauté the mushrooms, onion and garlic in the skillet until tender.
2. Add the stock; lower heat; simmer, uncovered, for 10 minutes.
3. Dissolve the cornstarch in the water; gradually add the cornstarch mixture to the skillet; stir to avoid lumps from forming until thickened.
4. Season with salt and pepper and serve.

YIELD: 2 cups
FAT GRAMS IN ENTIRE RECIPE: 1

Notes:

MUSHROOM AND LEEK SAUTÉ

Another fine gravy or sauce. The leeks are a little more delicate than the onions.

Cooking utensil: A non-stick skillet

---

2 Tbs. Fleischmann's Fat Free Low Calorie squeeze margarine
2 cups sliced leeks
1 pound fresh mushrooms, quartered
2 Tbs. tamari or soy sauce
2 Tbs. fresh parsley, chopped
Salt and pepper to taste

---

1. Heat the margarine in a skillet; add the leeks; sauté for 3 minutes.
2. Add the mushrooms and all ingredients except the salt and pepper; sauté until the mushrooms are tender.
3. Season to your taste and serve.

YIELD: 4 cups
FAT GRAMS IN ENTIRE RECIPE: 3

BTW: Try using this sauté as a sauce on sliced turkey or chicken breast which has been placed over fat free stuffing.

Notes:

_____

_____

_____

_____

_____

MUSHROOMS WITH PEPPERS

This is so pretty, it's a natural as a side dish. Put it on rice or toss in pasta and surprise! It's dinner!

Cooking utensil: A non-stick skillet or wok

1/4 cup dry white wine
1 onion, thinly sliced
1 green bell pepper, thinly sliced
1 red bell pepper, thinly sliced
1 pound button mushrooms, quartered
1 tsp. ground cumin
1 tsp. dried thyme leaves, crushed
1/2 tsp. paprika
1/4 tsp. cayenne pepper to taste
Salt and freshly ground pepper to taste
2 Tbs. fresh parsley, chopped

---

1. Heat the wine in the skillet; add the onion and peppers; sauté over medium heat until just tender.
2. Add the mushrooms and remaining ingredients, except the parsley; cook on medium heat, uncovered, stirring often, until the vegetables are tender.
3. Add the parsley; toss and serve.

YIELD: 5 to 6 cups
FAT GRAMS IN ENTIRE RECIPE: 2

BTW: You can stretch this sauce for pasta by adding 1 cup of defatted chicken stock; dissolve 2 Tbs. cornstarch in 1 Tbs. water; add this to the above recipe; and cook on low heat until thickened. You have enough sauce for pasta with no extra grams of fat in the sauce. Sprinkle some fat free grated Parmesan and all you need add to the gram count is the pasta you consume.

Notes:

RATATOUILLE WITH MUSHROOMS

Aha! Another ratatouille. This one, unlike those in the eggplant section of the book, has the added attraction of mushrooms.

Cooking utensil: An 8 quart non-stick pot

1/2 cup white wine or defatted stock
1 eggplant (1 1/2 pounds), unpeeled and cubed
1 large onion, chopped
1 green bell pepper, chopped
1 red bell pepper, chopped
1 pound zucchini, thickly sliced
1/2 pound button mushrooms, quartered
1 can (16 oz.) Hunt's Choice Cut tomatoes with juice
1 can (6 oz.) tomato paste
1/2 tsp. dried basil leaves, crushed
1/2 tsp. dried thyme leaves, crushed
1 tsp. dried oregano leaves, crushed
1 tsp. red pepper flakes
Salt and pepper to taste

---

1. Sauté the eggplant in the wine or stock in a large pot for 10 minutes.
2. Add the onion and peppers; lower the heat; cook until the onions are tender.
3. Add the zucchini and the remaining ingredients; simmer, uncovered, until the mushrooms and zucchini are tender.
4. Season to taste and serve.

YIELD: 10 to 12 cups
FAT GRAMS IN ENTIRE RECIPE: 5

Notes:

_____

_____

_____

QUICK CHICK WITH TOMATO AND MUSHROOMS

Don't you just love a recipe where you see the words, "add all remaining ingredients" right up there at the beginning of the instructions. It means *easy* ! And this one is.

Cooking utensil: A large non-stick skillet treated with Olive Oil Pam

---

2 chicken breasts (4 oz. ea.), skinless and boneless
Olive Oil Pam
1 medium onion, sliced
1 cup button mushrooms, sliced
1 tsp. garlic powder
1 can (16 oz.) whole tomatoes with juice, chopped
1 Tbs. mixed dried Italian seasonings
3 Tbs. dry white wine, optional
Salt and freshly ground pepper to taste

---

1. Spray the Pam in the skillet; over a high heat, sear the chicken for about 3 minutes on each side.
2. Add all remaining ingredients; cook, uncovered, on medium heat until juices from the tomatoes are reduced by half and thickened.
3. Test the chicken; when white through, add the wine, if desired.
4. Season to taste and serve.

YIELD: 2 chicken breasts with about 3 cups of sauce
FAT GRAMS IN ENTIRE RECIPE: 10

Notes:

SHRIMP AND BUTTON MUSHROOMS

If you have only 10 minutes to prepare a delightful dinner and you have some shrimp already peeled and cleaned, this will do it for you.

Cooking utensil: A non-stick wok

1/4 cup white wine or defatted stock
1 medium onion, in half and thinly sliced
1 clove garlic, minced
4 fresh basil leaves or 1/3 tsp. dried and crushed
1/2 pound mushrooms, thickly sliced
1 pound shrimp, peeled and deveined
1/4 cup white wine or defatted stock, additional, if needed
Red pepper flakes, salt and black pepper to taste

---

1. Sauté the onion and garlic in the wine or stock until crisp-tender.
2. Add the mushrooms and basil and continue to sauté until the mushrooms are crisp-tender.
3. Add the shrimp and sauté on high heat until the shrimp are pink; if dry, add the additional stock or wine.
4. Season to taste and serve on cooked pasta or rice.

YIELD: About 3 cups
FAT GRAMS IN ENTIRE RECIPE: 4

Notes:

CRAB AND MUSHROOM STIR-FRY

This is a pretty appetizer. It's simple to prepare and the colorful green scallions and red tomatoes, while retaining the delicacy of the crab, makes a delightful presentation.

Cooking utensil: A non-stick wok

1/4 cup dry white wine or defatted stock
1/2 pound button mushrooms, quartered
1/2 cup green onions
12 cherry tomatoes, halved
1/2 pound fresh or frozen crabmeat, flaked
3 Tbs. sweet vermouth or medium-sweet sherry
1 Tbs. fresh lemon juice
Steamed rice, cooked without oil or margarine

---

1. Stir-fry the mushrooms and onions in the wine over high heat for 1 minute.
2. Add the tomatoes, crabmeat, vermouth and lemon juice; stir-fry until heated through.
3. Serve on steamed rice.

YIELD: 3 cups
FAT GRAMS IN ENTIRE RECIPE: 3

BTW: If you can find fat free wonton wrappers in the frozen food section of your store, dig this: spray Pam or Mazola on a muffin tin; push the wrappers in the muffin holders, one to a muffin hole; spray again; place in oven at 350° until golden. They make little baskets which can be served at room temperature so you can make these ahead of time. Place the Crab and Mushroom Stir-fry in each basket and serve one to a guest.

Notes:

STUFFED MUSHROOMS

Choose large, firm mushrooms that won't fall apart when you stuff them. This appetizer has brought raves.

Cooking utensils: A 3 quart and a 2 quart non-stick saucepan

---

12 large fresh button mushrooms
1/2 cup white wine
2 tsp. beef bouillon granules
1/4 cup onion, minced
2 packets Butter Buds, prepared
1/2 cup packaged herb-seasoned stuffing mix

---

1. Wash the mushrooms; remove the stems; set stems aside.
2. Heat the wine and bouillon in a medium-sized saucepan; add the mushroom caps, top down; simmer, covered, for 2 to 3 minutes; remove the mushrooms; set aside; reserve the wine mixture.
3. Chop the mushrooms stems and combine with the onion, 1/2 cup Butter Buds and 1/4 cup wine mixture; cook, in separate saucepan, over medium heat until the vegetables are tender, about 2 to 3 minutes.
4. Stir in the stuffing.
5. Place about 1 Tbs. of stuffing in each mushroom cap; brush with Butter Buds liquid and place under broiler for about 2 to 3 minutes until hot.

YIELD: 12 stuffed caps
FAT GRAMS IN ENTIRE RECIPE: Traces

BTW: Appetizers and hors d'oeuvres can be easy and can be exciting and can be low fat. Apply all you enjoy in regular cookery to your low fat culinary talents.

Notes:

DUXELLES

As you already are quite aware, mushrooms are a useful way to fill a recipe with a meaty feel without the meat. One of the most important basics in a vegetarian kitchen and, I'm told, an important lesson in rudimentary culinary skills, is how to prepare duxelles. The variations are numerous: tomatoes; carrots; celery; garlic; dried tarragon, thyme or oregano; hoisin sauce; honey; hot chili pepper; cayenne.

Cooking utensil: A small non-stick skillet

---

2 Tbs. defatted stock
2/3 cup onions, minced
2 cups mushrooms, minced
1/4 tsp. salt
1/2 tsp. soy sauce

---

1. Sauté the onions in the stock until just transparent.
2. Add the mushrooms and the remaining ingredients; cook over medium heat until the mixture dries and looks like paste.
3. Use in other recipes or allow to cool and refrigerate or freeze.

YIELD: 1 cup
FAT GRAMS IN ENTIRE RECIPE: 2

BTW: The benefit of having the duxelles frozen, awaiting your desire to use it, is in the time savings. This "mushroom hash" may be added to Egg Beaters with onions, for a delightful brunch. It's great for stuffing squash or tomatoes or eggplant, and can act as a ground meat substitute in marinara sauce. In fact, spread on top of fat free cream cheese on melba toast or a toasted pita point it is delicious, and you may want to add a touch of smoked salmon to that to produce an artistic hors d'oeuvre.

Notes:

MARINATED MUSHROOMS

These mushrooms are easy to put together when you're looking for a neat addition to a salad, to give it an invigorating lift.

Preparation utensil: A bowl or tight-lidded jar

---

1 jar (5 oz.) button mushrooms
3 Tbs. fat free French or Italian salad dressing
1 Tbs. fresh parsley, chopped or 1 tsp. dried
Dash garlic powder
Dash hot pepper sauce, optional

---

1. Toss all the ingredients.
2. Refrigerate for at least 1 hour.
3. Serve chilled.

YIELD: 1/2 to 3/4 cup
FAT GRAMS IN ENTIRE RECIPE: 0

BTW: Add this to a relish tray when you're entertaining.

Notes:

Portobello Mushroom Sauté

The portobello mushroom is the meat of the mushrooms. While most mushrooms have a density and muskiness that lend a meat "feel" to a dish, the portobello is the steak. This recipe is the basic sauté that can be added to other recipes.

Cooking utensil: A non-stick skillet treated with spray-on oil

---

1 pound portobello mushrooms, thinly sliced
1 clove garlic, minced
1 Tbs. fresh parsley, chopped
1 Tbs. dry white or red wine

---

1. Place the mushroom in the skillet and sauté for 2 minutes.
2. Add the remaining ingredients; cook over high heat until the mushroom is cooked through, about 5 to 7 minutes.

YIELD: 2 cups
FAT GRAMS IN ENTIRE RECIPE: 3

BTW: With this sauté you have the perfect addition to The Marinara Sauce, any of your stir-fry dishes, your broth-based pasta sauces and an interesting baked potato topping. Add chopped tomato, thinly sliced onion, bell pepper or hot peppers...whatever you like to enhance the use of this appealing mushroom.

Notes:

Pasta With Shiitake Mushrooms

The smoky meatiness of this mushroom makes it ideal for Oriental dishes. Recently I've been seeing it, frequently, in Italian dishes because it's a wonderful flavor-mate with broth-based or tomato-based sauces.

Cooking utensil: A non-stick wok

1/4 cup white or red wine
1 clove garlic, minced
1/2 medium onion, thinly sliced
5 fresh Roma (plum) tomatoes, chopped
3/4 tsp. dried oregano, crushed
1/2 cup fresh parsley, chopped
1 Tbs. plus 1 tsp. chicken bouillon granules
1 cup water
Crushed red pepper flakes to taste
8 shiitake mushrooms, soaked, stems removed, thinly sliced
8 ounces pasta, cooked without oil
Salt and pepper to taste

---

1. Sauté the garlic and onion in the wine until tender.
2. Add all remaining ingredients except the pasta, salt and pepper; simmer, uncovered, stirring often, for about 15 to 20 minutes.
3. Add additional water, wine or defatted stock (or bouillon) if the sauce dries up.
4. Add the pasta and toss; season to taste and serve.

YIELD: About 8 cups
FAT GRAMS IN ENTIRE RECIPE: 4

BTW: If you don't have shiitake mushrooms, another kind will do. I find shiitake mushrooms are the easiest to keep on hand because they're dried and don't spoil. They're just there, in the pantry, ready to go any old time.

Notes:

SZECHUAN SHRIMP WITH SHIITAKE MUSHROOMS

Shrimp and mushrooms are always a natural. Make them shiitake mushrooms and you add an earthiness that is a little different and a lot good! No question about it...this dish is *hot* so have plenty of white rice at hand!

Cooking utensil: A non-stick wok treated with spray-on oil

---

1 pound shrimp, peeled and deveined
Pam or Mazola spray-on oil
3 green onions, chopped
3 slices fresh ginger
3 shiitake mushrooms, soaked, stems discarded, quartered
1 tsp. sugar
1 Tbs. Chinese rice wine
1 Tbs. light soy sauce
3 Tbs. Szechuan sauce

---

1. Sauté the shrimp in the Pam or Mazola until pink and curled; set aside.
2. Spray again with Pam or Mazola; sauté the onions, ginger and mushrooms over a medium heat until tender, about 2 to 3 minutes.
3. Add the sugar, rice wine, soy sauce and Szechuan sauce; stir continuously until the sauce is nearly dry.
4. Serve on steamed rice, cooked without oil or margarine.

YIELD: About 3 cups
FAT GRAMS IN ENTIRE RECIPE: 8

BTW: This recipe came from the label of the KA-ME Szechuan Sauce bottle. Of course, they're recommending 4 Tbs. peanut oil for sautéing. We've made the conversion for you but the KA-ME products are really fine and the recipe on their label calls for using all of their products for this dish. Be aware that different brands of Szechuan sauce or hot garlic sauce vary considerably, so try them to see if you're going to get what you expect. We found this brand in the Foreign Foods section of our supermarket.

ASIAN SHRIMP WITH SHIITAKE MUSHROOMS IN GARLIC SAUCE

If you looked at the previous recipe for Szechuan Shrimp with Shiitake Mushrooms and the Szechuan is just too hot for your taste, don't give up on shrimp with shiitakes. They still marry well. Here's a combo that's easier on those who like it not-so-hot!

Cooking utensil: A non-stick wok

---

3 Tbs. white wine or defatted stock
1 small onion, chopped
1 tsp. ginger root, grated
4 cloves garlic, sliced
5 to 6 shiitake mushrooms, soaked 30 minutes and sliced
1 cup frozen peas, thawed
1 pound shrimp, cleaned and deveined
1/2 cup defatted chicken broth or stock
2 tsp. soy sauce
1 Tbs. cornstarch
1 Tbs. water

---

1. Sauté the onion, ginger root and garlic in the wine or stock for 1 to 2 minutes.
2. Add the mushrooms and peas; stir-fry for 2 to 3 minutes.
3. Add the shrimp and stir-fry until the shrimp is pink and just curling.
4. Dissolve the cornstarch in the water; combine with the broth, soy sauce and salt.
5. Add the cornstarch mixture to the wok; heat until the sauce thickens.
6. Serve on steamed rice, prepared with no oil or margarine and with soy sauce for added oomph.

YIELD: 4 cups
FAT GRAMS IN ENTIRE RECIPE: 4

BTW: The addition of mung bean sprouts, bok choy or other Oriental vegetables can only enhance this dish.

PASTA AND SHIITAKE MUSHROOMS WITH ASPARAGUS AND WINE

Talk about some of the most divine ingredients and you're talking about this dish.

Cooking utensil: A non-stick wok or large non-stick skillet

1/4 cup dry white wine or defatted stock
1 pound fresh asparagus, peeled, diagonally sliced in 3/4 inch pieces
1/4 pound fresh shiitake mushrooms, sliced
4 cloves garlic, minced
1/2 cup fresh parsley, chopped
1/3 cup dry white wine, additional
1/4 tsp. crushed red pepper flakes
Salt and freshly ground pepper to taste
1/2 pound pasta, cooked without oil
Fat free grated Parmesan

---

1. Heat the wine or stock; sauté the asparagus about 1 minutes.
2. Add the mushrooms and garlic; reduce heat to medium and cook 3 minutes.
3. Add the parsley, wine and red pepper flakes; cook for 2 minutes more; season to taste with salt and pepper.
4. Place pasta in a large bowl; add the sauce and the Parmesan cheese.
5. Toss and serve.

YIELD: 6 cups
FAT GRAMS IN ENTIRE RECIPE: 6

Notes:

_____

_____

_____

_____

OKRA

Okra is known for its slidey, slippery, almost gooey feel. Yet it's a necessary ingredient in gumbo and other dishes from Louisiana and the Caribbean. In these dishes the stickiness of the okra thickens the stew. Okra is available fresh in the summertime or frozen, year round. They are bright green and about 2 1/2 to 3 inches long when they are at their best. Darker green or larger and the okra becomes fibrous.

1 pound of fresh or frozen okra will give you about 3 to 4 cups, trimmed and ready to cook.
3 to 4 cups of okra brings about 1 gram of fat.

If it's not in gumbo, the best recipe for okra is in a stew with tomatoes or you can buy them pickled in a jar in the supermarket, ready to add to a salad.

OKRA AND TOMATOES

Trim the okra by removing the stem piece.

Cooking utensil: A non-stick skillet

---

1 pound okra, trimmed, cut in 1/2 inch pieces
1 medium onion, chopped
1 rib celery, chopped
2 Tbs. Fleischmann's Fat Free Low Calorie margarine
1 can (14 1/2 oz.) diced tomatoes
1 clove garlic, minced
1/8 tsp. crushed red pepper flakes, optional
Salt and freshly ground pepper to taste

---

1. Place the okra, onion and celery in a skillet with the margarine; sauté on medium heat for about 10 minutes.
2. Add the tomatoes, garlic and red pepper; sauté for about 3 minutes; reduce heat; simmer for about 10 to 15 minutes or until the okra is tender.

YIELD: 5 to 6 cups
FAT GRAMS IN ENTIRE RECIPE: 2

SHRIMP AND OKRA GUMBO

The *roux* that we make in this recipe is an important basis of Cajun cooking. It sets up the thickening for a stew or gumbo. It's not necessary to brown the roux, but you do want to "stir-fry" the flour so that when you add the liquids the flour won't lump up. Stir the flour in the margarine and if too dry, gradually add stock as needed. That will give you a sufficient thickening agent for your gumbo. The filé powder is a flavoring that can be purchased in your supermarket where the seasonings are shelved.

Cooking utensil: An 8 quart non-stick pot

---

2 Tbs. Fleischmann's Fat Free Low Calorie margarine + 4 Tbs.
2 cups fresh okra, diced
4 Tbs. flour
2 Tbs. or more defatted chicken stock, as needed
1 onion, chopped
1 tsp. garlic minced
1 green bell pepper, chopped
2 ribs celery, chopped
1 can (14 1/2 oz.) diced tomatoes with juice
2 cloves garlic, chopped
1 Tbs. scallions, chopped
3 quarts water
1 Tbs. Worcestershire sauce
1 bay leaf
1/2 tsp. dried thyme, crushed
2 pounds shrimp, peeled and deveined
Salt and pepper to taste
Louisiana hot sauce to taste
Filé powder to taste

---

1. Add the okra to the margarine in a large pot; sauté for about 10 minutes, stirring constantly; if necessary; remove okra from pot; set aside.
3. Place the additional margarine in the pot, adding the flour gradually to make a roux; add the stock as needed to avoid sticking.
4. Add the rest of the vegetables and the okra; stir-fry until wilted; add the water and Worcestershire sauce; cook 1 to 2 hours, uncovered.
5. Add the shrimp; cook 30 minutes or until the shrimp is tender.

6. Season to taste; sprinkle the filé powder to taste; serve on steamed rice, prepared with no oil or margarine.

YIELD: 18 cups
FAT GRAMS IN ENTIRE RECIPE: 12

Notes:

OKRA AND BEAN GUMBO

Here's a touch of Louisiana that takes an awful lot of the work out of a gumbo. The wok may seem incongruous with Cajun cooking but it works!

Cooking utensil: A non-stick wok

1/4 cup white wine or defatted stock
1 cup onion, chopped
2 cloves garlic, minced
1/2 cup celery, diced
1 medium green bell pepper, chopped
2 cans (14 1/2 oz. ea.) diced tomatoes, with juice
Dash cayenne pepper, optional
1 tsp. dried thyme leaves, crushed
1 1/2 cups frozen okra, thawed
1 cup frozen peas
1 can (16 oz.) white kidney beans (cannellini)
Salt and pepper to taste
Louisiana hot sauce to taste

---

1. Sauté the onion and garlic in the wine or stock until tender.
2. Add the celery and bell pepper; cook until tender.
3. Add the tomatoes; increase heat until boiling; reduce heat; add cayenne and thyme; simmer 45 minutes.
4. Add the okra, peas and beans; cook until the peas are cooked through; do not overcook.
5. Season with salt, pepper and hot sauce and serve.

YIELD: About 6 cups
FAT GRAMS IN ENTIRE RECIPE: 2

BTW: Yes, I like rice with this dish. I put some of this gumbo right on top of the rice that's been cooked without oil or margarine. Try it without, but have that rice handy if you decide you like it better with rice, too.

Notes:

ONIONS AND OTHER BULBS

It's hard to say too much about onions, since they're an important part of almost all the recipes in this book and any other cookbook except those featuring desserts, only.

Garlic falls into this category of bulbs, as do scallions and chives. The union of the onion and the garlic clove is a marriage made in heaven. The two are inseparable in so many cultures, sautéed in oil, butter or, of course, in *our* culture, sautéed in wine or stock. And they're wonderful roasted, grilled, stewed, baked.

The most common onions in the supermarket are the yellow onion, white onion (a little milder than the yellow), shallots (a much more gentle onion flavor and faster-cooking), red or Bermuda onion (a strong flavored, sweeter onion), the Vidalia (an extremely mild onion of the white family) which is great for chopping in mixed salads like potato or bean salad.

The scallions (green onions, as they are sometimes called) and chives are used interchangeably in many areas. The chive is a thinner plant that can be grown on a windowsill and snipped with a pair of scissors anytime you want to add it to a potato or salad. There is also a garlic chive that combines the taste of both the onion and the garlic.

Buy these bulbs firm with no soft spots. If stored at home, an onion that starts sprouting should be discarded. Storage is best in a cool place, 40° to 50° F. This is rather difficult to accomplish unless you have a root cellar. We store our onions in the pantry, but use them so quickly we don't run the risk of having them age before use. Refrigerator storage works well, also, and cuts down on the tearing associated with chopping this aromatic bulbs.

Peeling an onion is simply a matter of cutting both ends off and using a paring knife to cut one slit through the skin. The rest of the skin will easily peel off.

When cutting onions, I like to cut from the tip to the stem end. Then, if slicing I lay the onion on the flat half and slice from the tip to the stem. If chopping, I then turn the onion and slice in the other direction. It's simple and fast. The only time I slice the onion in half through its middle is when I'm slicing rings. Chopped onions freeze well. This is a great time-saver on busy days. Chop up a bunch, place in a freezer bag with a zip-lock, and take out what you need when you need it.

The fat in an onion is so small an amount that it qualifies as traces.

With garlic, the easiest way to remove the skin is to mash the garlic with the flat part of the knife. The peel will break and the garlic is ready to slice or chop, the same way as the onion, from one tip to the other.

Recipes will usually advise, in the ingredients, whether the green end or the white bulb of the scallion should be used. When there is no recommendation, let your conscience be your guide.

1 pound of onions (2 onions, 1 medium and 1 large), will make about 4 cups sliced. The 4 cups will cook down to about 2 cups. 1 pound of scallions will trim down to about 2 to 2 1/2 cups, chopped, that will cook down to about 1 cup.

Garlic is purchased by the bulb and 1 teaspoon minced is equal to 1 clove. Garlic is available in jars in the supermarket, with all the mincing done for you. The jar is kept refrigerated, once opened. Read the label...some of the jarred, minced garlic is packed in oil. Polaner and Spice World produce an oil-free, minced garlic. It tastes just as good as the fresh. The only problem is, you can't roast minced garlic!

1 pound of garlic, untrimmed, has 2 grams of fat. 1 ounce of garlic has about 1/10 of a gram of fat.

HOT ORIENTAL SHRIMP WITH SHALLOTS

Every now and then you're looking for a nibble for cocktail hour that's different from the high fat Pigs-in-Blankets. This is a winner. The Oriental Chili Sauce with Garlic called for in this recipe is available in the Foreign Foods section of your supermarket or, if not, you will definitely find it in a nearby Oriental specialty store. These shrimp are hot!

Cooking utensil: A non-stick wok

1 Tbs. white wine or defatted chicken stock
3 Tbs. shallots, minced
1 1/2 pounds shrimp, peeled and deveined
1 Tbs. Oriental Chili Sauce with Garlic
3 Tbs. fresh lemon juice
Salt and freshly ground pepper to taste

1. Heat the wine or stock in your wok; add the shallots; cook 1 minute; add the shrimp; cook for about 4 minutes or until pink.
2. Place the shrimp in a bowl with the Chili Sauce and lemon juice; season with salt and pepper; refrigerate for at least 2 hours.
3. Drain shrimp and serve with toothpicks.

YIELD: About 30 to 40 shrimp, depending on the number per pound
FAT GRAMS IN ENTIRE RECIPE: 6

Notes:

SWEET AND SOUR SHRIMP

Cooking utensil: A 3 quart non-stick saucepan

1/2 cup sugar
1 Tbs. cornstarch
1 can (13 1/2 oz.) pineapple chunks, reserve liquid
1/2 cup vinegar
2 tsp. soy sauce
2 ribs celery, sliced
4 green onions with tops, sliced
1/2 medium green bell pepper, thinly sliced
1 large tomato, cut in eighths
1/2 pound shrimp, peeled and deveined
Soy Sauce to taste
Steamed rice, cooked without oil or margarine

---

1. Combine the sugar and cornstarch in a saucepan.
2. Add enough water to the pineapple juice to measure 1 cup; stir together the pineapple juice liquid, vinegar and soy sauce; gradually add to the sugar and cornstarch mixture; cook over low heat until thickened, stirring constantly.
3. Stir the pineapple, celery, onions and green pepper into the sauce mixture.
4. Fold in the tomato and shrimp; cook until the shrimp are pink and curled.
5. Season with soy sauce to taste and serve with the rice.

YIELD: About 4 cups
FAT GRAMS IN ENTIRE RECIPE: 3, without the rice

Notes:

Lox And Onion And Eggs

Whoever thought that this dish could be prepared low fat? Now with egg substitutes available, it's a done deal.

Cooking utensil: A large non-stick skillet

---

1 small onion, in half and thinly sliced
1/4 pound smoked salmon, thinly sliced
1 Tbs. Fleischmann's Fat Free Low Calorie margarine
1 1/2 cups Egg Beaters

---

1. Place the onion and the smoked salmon in a non-stick skillet with the margarine; sauté until the onion is tender.
2. Add the Egg Beaters to the skillet and scramble with the onions and smoked salmon.

YIELD: 2 3-egg omelets
FAT GRAMS IN ENTIRE RECIPE: 5

BTW: Don't forget to toast the onion bagels and put the fat free cream cheese on the table.

Notes:

Mexican Omelet

The last recipe reminded me of this omelet that also uses onions to enhance the flavor of the eggs.

Cooking utensil: A large non-stick skillet

1/2 large onion, chopped
1/2 green bell pepper, chopped
I Can't Believe It's Not Butter spray
2 cups Egg Beaters
4 oz. Healthy Choice processed loaf cheese, broken up
1 can (10 oz.) Rotel (diced tomatoes and chilies)

---

1. Place onion and bell pepper in a large non-stick skillet; spray the margarine; sauté the vegetables over medium-high heat until tender.
2. Add the eggs and the cheese; scramble; cook until the cheese melts.
3. Place the omelets in plates; spoon on some of the Rotel; serve.

YIELD: 4 2-egg omelets
FAT GRAMS IN ENTIRE RECIPE: 1

BTW: This is particularly good with fat free corn or flour tortillas and Quick Chili Beans or Jim's Beans.

Notes:

CRISPY SPICY BAKED ONION RINGS

Don't you love onion rings? I don't know anyone who doesn't enjoy biting into a crispy, pungent onion ring, whether it's with a hamburger or on top of a casserole. Now, at last, you can prepare some onion rings that are delicious and easily substitute for the fried kind.

Baking utensil: A baking sheet

1 very large sweet onion, sliced in rings 1/4 inch thick
1 box (7 oz.) corn flakes, crushed
1 tsp. Creole Seasoning
2 tsp. sugar
1/2 to 1 cup Egg Beaters

Preheat the oven to 375°

1. Combine the corn flakes, Creole Seasoning and sugar.
2. Dip each ring into the Egg Beaters; dredge each ring in just enough of the corn flake mixture to cover that ring (if you dredge the rings in the full quantity of the mixture, the flakes clump); place on the baking sheet.
3. Bake 20 to 25 minutes or until crisp.
4. Serve at once.

YIELD: About 30 rings
FAT GRAMS IN ENTIRE RECIPE: Traces

BTW: These are amazingly satisfying. The crispiness of the corn flakes captures the feel of the fried version. Don't hesitate to use these on top of the Broccoli Rice Casserole. Surprisingly, the rings don't get soggy.

Notes:

ONION TOMATO SOUP

Here's a quickie soup you can serve in a cup as a light appetizer or as a cozy pick-me-up on a cold winter's night.

Cooking utensil: A 3 quart non-stick saucepan

---

1 Tbs. Fleischmann's Fat Free Low Calorie squeeze margarine
2 cups onion, thinly sliced
1 can (10 3/4 oz.) Campbell's Beef Consommé, undiluted, defatted
1 soup can water
1 can (10 3/4 oz.) Campbell's Tomato Soup, undiluted
1 soup can skim milk
Salt and pepper to taste

---

1. Place the margarine in a saucepan; add the onion and sauté until tender.
2. Add the consommé and the water; simmer, covered, 15 minutes.
3. Add the remaining ingredients and heat through over medium heat, do not boil.
4. Season to taste and serve.

YIELD: About 5 cups
FAT GRAMS IN ENTIRE RECIPE: 4

Notes:

GARLIC, POTATO AND CELERY SOUP

When you combine the bland potato with the roundness of the garlic flavor and throw in the bitey celery, how can this be anything other than a winner?

Cooking utensil: A 6 to 8 quart non-stick saucepan

1/4 cup defatted stock
1 medium onion, chopped
6 to 8 cloves garlic, peeled and whole
8 to 10 ribs celery, sliced
1 Tbs. fresh parsley, chopped
2 medium potatoes, peeled and diced
8 to 10 cups water
1 to 2 Tbs. vegetable bouillon granules
Salt and freshly ground pepper

---

1. Sauté the onion in the stock until tender.
2. Add the garlic and cook 2 to 3 minutes.
3. Add remaining ingredients; simmer, covered, for 30 minutes.
4. Remove from heat, season to taste and place in a blender or food processor; purée.
5. Return to pot; heat through and serve.

YIELD: About 10 cups
FAT GRAMS IN ENTIRE RECIPE: 1

Notes:

_____

_____

_____

_____

_____

ONIONS, MUSHROOMS AND PEPPERS WITH PASTA

Another of the stir-fry pasta dishes for a quick turnaround when everyone is clamoring for dinner.

Cooking utensil: A non-stick wok

---

1 large onion, in half and sliced
1 Tbs. garlic, minced
1/2 green bell pepper, thinly sliced
1/2 red or yellow bell pepper, thinly sliced
1/2 cup dry white wine or defatted chicken stock
1/2 pound mushrooms, thickly sliced or quartered
1 large or 3 Roma (plum) tomatoes, chopped
1/2 cup defatted chicken stock additional
1/2 tsp. dried basil, crushed
1/2 tsp. dried thyme, crushed
1 tsp. dried oregano, crushed
1/2 cup fresh parsley, chopped
3 slices fat free Swiss cheese, broken up
3/4 pound pasta, cooked
Crushed red pepper flakes to taste
Salt and freshly ground pepper to taste
Fat free grated Parmesan

---

1. Sauté the onion, garlic and bell peppers in the wine or stock until crisp-tender.
2. Add the mushrooms, tomatoes, additional stock and herbs; simmer, uncovered, stirring occasionally, until the mushrooms are tender.
3. Lower the heat; add the Swiss cheese and simmer on low heat until the cheese melts and makes a creamy sauce.
4. Add the pasta to the sauce; toss gently and season to taste.
5. Sprinkle with Parmesan cheese and serve.

YIELD: About 12 cups
FAT GRAMS IN ENTIRE RECIPE: 8

Btw: If you happen to have some cooked turkey or chicken, add the poultry after the herbs, stir once or twice, and continue with the recipe. A spicy turkey or chicken sausage does well added to this dish. Use your imagination.

BAKED HERBED FISH

The classic baked fish looks so elegant, is so simple to prepare, and goes beautifully with any accompaniment.

Baking utensil: A 9 x 13 baking dish

---

2 pounds red snapper or halibut, filleted
I Can't Believe It's Not Butter spray
1/2 tsp. salt
1/2 tsp. marjoram
1/2 tsp. dried thyme leaves, crushed
1/4 tsp. garlic powder
1/8 tsp. white pepper
2 bay leaves
1/2 cup onion, chopped
1/2 cup white wine
Lime or lemon wedges
Hungarian sweet paprika

Preheat oven to 350°

1. Rinse the fish with cold water and pat dry; place in baking dish; spray the margarine on both sides of the fish; set aside.
2. Combine all dry seasonings; sprinkle evenly on one side of fish; top with the bay leaves and onion, sprinkle with the paprika; pour the wine over all.
3. Place in the oven and bake, uncovered, for 20 to 30 minutes or until the fish flakes when prodded with a fork.
4. Serve on a platter with the lemon or lime wedges.

YIELD: 32 ounces, enough for 4 healthy servings
FAT GRAMS IN ENTIRE RECIPE: 14, if snapper; 22, if halibut

Notes:

_____

_____

PEAS

Although beans and peas make up the category we know as legumes, the fresh green peas are in a vegetable class in most people's minds. And then, of course, we have the delightful, crunchy pods, or snow peas, that add so much color and crunch to Asian food. Sugar snaps add a sweet, crispy touch to vegetable dishes and are now available frozen. When buying peas, most of us don't have the time to shell them if they are purchased fresh in the pods, so we'll concentrate on the snow peas, sugar snaps and frozen peas. The recipes for frozen peas will work just as well as fresh.

1 pound of frozen peas has 1 gram of fat. Sugar snaps and snow peas have about 1/2 gram in the pound.

Frozen peas need a run under cold water to thaw for use in salads. They can be introduced to recipes, like stews and soups, still frozen.

Snow peas do not freeze well. They get soggy. Try to find them fresh and look for bright green and firm. Limp snow peas will not add the zip to the dish you're anticipating. To trim the snow peas, snip off the stem end, pulling off the string that runs down the side, snip off the opposite tip of the pod.

Sugar snaps freeze very well and are certainly an asset to many vegetable dishes. You can just pull them out of the freezer, place them in a strainer or colander under cold, running water and in no time they're thawed, ready to add to any dish to give it a little extra crispy sweetness.

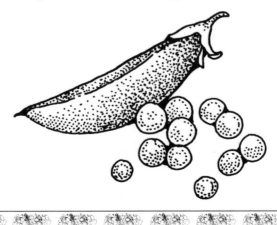

ENGLISH PEAS

The classic dish for peas and a great part of a vegetable plate for dinner.

Cooking utensil: A 3 quart non-stick saucepan

---

1 package (10 oz.) frozen green peas
1 Tbs. Fleischmann's Fat Free Low Calorie margarine
1/4 tsp. sugar
Salt and freshly ground pepper

---

1. Rinse the peas with cold water; place peas and margarine in a saucepan with sugar; cook over low heat until heated through.

YIELD: About 2 cups
FAT GRAMS IN ENTIRE RECIPE: 0

Notes:

GREEN PEAS WITH MUSHROOMS

Here's an easy side dish or additional veggie for a vegetable plate.

Cooking utensil: A large non-stick skillet

---

2 Tbs. Fleischmann's Fat Free Low Calorie squeeze margarine
1 medium onion, sliced
1/2 tsp. garlic, minced
1/2 pound mushrooms, thickly sliced
2 packages (10 oz. ea.) frozen peas, thawed
1/2 tsp. chicken bouillon granules

---

1. Heat the margarine in a skillet or saucepan; add the onion and garlic; sauté until crisp-tender.
2. Add the mushrooms and cook until tender.
3. Add the peas and bouillon; simmer gently until heated through; serve.

YIELD: 6 cups
FAT GRAMS IN ENTIRE RECIPE: Traces

BTW: These peas do well with seasonings like cumin and turmeric. Spice the dish up with some exotic herbs and serve on brown rice and you've got dinner. If you prefer the more Asiatic spices, add more garlic and think of five spice powder and soy.

Notes:

PEAS AND WATER CHESTNUTS

A quick-fix Asian dish to serve on steamed rice.

Cooking utensil: A non-stick wok

1/4 cup white wine or defatted stock
1 small onion, thinly sliced
1/2 tsp. garlic, minced
1/2 cup celery, minced
2 packages (10 oz. ea.) frozen peas, thawed
1 can (8 oz.) water chestnuts, sliced
1 cup bean sprouts
1 1/2 tsp. chicken bouillon granules
1/4 cup water, as needed
Soy sauce to taste

1. Sauté the onion, garlic and celery in the wine or stock until crisp-tender.
2. Add the peas and remaining ingredients, except the water; stir-fry over medium-high heat until all the veggies are cooked through and still crisp, about a minute or 2; add the water, a little at a time, only if necessary to avoid sticking.
3. Season with soy sauce and serve on steamed rice that's been cooked without oil or margarine.

YIELD: 4 cups
FAT GRAMS IN ENTIRE RECIPE: Traces

BTW: Here again, it's easy to add any leftover turkey or chicken, cut in strips to make a heartier dish.

Notes:

SNOW PEAS, WATER CHESTNUTS AND MUSHROOMS

These flavors are all extremely delicate. The mushrooms are added to present a tender alternative to the crunchy water chestnuts and crispy snow peas.

Cooking utensil: A non-stick wok

---

1 cup button mushrooms, sliced
1/4 cup wine or defatted stock
1 pound fresh snow peas, trimmed
1 small shallot, minced
1/2 cup water chestnuts, sliced
Salt and freshly ground pepper to taste

---

1. Heat the wine or stock; add the mushroom and sauté for about 2 minutes.
2. Add the rest of the ingredients and stir-fry until all ingredients are heated through.
3. Season to taste and serve.

YIELD: 5 cups
FAT GRAMS IN ENTIRE RECIPE: Traces

Notes:

Sugar Snaps, Mixed Veggies And Pasta

I love pasta with vegetables. The easiest vegetables to use are the frozen bags and boxes. The recipe that follows is a ten minute fix and a ten minute cook-time. All you need to have prepared beforehand is some leftover marinara sauce (of course, the store-bought fat free will do!) and cooked pasta to add to the pot. I use my wok for throwing this together.

Cooking utensil: A non-stick wok

---

1 package (10 oz.) frozen kale
1/2 bag frozen mixed vegetables
1/2 bag frozen sugar snap peas
1/2 cup defatted chicken stock
1 tsp. garlic, minced
1 medium onion, in half and sliced
1 cup fat free marinara sauce
1/2 pound pasta, cooked without oil
Fat free grated Parmesan

---

1. Cook the frozen kale in the microwave or stove-top according to directions; meanwhile, place other frozen vegetables in a strainer or colander and thaw with cold, running water.
2. Heat the stock; add the onion and the garlic; sauté for about 5 minutes.
3. Add the kale and other vegetables in the wok; toss and heat through over high heat, stirring often, about 5 minutes.
4. Add the marinara sauce and heat through, about 2 minutes; add the pasta and heat through, about 2 minutes more.
5. Sprinkle with grated Parmesan and serve.

YIELD: About 12 cups, determined by amount of vegetables and pasta.
FAT GRAMS IN ENTIRE RECIPE: 6 grams in this recipe
> **Check labels for grams in veggies**

BTW: Don't forget The Marinara Sauce, which is virtually fat free.

Notes:

PEPPERS

What a treat peppers are! They're so attractive in red, green, yellow and orange. They're crunchy, they're sweet, they're hot. They help to add zip to a recipe or they round out the flavor. They're delicious cooked or raw. They even taste good roasted and jarred. Buying peppers is simply a matter of finding firm peppers, with no blemishes or soft spots. They store well in the refrigerator for at least a week. They should always be in the refrigerator for a quick veggie dish or to throw into a salad.

You'll get about 3 bell peppers in a pound which will slice into 4 cups after cleaning and trimming. Remove the stem and core. Trim the membranes, which may be bitter, and then slice, dice or chop the meat with the skin. All the recipes in this book calling for peppers, sliced, diced, chopped, refer to peppers that have been cleaned and trimmed.

The fat in a whole medium pepper is about 1/10 of a gram. This is a food that the low fat lover can love.

Hot peppers vary slightly in size but are usually about 3 to 6 inches long. There are also round cherry peppers that are a nifty addition to appetizer trays or Antipasto. Hot peppers can be added, raw, minced, to foods as you've seen in some of the recipes, and are often used pickled, such as jalapeños, that are so prevalent in Mexican food. You can also find canned chili peppers, already chopped or sliced. Whenever working with hot peppers, raw or pickled, be sure to wash the utensils and your hands well, afterward. The capcaicin that leaches onto your fingers can burn your eyes, your face or any mucous membrane.

Broiling or charring bell peppers intensifies the flavor and it's easy enough to do. Place the peppers on a pan and broil them until the skin blisters. Rotate them with a pair of tongs to keep the charring uniform. When black, remove them from the broiler and place them in a paper bag for 15 to 20 minutes. When you take them out of the bag the skins will slip off. The same results can be accomplished with a gas stove, by placing the pepper on the burner and turning it as it scorches.

Grilling bell peppers along with other vegetables on an outdoor grill in summertime is a delicious variation of the stewed, sautéed and stir-fried flavors we know so well. And there are other ways, besides eating them from the grill, you'll enjoy.

PASTA WITH GRILLED PEPPERS

If you're into doing a bunch of grilling in the summer, you probably have leftover vegetables from the grilling basket on occasion. If not, next time you grill, toss extra vegetables on the grill explicitly for this use. The flavor of the grilling gives a delicious twist to this dish.

Cooking utensil: A non-stick wok

1/2 cup defatted chicken stock
2 tsp. garlic, minced
1 pinch salt
1 cup green bell peppers, grilled and sliced
1 cup red or yellow bell peppers, grilled and sliced
1 cup onions, grilled and sliced
8 or more cherry tomatoes, grilled and halved
2 Tbs. white wine
1 cup fat free marinara sauce
3/4 pound pasta, cooked without oil
Salt and freshly ground pepper to taste
Fat free grated Parmesan

---

1. Heat the stock; sauté the garlic for 2 minutes with the salt.
2. Add the vegetables; cook uncovered over medium heat, until heated through, about 3 to 5 minutes; add more stock if necessary to avoid drying.
3. Add the wine and cook for 2 minutes; add the marinara sauce and heat through.
4. Add the pasta; cook over medium heat, tossing frequently until heated through.
5. Season will salt and pepper; sprinkle with grated Parmesan and serve.

YIELD: About 10 cups
FAT GRAMS IN ENTIRE RECIPE: 9

Notes:

PEPPER AND POTATO BAKE

This is a takeoff on Bari's Shake and Bake Potatoes that you'll find in the potato section of this book. It's a great vegetable to serve when entertaining because you don't have to stir. The oven does the cooking for you.

Baking utensil: A non-stick baking pan 8 x 8 or 9 x 9

---

1 1/2 pounds mixed red and green bell peppers, cut in 1 inch squares
1 pound small redskin potatoes, scrubbed, cut in half and each half in thirds
2 large sweet onions, in half, each half quartered
1 tsp. olive oil
2 Tbs. Fleischmann's Fat Free Low Calorie squeeze margarine
1 Tbs. mixed Italian seasonings
2 tsp. garlic powder
Salt and freshly ground pepper

Preheat the oven to 425°

1. Combine the peppers, potatoes and onions in a large bowl, then divide into thirds; set aside.
2. Combine the olive oil, the margarine and the seasonings.
3. Use a 1-gallon plastic storage bag; place the first third of the vegetables in the bag with 1/3 of the margarine mix; coat the vegetables; place them in a shallow baking pan.
4. Repeat with each third of the remaining vegetables and margerine mixture; bake for about 30 minutes or until the potatoes are cooked through.

YIELD: About 14 cups mixed cubed vegetables
FAT GRAMS IN ENTIRE RECIPE: 6

Notes:

_____

_____

SZECHUAN CHICKEN WITH GREEN PEPPERS

Here you have one of David's favorites. The chicken marinates for at least 20 minutes before you can continue with the preparation of the dish. My recommendation is to put together the marinade, cut the chicken and peppers, put the chicken in a bowl with the marinade, take some rice out of the freezer and place it in the microwave or put it on to boil. The rest is easy. Preparation time is about 15 minutes. Cook-time is about 10 minutes.

This dish is *hot!*

Cooking utensils: A dish for the microwave and non-stick wok

---

2 Tbs. Chili Purée with Garlic
1 tsp. white rice vinegar
1/2 tsp. sugar
1 Tbs. light soy sauce
1 tsp. sesame oil
1 Tbs. sherry or white wine
1 clove garlic, minced
1 Tbs. cornstarch
2 chicken breast halves (4 oz. ea.), skinless, boneless, cubed
2 medium green bell peppers, cut in 3/4 inch squares
Pam or Mazola spray-on oil

---

1. Combine the Chili Purée with Garlic with the vinegar and sugar; set aside.
2. Combine the soy sauce, sesame oil, sherry, garlic and cornstarch; marinate the chicken cubes in the soy sauce mixture for 30 minutes.
3. After the chicken has marinated for 30 minutes, discard the marinade; place the chicken in a baking dish in one layer and microwave on high for 3 1/2 minutes; stir and microwave for 1 1/2 minutes more or until cooked through; set aside.
4. Place the green peppers in a wok that's been treated with the spray-on oil; stir-fry the peppers for 1 minute.
5. Add the chicken, along with the Chili Purée mixture and stir-fry until both the chicken and peppers are thoroughly tossed with sauce and heated through.
6. Serve on steamed rice, cooked without oil or margarine.

YIELD: About 5 cups
FAT GRAMS IN ENTIRE RECIPE: 14

SHRIMP WITH BASIL AND HOT CHILIES

This dish is divine. It's aromatic and hot, the basil and chilies complimenting each other with an explosion of flavor with the delicate shrimp to balance the show. It's soupy, so have plenty of steamed rice on hand.

Cooking utensil: A non-stick wok

---

1 pound shrimp
1 bunch fresh basil, 2 leaves
2 cloves garlic, minced
2 or 3 red or green chilies (serrano or fresh jalapeño), seeds removed,
   thinly sliced
4 green onions, white part, minced - green part, in 1 inch cuts
1 tsp. peanut oil
1/2 cup +2 Tbs. defatted chicken stock
2 Tbs. fish sauce
2 Tbs. soy sauce
1 tsp. sugar
Hot steamed rice, cooked without oil or margarine

---

1. Wash and dry the basil; set aside.
2. Heat the wok over high heat; add the oil and 2 Tbs. stock, the white part of the scallions, the garlic and chilies; cook for 10 seconds.
3. Add the shrimp; stir-fry 20 seconds.
4. Add the fish sauce, the soy sauce, sugar, remaining stock and the green part of the scallion; bring to a boil; stir in the basil; cook for 20 seconds.
5. Serve with steamed rice.

YIELD: 4 to 5 cups
FAT GRAMS IN ENTIRE RECIPE: 9

Notes:

CHILI CON QUESO

Every now and then you come up with a recipe that everyone asks for when they know you're cooking. This is one of those recipes for me.

Cooking utensil: A microwave oven-proof bowl or 3 quart non-stick saucepan

---

1/2 onion, minced
1/2 green bell pepper, minced
1 package (2 lbs.) Healthy Choice Pasteurized Process Cheese
  Product (loaf cheese) broken up into 8 to 10 pieces
2 cans (10 oz.) Rotel Diced Tomatoes and Green Chilies, reserve juice
Pickled jalapeño peppers, sliced, to taste
Baked corn chips

---

1. Place all ingredients, except the reserved juice from the Rotel and the pickled jalapeños in a large microwave-proof bowl; heat on high, covered, for 5 minutes, stirring occasionally. If you cannot use the microwave, cook stove-top following directions with a slight adjustment for time.
2. Check at 5 minutes, stir well; if lumps of cheese remain, cook for 5 minutes more on high; check again; if too dry, add some of the reserved juice, sparingly, until the right consistency.
3. Cook at 3 minute intervals until smooth and thick enough to cling to a baked corn chip, and not so thick that the corn chip will break when dipped.
4. Serve with the jalapeño peppers available for making it hotter.

YIELD: About 5 to 6 cups
FAT GRAMS IN ENTIRE RECIPE: 0

Btw: This stuff is so good it will make a Mexican buffet a fiesta! Serve it with fat free tortillas and beans (Jim's Beans, Quick Chili Beans), Mexican rice (Red Rice) and the salsa of your choice. We like Old El Paso Thick & Chunky Salsa and Utz Baked Corn Chips. If not available, Pace Thick & Chunky and Tostito's brands will make you happy, too. Look at the recipe for Salsa, if you would like to prepare it yourself. This dip can be used on baked potatoes, nachos, chili and taco salads.

POTATOES

Potatoes, along with pasta and bread were the foods I missed most when I was subjected to the old-fashioned, carbohydrate-poor diets. Now we can eat these many-faceted beauties to our hearts' content.

There are baking potatoes, usually Idaho potatoes that have a thick skin that allows for making the skin a shell to hold all the goodies we're going to plop in there; there are white potatoes, the skins so thin they slough right off when the potato's been boiled so they make great mashers. Then there are Yukon gold potatoes with a dense, velvety pulp, good for stew, boiling or mashing; redskin potatoes that merely need scrubbing and cubing and they are perfect for potato salad with the skins on, boiled with the skins on, or tossed with Fleischmann's Fat Free Low Calorie margarine and parsley, then roasted. Sweet potatoes, a total world of difference and utter joy, just baked and sprinkled with Molly McButter, or dressed up with apples and sugar and cinnamon. We probably could play with a book based entirely on baked potatoes and the toppings we could fix...fat free. We'll cover a few of those for you, along with some other potato recipes that we love.

We weighed a potato recently and were shocked at the size referred to in magazines and cookbooks and the FDA. A 4 ounce potato is about the size of a half-cup! When you think of a potato it's usually about 10 to 12 ounces. Redskins run about 4 to 6 in a pound. Buy them firm, with no sprouts, no bruises and no mold. Do not buy potatoes with a greenish cast. Storage should be in a dark, cool place, preferably in a net, and will keep for about one to two weeks. Do not store in plastic bags or the refrigerator. Use your vegetable brush for scrubbing, with some mild detergent, rinsing thoroughly. If you're going to peel the potatoes just scrub well with the brush, and then peel. Scrubbing should be performed just before cooking.

A pound of potatoes has less than 1/2 gram of fat. Pretty good, huh?

BOILING POTATOES

Cooking utensil: An 8 quart non-stick pot

1 pound white potatoes, peeled
Water to cover
Salt to taste (about 1 tsp. per quart of water)

1. If the potatoes are not uniform in size, cut them into pieces that are about the same size so that they'll cook evenly.
2. Place them in a large pot with plenty of water, while the water is cold; bring to a boil; keep water rolling for about 20 minutes for fully-cooked potatoes.
3. Test them with a fork; when the fork pierces the potato, it's done. Do not overcook or you'll have paste!

YIELD: 4 small potatoes
FAT GRAMS IN ENTIRE RECIPE: Traces

BTW: For an extra bonus in flavor, use defatted stock or water that's been doctored with 1 Tbs. chicken bouillon granules, instead of salted water.

Notes:

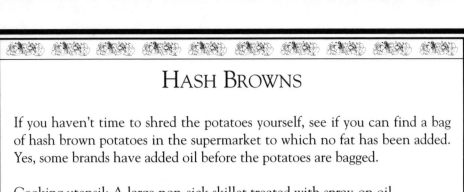

HASH BROWNS

If you haven't time to shred the potatoes yourself, see if you can find a bag of hash brown potatoes in the supermarket to which no fat has been added. Yes, some brands have added oil before the potatoes are bagged.

Cooking utensil: A large non-sick skillet treated with spray-on oil

---

1 pound shredded potatoes
1 large onion, thinly sliced
Salt and pepper to taste

---

1. Treat a large skillet with the spray; heat the skillet.
2. Add the potatoes and the onion and mash down so you have a thin layer; brown on one side, about 10 minutes; turn with a plastic spatula and brown on the second side, about 5 minutes more.
3. Season with salt and pepper and serve.

YIELD: 2 1/2 to 3 cups
FAT GRAMS IN ENTIRE RECIPE: About 4 (depends on how skimpy you spray with Pam or Mazola)

BTW: Another likely addition to this potato is 1/2 green or red bell pepper, finely chopped.

Notes:

ITALIAN POTATO AND PASTA STEW

This stew is good the first day, but great the second day. Spend about 20 minutes peeling and chopping and the stew cooks itself after that. We like it with brown rice. There's plenty of time to cook the rice while the stew's bubbling or pull it out of the freezer and steam it in the microwave.

Cooking utensil: An 8 quart non-stick pot

---

1 large onion, chopped
1/3 cup celery, chopped
1/4 cup red wine or defatted stock
4 cloves garlic, minced
2 cups canned plum tomatoes with juice, chopped
1/3 cup fresh parsley, chopped
1/2 cup carrots, sliced
2 cups redskin potatoes, scrubbed and diced
1 cup raw macaroni
2 cups cooked lima beans
8 cups vegetable broth
1 Tbs. dried basil, crushed
1 tsp. dried chives
2 tsp. dried oregano, crushed
1/2 tsp. cayenne pepper
2 cups brown rice, cooked
Salt, pepper and hot sauce to taste

---

1. Sauté the onion, celery and garlic in the wine until it softens; do not brown it; add more wine or stock if necessary.
2. Add tomatoes, parsley and carrots; cook another 5 minutes, stirring often.
3. Add the remaining ingredients, except the rice and bring to a full boil; reduce heat and simmer, uncovered, until the vegetables are soft, about 20 minutes.
4. Run a cup or two through the blender or food processor, to purée it, and add it back to the stew.
5. Adjust the seasonings to taste; serve on brown rice or add the rice directly to the stew for a thicker consistency and a mouthfeel like barley.

YIELD: 8 cups
FAT GRAMS IN ENTIRE RECIPE: 8

MASHED POTATOES

There are times, like the holidays, when mashed potatoes are very important. In fact, how does any kid grow up without having had a hand at playing with the mashed potatoes and peas and gravy, making roadways and mountains and important creative things like that? For a long time mashed potatoes, with the milk and butter was off-limits for weight watchers and people on restrictive diets...but no more. Try these and smile.

Cooking utensil: An 8 quart non-stick pot

Boiling water (about 2 quarts) with 2 tsp. salt
2 pounds white or Yukon gold potatoes, peeled, cubed or sliced
1/2 to 3/4 cup skim milk
Molly McButter to taste
Salt and freshly ground pepper to taste

---

1. Place the potatoes in the boiling water to cover; cook, uncovered, on high heat, the water rolling, until the potatoes can be easily penetrated with a fork, about 10 to 15 minutes.
2. Drain and place the potatoes in a warm bowl; use a potato ricer, masher or an electric beater to mash the potatoes.
3. Add the milk, gradually, to the consistency that pleases you.
4. Add the Molly McButter, salt and pepper to taste.

YIELD: 4 cups
FAT GRAMS IN ENTIRE RECIPE: Traces

Btw: The wonder of these potatoes is the difference between these and the original that Mother used to make. With whole milk and butter, there would be between 28 and 39 grams of fat! And just think of these potatoes that taste like the real thing with the Thick Mushroom Gravy. Fat free sour cream is an interesting change from the milk. Another neat modification of the original potato is using redskins, scrubbing and cubing them, instead of peeling them.

Notes:

MASHED POTATOES WITH ONIONS

While we're mashing potatoes, there's a delightful way to serve them that you'll enjoy. This presentation is dressier and tastier than the original recipe, if you can believe that. The dish can be prepared with the white potato base or the yellow and is great with the redskin potatoes, mashed, too. Add the cheese on occasion, if you like.

Cooking utensils: A non-stick skillet and a non-stick oven-proof baking dish

---

4 cups Mashed Potatoes
1 large onion, thinly sliced
2 to 3 Tbs. Fleischmann's Fat Free Low Calorie squeeze margarine
1/4 to 1/2 cup fat free shredded cheddar, optional

Preheat oven to 325° if you choose to bake this potato dish.

1. Place the potatoes in an oven-proof bowl; set aside.
2. Place the onion in a skillet with the margarine; cook over a medium-low heat until the onion is soft; increase the heat and brown slightly.
3. Pour the onion mixture over the potatoes; serve.

OR

3. Pour the onion mixture over the potatoes; sprinkle the cheese over the top; bake at 325° until the cheese melts and serve.

YIELD: 5 cups
FAT GRAMS IN ENTIRE RECIPE: Traces

BTW: Sour cream works well with this recipe as an alternative to the milk.

Notes:

PARSLEY PARMESAN POTATO PATTIES

So you prepared mashed potatoes and, as a good hostess does, you made enough for half-again as many people as the number of guests. Now, what do you do with the leftovers? Why not make tasty patties the following evening. They're so good, you won't even recognize that they are leftovers.

Cooking utensils: A non-stick skillet and a baking sheet treated with spray-on oil

---

2 Tbs. defatted stock
1/2 cup fresh parsley, chopped
4 cups Mashed Potatoes (freshly made or leftover)
1 cup onion, chopped
1/4 cup Egg Beaters
1/4 cup fat free grated Parmesan (or more to taste)
Paprika, pepper and salt to taste

Preheat oven to 375°

1. Sauté the onion and parsley in the stock until crisp-tender.
2. Combine with the mashed potatoes, the Egg Beaters and Parmesan cheese.
3. Spray a baking sheet with Pam or Mazola; set aside.
4. Form the potato mixture into 2 inch balls, flatten into patties and place on baking sheet; bake for about 15 to 20 minutes or until golden brown.

YIELD: 15 to 18 patties
FAT GRAMS IN ENTIRE RECIPE: 3

Notes:

SAGE POTATOES

Cooking utensil: A non-stick wok

2 Tbs. Fleischmann's Fat Free Low Calorie squeeze margarine
1 medium onion, sliced
1 Tbs. fresh sage leaves or whole dried leaves, crushed
2 pounds potatoes, scrubbed, sliced
1 can (16 oz.) tomatoes with juice, sliced
2/3 cup dry white wine
1 package (10 oz.) frozen peas, thawed
Salt and freshly ground pepper to taste

1. Sauté the onion and sage in the margarine until the onion is tender.
2. Add the potato and toss with the onion for 1 minute; add the tomatoes and wine; simmer, covered, over low heat until the potatoes are tender, stirring occasionally.
3. Add the peas and cook 5 minutes more.
4. Season to taste and serve.

YIELD: 8 cups
FAT GRAMS IN ENTIRE RECIPE: 1

Notes:

FRENCH POTATO SOUP

Serve this soup cold and it's Vichyssoise, a delicate, cold soup for summer-time pleasure. Serve it hot, in the winter, with some crusty fat free sour-dough and it'll warm you up. Either way, it's a darned good soup.

Cooking utensil: An 8 quart non-stick pot

1/4 cup white wine or defatted stock
3 leeks (white part only), cleaned and sliced
1 onion, sliced
4 medium potatoes, peeled and thinly sliced
4 cups defatted chicken stock, additional
2 cups skim milk
2 Tbs. Butter Buds
Salt and freshly ground pepper to taste
Chopped chives or parsley, as a garnish

---

1. Sauté the onion and leeks in 1/4 cup wine or stock until tender.
2. Add the potatoes and additional stock; simmer until the potatoes are very tender.
3. Remove the vegetables and purée in the blender or food processor; return the vegetable purée to the soup.
4. Mix the milk with the Butter Buds and add to the soup; cook over low heat until heated through.
5. Season to taste and serve hot or chill overnight to serve, very cold, as Vichyssoise.
6. Before serving, garnish with chives or parsley.

YIELD: About 8 cups
FAT GRAMS IN ENTIRE RECIPE: Less than 1

Notes:

THE BAKED POTATO

In about 1958, I moved from New York to Dallas, Texas. We had lived there only a week or two when we went to a restaurant and I ordered a baked potato. In New York, back then, a baked potato was just that. You were served some butter, usually glopped in the middle, and then you added salt and pepper. But the baked potato in Dallas arrived with butter, grated cheddar cheese and sour cream, with chopped chives on top! They even wanted to know it we wanted crumbled bacon! That was then...this is now...and baked potatoes come with just about everything you can imagine. The idea in this book is to keep *everything* low fat. Here we go!

---

1 large baking potato, scrubbed
1 Tbs. Fleischmann's Fat Free Low Calorie squeeze margarine
2 Tbs. fat free sour cream
1 Tbs. chopped chives or scallions
1 1/2 Tbs. McCormick Bac'N Pieces

Preheat oven to 425°

1. Prick holes in the potato with a long-pronged fork; bake the potato for 1 hour; test with a fork to see if the potato is tender inside, if not, bake an additional 15 minutes.

OR

1. Prick holes in the potato with a fork; bake in the microwave for 5 minutes; turn over and bake another 5 minutes; remove from microwave and bake for about 30 minutes in the oven ; proceed as in step 1.
2. When the potato is baked sufficiently, slit the potato from end to end; fluff the pulp with a fork and add the margarine.
3. When the margarine melts, spread it around the potato and add the sour cream, top with the chives or scallions and then top with the Bac'N Pieces.
4. This is so pretty you may want to frame it, but it's better if consumed.

YIELD: 1 baked potato with all the toppings
FAT GRAMS IN ENTIRE RECIPE: 1

RESTUFFED BAKED POTATO

The potatoes in this recipe require oven baking. Although the half-microwaved and half-baked will have a skin thick enough for dressing with the goodies, in this recipe the potatoes need a thicker, stiffer skin.

Baking utensil: A non-stick baking sheet

---

6 medium to large baking potatoes, scrubbed
3/4 to 1 cup fat free sour cream
1 packet Lipton's Onion Soup Mix
6 oz. Healthy Choice Processed loaf cheese, broken into small pieces

---

Preheat oven to 425°

1. Prick the potatoes with a fork; place them in the oven and bake for 1 to 1 1/4 hours; test for doneness.
2. When fully baked, slice the potato in half, lengthwise, remove the pulp carefully, do not rib the skin of the potatoes.
3. Place the pulp in a bowl; combine with the sour cream and the soup mix; add 4 ounces of the cheese, reserving 2 ounces; toss.
4. Replace this mixture into the potato skins; place the halves on a baking sheet and return to the oven; bake for about 10 minutes or until the cheese is melted and the potato is hot through; place the reserved cheese on top of the potatoes and bake for 5 minutes more or until the cheese melts.

YIELD: 12 potato halves
FAT GRAMS IN ENTIRE RECIPE: 2

BTW: McCormick Bac'N Pieces can be added to the pulp mixture along with the onion soup and cheese. These potato halves freeze very well and a few can be prepared at one time and then used for a meal or a minimeal, anytime.

Notes:

CARROT-STUFFED BAKED POTATOES

Stuffing the potato with carrots and horseradish give it an exciting new flavor and a crunch, too.

Baking utensil: A non-stick baking sheet

1/4 cup Butter Buds, prepared
4 baked potatoes
1 raw carrot, crated
1/4 cup fresh parsley, chopped
1/4 cup onion, minced
1/2 tsp. horseradish
2/3 cup fat free sour cream
Salt and pepper to taste
Fat free grated Parmesan
Paprika

Preheat the oven to 350°

1. Prepare the Butter Buds and refrigerate for at least 4 hours prior to use; this will cause it to thicken.
2. Slice the potatoes in half, lengthwise; scoop out the pulp; whip the potatoes with the carrots, parsley, onion, horseradish sour cream and thickened Butter Buds liquid.
3. Season to taste with the salt and pepper; top with the grated cheese and sprinkle paprika on top of that.
4. Bake for 15 minutes or until the cheese melts.

YIELD: 8 potato halves
FAT GRAMS IN ENTIRE RECIPE: 3

Notes:

_____

_____

_____

BARI'S OWN SHAKE AND BAKE

You won't believe how good these quickie potatoes are until you've baked them.

Baking utensil: A non-stick baking sheet

---

1 Tbs. mixed Italian seasonings
1 tsp. garlic powder
1/2 tsp. seasoned pepper
1 tsp. canola oil
4 medium redskin potatoes, scrubbed, cut in 1/2 inch cubes

Preheat the oven to 350°

1. Mix together the dry ingredients; place this mixture in to gallon-sized plastic bag; add the canola oil; squeeze the oil with the herbs to blend, thoroughly.
2. Add the potato cubes to the bag; shake the bag to evenly coat the potato.
3. Place in a single layer on a baking sheet for 20 to 25 minutes or until the potatoes are golden and crunchy on the outside and tender on the inside.

YIELD: About 4 cups
FAT GRAMS IN ENTIRE RECIPE: 5

BTW: Now you'll never be tempted by French fries...you'll have these instead!

Notes:

BAKED POTATO WITH ROSEMARY

If you love garlic and the delightful flavor of rosemary, you'll flip over this baker.

Preparation utensil: Aluminum foil

---

4 baking potatoes
2 cloves garlic, minced
4 sprigs rosemary, 1/2 inch long
1/2 medium onion, sliced
Fat free Italian salad dressing
Freshly ground pepper

Preheat the oven to 425°

1. Remove a 1 inch wide by 1 inch deep "V" shaped wedge, lengthwise across each potato.
2. Into this crevice, insert a sprig of rosemary, 1/4 of the onion slices, 1/4 of the garlic and a grind or two of pepper.
3. Replace the potato wedge; pour the salad dressing on each potato and into the wedged area; wrap each potato in aluminum foil; bake for 1 hour.
4. Test for doneness; when the potato is soft, remove the foil and serve.

YIELD: 4 baked potatoes
FAT GRAMS IN ENTIRE RECIPE: 1

Notes:

_____

_____

_____

_____

_____

POTATO SALAD

We like our potato salad prepared with redskin potatoes. It provides the extra nutrients you acquire in the skins and we think they're prettier than the plain white. If you don't have redskins on hand, use the white or Yukon gold potatoes, peeled, instead.

Preparation utensil: A large bowl

---

1 1/2 pounds small redskin potatoes, cut in 1/2 - 3/4 inch cubes
4 ribs celery, minced
1/4 medium onion, minced
1/2 red bell pepper, minced
3/4 cup fat free mayonnaise
1/4 cup vinegar
1 1/2 Tbs. Dijon mustard
3/4 tsp. salt
Seasoned pepper to taste
Dill weed to taste

---

1. Scrub the potatoes, cut into cubes; place in cold, salted water; bring to a boil; cook uncovered over high heat until the potatoes are firm, but can be pierced with a fork (if soft, the potatoes will fall apart when you mix them with the other ingredients), about 15 minutes; drain and set aside to cool.
2. Combine the celery, onion, bell pepper; set aside.
3. Combine the mayonnaise, vinegar, mustard and salt.
4. Place potatoes, minced vegetables in a large bowl and toss with the mayo mix.
5. Season to taste with seasoned pepper and dill weed; refrigerate for at least 3 to 4 hours before serving.

YIELD: 5 to 6 cups
FAT GRAMS IN ENTIRE RECIPE: 1

BTW: The dill weed adds a particularly fresh flavor to the salad.

Notes:

KATHY'S GREEK POTATOES

This recipe is from Kathy Giordano, one of our dearest friends, and a practiced low fat mavin. And, by the way, one heck of a good cook.

Baking utensil: A large non-stick roasting pan

---

1 Tbs. powdered oregano
1 Tbs. garlic powder
Juice of 1 lemon
4 medium potatoes, peeled and quartered
Salt and freshly ground pepper to taste
2 cans (10 oz. ea.) defatted or fat free chicken broth

Preheat oven to 350°

1. Toss the potatoes with the oregano, garlic and lemon juice, salt and pepper; place in a roasting pan; add broth to cover halfway up the potatoes.
2. Bake for 1 to 1 1/2 hours or until potatoes can be pierced with a fork.
3. The liquid in the pan may be reduced to 1/2 to use as a sauce.

YIELD: 3 to 4 cups
FAT GRAMS IN ENTIRE RECIPE: TRACES

Notes:

THE BAKED YAM

A yam is loaded with beta-carotene and vitamins C and B. Usually this root is doctored with sugar and such, but is delightful as a simple baked potato without the extra sweets. Here's how.

---

1 large yam
Molly McButter

---

1. Scrub the skin very well; remove any root hairs and cut off the ends.
2. Place it on a paper towel in the microwave; cook on high for 5 minutes.
3. Turn it over and cook it for about 3 minutes; check for doneness; when you squeeze it and it's soft inside the potato is done.
4. Put the potato in a plate and slice it open, lengthwise; sprinkle in Molly McButter for a salty, buttery taste or Fleischmann's fat free squeeze margarine for sweet butter taste.

YIELD: 1 potato
FAT GRAMS IN ENTIRE RECIPE: Less than 1

BTW: I like freshly ground pepper on mine...some people like cinnamon.

Notes:

SIMPLE CANDIED YAMS

What is Thanksgiving without candied sweet potatoes? In my family it wouldn't be the same holiday. Years ago we dropped the butter from this recipe and no one missed it. See what you think.

Cooking utensils: A 4 quart saucepan and a non-stick baking pan 9 x 13

---

6 yams or sweet potatoes, peeled and sliced in 1/2 inch rounds
Molly McButter
1/2 cup lite maple syrup
2 - 3 Tbs. brown sugar, crumbled
Ground cinnamon, optional

Preheat the oven to 350°

1. Boil the potato slices until just tender, about 15 minutes; drain.
2. Place slices in an oblong, non-stick baking pan; sprinkle with Molly McButter, followed by syrup and a sprinkling of the brown sugar and cinnamon; bake for 1/2 hour.

YIELD: About 12 cups
FAT GRAMS IN ENTIRE RECIPE: 3

Notes:

KAREN'S CANDIED YAMS WITH APPLES

If you love apple pie and you love sweet potatoes, this is to die for! Karen Stefanik, a very, very special lady, and our sister-in-law, prepared this for us and if I try really hard I can shut my eyes and conjure up the taste.

Baking utensil: A non-stick baking pan 9 x 13 or a 2 quart casserole dish, treated with spray-on oil

---

2 cans (29 oz. ea.) yams, drained and in chunks
1 Tbs. lemon juice
1 cup brown sugar (loosely packed)
1 can (21 oz.) apple pie filling
Cinnamon to taste

Preheat the oven to 350°

1. Place the potatoes on the bottom of the casserole, leaving 1 inch at the top for the other ingredients; sprinkle lemon juice on top.
2. Crumble the sugar over the potatoes; cover with the apple pie filling.
3. Sprinkle the cinnamon on top; bake for 40 minutes or until bubbling.
4. Serve hot.

YIELD: About 12 cups
FAT GRAMS IN ENTIRE RECIPE: 1

BTW: You will enjoy this as a leftover, too. The potato and apple flavors blend and reheat to make a delicious taste treat.

Notes:

SALAD GREENS

Where, oh, where would we be without salad?

And where would our salads be without the greens?

For years the American salad lover based salad on head lettuce or iceberg...you know, the round head that's crispy but lends no flavor or nutritional value to the salad. The greens were then doused in gobs of fatty dressing and then that soggy mess was downed as the preliminary course to the steak and potatoes. We're wiser now, right?

We know that romaine, escarole, arugula and radicchio, all those lovely fresh greens now available to us are blessed with some nutrients like vitamins A. The flavors vary and your choices are a result of what titillates your own taste buds. Romaine is available in all supermarkets, has a long leaf and a hearty flavor with lots of crunch. It's superb as a base lettuce for a salad and is used, alone, in Caesar Salad and often in Greek salad. Bibb lettuce is round and loose-leafed, has a much softer leaf and a delicate flavor. Arugula has a small, serrated leaf and a peppery taste. Escarole looks somewhat like short Romaine, with a thicker, wavy leaf and a bitter taste. Radicchio is red and white, very colorful in a mixed green salad because of the contrast and has a bitter flavor. Watercress has a small, dark green leaf on a stem and a spicy flavor. These lettuces can be purchased as a "mixed bag" in most supermarkets in plastic bags, cleaned and ready to use. They call it the European Mix in some stores. The cost is somewhat prohibitive for frequent use, but the mix makes an impressive statement as the beginning of an important dinner. Most of the individual greens are available for you to mix your own.

We're not going to get into spinach in this section. It's so important as a stand-alone vegetable that I am treating it just that way...that section follows this one. However, it is important to add this one note regarding spinach when we talk about salad greens. Spinach is delicious raw, especially the young, tender leaves. It can be the whole salad with some thinly sliced purple onion, or it can be added to a mixed green salad. Either way, it's a taste treat.

Please be sure to wash your greens with plenty of water to assure removing sand and soil. Instructions on cleaning can be found in GREENS earlier in this section. Use a salad spinner or paper towels to pat the leaves dry. Too much water left on the leaves can ruin a beautiful salad.

A pound of the greens mentioned above averages from 1/2 to 1 gram of fat.

Enjoy these greens to your heart's content. It's the stuff you put on them that usually adds the fat grams. And yet there are some very good dressings that can make you happy.

Some tricks to be aware of in your quest for a satisfying dressing include buying a "light" dressing and spilling off the fat, carefully, that's sitting at the top of the rest of the liquid. Measure it with a spoon as you dump it so you know how many grams you've deducted from the total count in the entire bottle. Another way to accomplish this is to suck the dressing up into a gravy syringe. The fat will rise to the top and you can use the dressing from the bottom, as you squirt it out. You might want to add some vinegar to the dressing to liven up the taste a bit. Use red or white wine vinegar or balsamic.

As mentioned earlier in this book, you will avoid most of the fat in dressing, in restaurants where you cannot order fat free, by ordering the dressing "on the side" and then dipping your fork tip into the dressing to accumulate just enough on the fork to flavor the mouthful. You will eventually prefer this method of eating salad because you can really taste the delicate lettuce characteristics when the salad is not drenched in dressing. An alternative to this method is ordering a wine or balsamic vinegar (balsamic is much milder) and the oil separately, adding a teaspoon of oil to dispel the sharp vinegar taste and thereby fixing your own dressing at the table.

There are a few dressings that we enjoy that are fat free and we'll give you a chance to try them yourself in the following pages.

ANTIPASTO

We like our antipasto on a base of Romaine lettuce. There are so many different variations of marinated vegetables to enjoy...let your imagination run wild. In fact, the antipasto can be an individual salad with lettuce as a base or platters of exciting appetizers to nibble on. The Marinated Artichoke Hearts should find their way to the platter along with some store-bought goodies. Here's one way to do this. You change the additions to suit your own tastes. We're doing this as a salad rather than a smorgasbord.

Romaine lettuce leaves, chilled to crisp
Marinated Artichoke Hearts
Marinated Mushrooms
Marinated Mixed Beans
Roasted or grilled peppers
Pickled Beets
Jarred pickled okra
Any assortment of fresh vegetables
Tuna salad or turkey or chicken salad, prepared with fat free mayonnaise
Potato Salad

---

1. Remove the leaves from the Romaine, clean and chill them for an hour or so; lay them out on the platter or platters so that they overlap slightly.
2. Place the pickled and marinated vegetables in mounds in an array of shades: beets near the okra, colorful peppers around the artichoke hearts and mushrooms with the carrot sticks, celery sticks, broccoli flowerets and cherry tomatoes or halved plum tomatoes as color accents. The turkey, tuna, chicken or potato salads, which are all very pale should be strategically placed so that their delicate hues enhance the brightness of the reds and greens of the vegetables.
3. Serve with breadsticks or crackers.

YIELD: That really depends on what you choose
FAT GRAMS IN ENTIRE RECIPE: Add the different foods you're
serving and estimate accordingly

BTW: The benefits of serving an antipasto like this are many-faceted among which the most important is the variety, insuring that everyone can find foods to enjoy.

TACO SALAD

If you enjoy Mexican food, you'll thank me for this salad. No need for a fried taco shell. Heat up some corn tortillas, instead. They're fat free. Or, you might like to crunch on some heated, baked tortilla chips along with the salad.

---

2 cups iceberg lettuce
2 celery ribs, sliced
1/2 medium green bell pepper, sliced
1/2 cup Bean Dip
1/2 cup Chili Con Queso or fat free grated cheddar
1/2 cup fresh tomato, chopped
1 scallion, green top only, chopped

---

1. Place lettuce, celery and bell peppers in a salad bowl.
2. Heat the Bean Dip to room temperature.
3. Place over the salad fixings.
4. Heat the Chili Con Queso so that it is melted enough to spoon over the beans.
5. Top with the tomato and the scallion.

YIELD: 1 salad, about 6 cups
FAT GRAMS IN ENTIRE RECIPE: 2

Notes:

ANYTIME SUPPER SALAD

Very often we opt for a dinner that is a huge salad. We change some of the extras at each sitting, but the basics are always the same. After looking at our basics you'll decide which will be your "every-time" salad starters and which will become your infrequent, but welcome, add-ons.

---

6 cups assorted greens, in mouth-sized pieces
3 celery ribs, diagonally sliced
1 green bell pepper, thinly sliced
1 large carrot, diagonally sliced
1/2 cucumber, thinly sliced
1 can (16 oz.) red kidney beans, drained and rinsed
4 radishes, thinly sliced
1/4 purple onion, thinly sliced
3 plum tomatoes, sliced in the round

---

1. Toss all ingredients, except the tomatoes.
2. Add the salad dressing and toss lightly to cover.
3. Place tomatoes on top (they might break apart if added before tossing).

YIELD: 2 salads, about 6 cups each
FAT GRAMS IN ENTIRE RECIPE: About 2

BTW: Now the fun begins...in addition to the salads and pickled vegetables you can fix yourself, take a look at the hearts of palm, the water-packed artichoke hearts, frozen veggies you can thaw by running under cold water, the canned water-packed tuna, the leftover cooked chicken or turkey breast, the shredded fat free cheeses...and on and on. Don't limit yourself, as long as you are aware of the fat grams you're ingesting. Change the add-ons often. You deserve a treat!

Notes:

YOUR OWN HONEY DIJON RANCH

There are many really tasty, satisfying salad dressings out there on your grocers' shelves...but sometimes you want a change. Most of the people to whom this dressing has been served are not aware it's fat free.

Preparation utensil: A small bowl

1/2 cup Hidden Valley Fat Free Ranch
1 tsp. honey
2 tsp. Dijon mustard to taste
1 Tbs. white wine vinegar

---

1. Combine all ingredients; stir till smooth.
2. Serve chilled.

YIELD: 2/3 cup
FAT GRAMS IN ENTIRE RECIPE: 0

Notes:

Russian Dressing

This is a dressing I dearly loved in my younger days and could not eat when I was relegated to the "lemon juice, only, for salad dressing" diets. It's a snap to prepare and stores well in a tight-lidded jar for about a week in the refrigerator.

Preparation utensil: A small bowl

1/2 cup fat free mayonnaise
2 Tbs. Heinz Chili Sauce
1/2 tsp. Dijon mustard
1 tsp. prepared horseradish (more to taste)
1/2 tsp. garlic powder
2 Tbs. red wine vinegar
Freshly ground pepper to taste

---

1. Combine the first 5 ingredients.
2. Add the vinegar slowly, stirring as you do, to keep the mixture smooth.
3. Adjust ingredients and pepper to taste. Keep refrigerated.

YIELD: About 2/3 to 3/4 of a cup
FAT GRAMS IN ENTIRE RECIPE: Traces

BTW: This dressing is mild enough, if you go easy on the horseradish, for kids if you want to toss the salad with the dressing, beforehand. Try this dressing on a salad with boiled or grilled shrimp. A natural winner.

Notes:

JIM'S HONEY VINAIGRETTE

Jim Mann, our dear friend from Arkansas, came up with this one. It's especially good on spinach salad; he loves it with cucumber and onions.

Preparation utensil: A small bowl

1 cup fat free Italian bottled salad dressing
1/4 cup honey
Pinch of ground nutmeg
Pinch of paprika
1 Tbs. Dijon mustard

1. Combine all of the ingredients.
2. Refrigerate.

YIELD: 1 1/4 cups
FAT GRAMS IN ENTIRE RECIPE: 0

Notes:

SPINACH

Spinach is one of my favorite vegetables. There are so many ways to use this green. It matters in some recipes, whether you use the fresh or the frozen, but so many times just having a few packages of the Birds Eye or Green Giant frozen version can make a dinner out of a side dish.

Do not be deceived by the quantity of fresh spinach called for in some recipes where wilting or cooking is called for. This stuff literally collapses. 2 to 3 pounds fresh, untrimmed spinach, which measures approximately 28 to 48 cups, loosely packed, cooks down to about 2 measly cups. The variance is a result of differences in water content and the variety of the particular spinach.

A pound of spinach, untrimmed, has about 1 gram of fat. The frozen spinach, chopped or leaf, delivers 1/2 gram in the 10 ounce package.

There is no need to remove the stems from baby spinach leaves because they are so tender. Larger leaves may demand stemming and sometimes, slicing or tearing. Cleaning spinach is time consuming, but if not diligently conducted, the sand and grit will ruin a lovely dinner. The easiest way to buy spinach is at the discount, warehouse-type, store in the 2 1/2 pound plastic bag. Even though the labeling states that the spinach has been cleaned, I have found soil stuck to the leaves, so give it a careful scrutiny and rinse the leaves before use. If you don't use the whole bag within a few days, steam or wilt the spinach before it goes bad. You can store it for a few more days in the refrigerator, cooked, and you can also freeze it for use within the next three months or so.

WILTED SPINACH

It is so easy to wilt fresh spinach that it occurs in less time than it takes for me to tell you how. The only thing that you want to be careful about is overcooking it. Then you end up with spinach similar to the canned stuff.

Cooking utensil: A 3 quart non-stick saucepan or a non-stick wok

---

1/2 cup defatted stock or water with 1 tsp. bouillon granules
2 pounds leaf spinach, cleaned and stemmed
Garlic powder
Crushed red pepper flakes, optional

---

1. Bring the stock or water with bouillon to a boil.
2. Add the spinach and sprinkle garlic powder and pepper (if desired) on the spinach; toss as the spinach wilts.
3. When the color has gone from medium green to dark green and the leaves have collapsed, the spinach is wilted.

YIELD: About 2 cups
FAT GRAMS IN ENTIRE RECIPE: 2

BTW: This procedure readies the spinach for immediate consumption or for use in a number of different recipes. If the spinach is not available or you're caught short-handed, use one of the frozen substitutes. Where a recipe calls for the frozen, of course, you can always use the fresh and wilt it without the seasonings. A spray of Olive Oil Pam or 1/2 tsp. of the real olive oil adds a fine touch to an already delicious side dish.

Notes:

SPINACH AND CAPPELLINI

Because the spinach is so delicate a flavor I prefer a thin spaghetti. You may use any pasta with this from vermacelli to linguine.

Cooking utensil: A non-stick wok

---

1 1/4 cups defatted chicken stock
8 ounces fresh spinach (about 6 to 7 cups), cleaned and trimmed
1 tsp. garlic powder
1 tsp. celery seed
1 tsp. dried oregano, crushed
Crushed hot red pepper flakes, optional
1 Tbs. cornstarch
1 Tbs. water
2 slices fat free Swiss cheese
4 cups cappellini or other very thin spaghetti, cooked without oil
Fat free grated Parmesan

---

1. Bring the stock to a boil.
2. Add the spinach, garlic, celery seed, oregano and pepper flakes (if desired); cook over high heat until the spinach wilts; reduce the heat to low.
3. Combine the cornstarch and the water to blend; add to the spinach, slowly, while stirring to avoid lumping.
4. Add the Swiss cheese and melt over low heat; by the time the cheese melts, the starch will thicken the sauce.
5. Add the spaghetti to the pot and toss to cover the pasta with sauce.
6. Heat through and serve.

YIELD: 5 cups
FAT GRAMS IN ENTIRE RECIPE: 5

Notes:

Spinach And Pasta With Cilantro

If you're excited by the seasonings of Burmese and Thai foods, this dish has a good chance of making you happy. Similar to the previous recipe in that it's a combination of spinach and pasta...there the resemblance ends.

Cooking utensil: A non-stick wok treated with spray-on oil

1/2 pound shrimp, peeled and deveined, minced
1 tsp. garlic powder
1 cup defatted chicken stock
1 pound fresh spinach, cleaned and trimmed
2 tsp. fresh garlic, minced
1 medium onion, in half and thinly sliced
3 Tbs. cilantro, chopped
4 cups thin spaghetti, cooked
1/2 tsp. sesame oil

---

1. Add the minced shrimp and garlic powder to the sprayed wok; cook over high heat until the shrimp is pink and is golden from the garlic powder; set aside.
2. Add the stock to the wok; bring to a boil.
3. Add the spinach, garlic and onion; cook over high heat until the spinach is wilted and the onion is translucent.
4. Add the cilantro and the shrimp; cook, tossing for 30 seconds.
5. Add the spaghetti and sesame oil; toss.
6. Heat through and serve.

YIELD: 8 cups
FAT GRAMS IN ENTIRE RECIPE: 9

BTW: This dish takes about 30 minutes to prepare. Serve with some hot pita bread and if you like your food spicy, have some Sambal (crushed red chili sauce, available in Oriental markets) handy to heat things up. Just a little dab'll do ya!

Notes:

Spinach Salad

Wash your spinach leaves with care. Try to find young leaves, loose, in your grocer's produce aisle. You'll probably have more success this way, finding young, tender leaves. Use this recipe as an idea for a base salad and go on from here with your own additions and embellishments.

Preparation utensil: A large bowl

---

1 pound fresh spinach leaves, trimmed
1/2 pound fresh mushrooms, sliced
1/4 purple or Vidalia onion, very thinly sliced
1/2 cup balsamic vinegar
1 tsp. canola oil
1/2 tsp. sugar
1 tsp. apricot or orange marmalade
1/4 tsp. salt
Freshly ground pepper to taste

---

1. Use the leaves whole unless they're larger than 2 1/2 inches long; place them in a large bowl.
2. Add the mushrooms and onion; set aside.
3. Combine the vinegar and canola oil; add the other ingredients.
4. Pour dressing on top of the spinach salad and toss.

YIELD: 2 salads, about 7 to 8 cups each
FAT GRAMS IN ENTIRE RECIPE: 6

BTW: Try adding some white beans such as cannellini or white northern. Thinly sliced water-packed, or fat free marinated, artichoke hearts work as a delicate addition. An imitation bacon bit will introduce a smoky flavor, as will a piece of smoked turkey, chunked. Grilled breast of chicken is a hearty add-on, too.

Notes:

_____

_____

WILTED SPINACH SALAD

In this recipe you're not going to cook the spinach...wilt, is the key operative. It's an interesting warm (room temperature) salad that I love. See what you think.

Cooking utensil: A small non-stick skillet

Preparation utensil: A large bowl and a colander

---

1 pound cremini or button mushrooms
1 large onion, thinly sliced
1 clove garlic, minced
1/4 cup defatted stock or dry red wine
1 Tbs. fresh parsley, chopped
1/2 tsp. sugar
1 tsp. fresh lemon juice
1/2 tsp. sesame oil
1/4 cup balsamic vinegar
2 pounds fresh spinach, trimmed
Boiling water (about 2 quarts)
Freshly ground pepper

---

1. Sauté the mushrooms, onion and garlic in the stock or wine; add the parsley; cook until the onion and mushrooms are tender; set aside.
2. Combine the sugar, lemon juice, oil and vinegar; set aside.
3. Place the spinach in your colander in the sink; pour the boiling water over the spinach until it collapses; shake to remove excess water.
4. Place the wilted spinach in a bowl; add the onion mixture and the oil and vinegar mixture.
5. Toss gently and serve.

YIELD: 2 salads, about 3 cups each
FAT GRAMS IN ENTIRE RECIPE: 5

BTW: If you're looking for a truly elegant salad, here it is.

Notes:

KIMMIE'S SPINACH LASAGNA

You've got to love spinach lasagna. Everyone loves spinach lasagna. This one is a contribution from the younger daughter, Kim, who really knows her way around the kitchen. She uses a limited number of ingredients in this recipe, all of which should be in stock in your pantry and fridge. We keep fat free ricotta in the refrigerator all the time. It lasts a month or so and during that time I will make a lasagna. Lasagna is a great do-ahead meal for guests. Frozen and thawed, you're serving in 45 minutes. A salad or cup of minestrone, while the microwave or oven is heating up the lasagna, and you're good to go.

Baking utensil: A non-stick lasagna pan or 9 x 13 pan treated with spray-on oil

---

5 cups fat free marinara sauce (The Marinara Sauce)
16 to 18 lasagna noodles, cooked and drained
8 ounces fat free ricotta or cottage cheese
1 package (10 oz.) frozen spinach, cooked and squeezed dry
Fat free mozzarella, shredded

Preheat the oven to 350°

1. Spoon about 1/4 of the marinara sauce in the bottom of the pan.
2. Place a single layer of noodles on top of the marinara.
3. Combine the ricotta or cottage cheese and the spinach; layer 1/2 the spinach mixture on top of the noodles.
4. Repeat with a layer of sauce and a layer of noodles, followed by the spinach mixture.
5. Top with marinara, noodles and at last marinara on top.
6. Cover and bake for about 30 to 35 minutes or until bubbling.
7. Sprinkle mozzarella on top; bake for an additional 7 to 10 minutes or until mozzarella is melted.
8. Give the lasagna about 10 minutes out of the oven before you cut it into pieces.

YIELD: A 9 x 12 lasagna, about 6 large pieces
FAT GRAMS IN ENTIRE RECIPE: 7

BTW: The reason I prefer preparing a lasagna a day or so ahead of time is that the lasagna sets up when cold. It can be sliced, easily, when cold, and heated in slices for faster, more controlled warming through. In addition, when the lasagna is hot, it tends to slide when cut.

SIMPLE SPINACH LASAGNA WITH LENTILS

When I tried this lasagna I was surprised by the ease with which it is prepared. The noodles are *uncooked* when you layer them in the pan. They cook while baking with the other ingredients. This is a trick I learned from Lou Cimaglia who, with a solid Italian ancestry, really ought to know. Layering the noodles (which do have a tendency to stick together) is no more difficult than dealing cards! You'll love it!

Baking utensil: A non-stick lasagna pan or 9 x 13 pan treated with spray-on oil

---

2 containers (15 oz. ea.) fat free ricotta
1/2 cup Egg Beaters
2 packages (10 oz. ea.) frozen spinach, chopped, thawed and squeezed dry
8 ounces mozzarella, shredded and divided
1 Tbs. dried Italian seasoning
1/4 tsp. dried thyme leaves, crushed
5 cups fat free marinara sauce (The Marinara Sauce)
1 pound lasagna noodles, uncooked
3 Tbs. lentils, uncooked, picked and dry
A 9 x 12 non-stick baking pan

Preheat the oven to 350°

1. Combine the ricotta, Egg Beaters, spinach, 4 Tbs. of the mozzarella, Italian seasoning and thyme; set aside.
2. Cover the bottom of the pan with 1 cup of the marinara sauce; follow with a single layer of noodles (remember, they're uncooked).
3. Follow with 1/3 of the ricotta mixture; sprinkle 1 Tbs. of the raw lentils evenly over the mixture; cover with another layer of marinara, followed by the noodles, and repeat, ending with the noodles.
4. Spoon the last cup of marinara on top of the noodles.
5. Bake, covered, for 1 hour; sprinkle on the remaining mozzarella and bake uncovered for 10 minutes or until the mozzarella is melted.
6. Allow the lasagna to stand for about 10 minutes before slicing or cool and refrigerate. Reheat and serve the second day.

YIELD: A very deep 9 x 12 lasagna, about 8 pieces
FAT GRAMS IN ENTIRE RECIPE: 7

Janice Marshall's Spinach Balls

There are times when you're planning for guests and you want something other than dips and chips (baked or not!). You know that you want your appetizers and hors d'oeuvres to be as healthy as the meal that follows will be...and I've got just the finger food for you. We can thank Janice Marshall, San Antonio, for this one.

Baking utensil: A baking sheet, treated with spray-on oil and a small non-stick saucepan

---

2 packages (10 oz. ea.) frozen chopped spinach, cooked and well-drained
2 1/2 cups Pepperidge Farm Herb Stuffing Mix
1/2 cup onion, finely chopped
1 cup Egg Beaters
2 Tbs. prepared Butter Buds
1/2 cup fat free grated Parmesan
1/2 tsp. pepper
1/2 tsp. salt
1/4 tsp. dried thyme leaves, crushed
1/2 tsp. garlic powder
6 slices fat free Swiss
4 Tbs. white wine

Preheat the oven to 375°

1. Combine all ingredients except the Swiss cheese and wine.
2. Shape into balls, about 1 1/2 inches to 2 inches in diameter; place on the baking sheet.
3. Bake for 10 to 12 minutes.
4. In the meantime, heat the wine in a small skillet; add the cheese slices and melt the cheese, slowly.
5. When you remove the spinach balls from the oven, place them on a platter; dribble some of the cheese mixture on each ball. The cheese mixture will firm up and look like a glaze.

YIELD: 30 to 32 balls
FAT GRAMS IN ENTIRE RECIPE: 3

TOMATOES

Is there any fruit (that's really what the tomato is!) or vegetable that we use in our recipes more than tomatoes? Only onions and garlic! And the three together are heaven! Add some herbs and put the mixture on anything from rice to pasta to potatoes to mixed vegetables. So many of the recipes in this book feature tomatoes, even if the tomato was not the "star" of the dish, you'll have no problem seeing how to use them to their best advantage.

There are a few varieties of tomatoes we call for most often in our recipes: the Roma or plum tomato, a dense, hearty tomato, that we've even grown on our apartment balcony! This tomato is especially good in any sauce recipes. The salad tomato which is the common variety you see in the supermarkets year-round. In summer they're lush and delicious and in winter they're hothouse grown and run to tasteless. And then there are the cherry tomatoes that do so well in salads and antipasto.

In canned tomatoes, the stores have started carrying pre-diced, canned tomatoes that cut down on time for those hurried at kitchen-time. They're a great time-saver and the quality of the tomato seems on a standard with the canned whole tomatoes. Plum or Roma tomatoes are available in cans, too, which work so well in Italian dishes. The sauces are available in varying sized cans from the 8 ounce on up. When a recipe calls for tomato sauce and all you have is paste, mix the paste with twice the amount of water (1 can of paste, mixed with 2 cans of water) and use, measure for measure, instead of the sauce. Purée can be used, as well, by adding half again as much water as the amount of purée...then go on with the recipe.

2 large tomatoes or 8 to 9 plum tomatoes equal approximately 1 pound. That pound will chop to about 2 cups of tomato, 1 1/2 without skin or seeds.

A pound of raw, untrimmed tomatoes has less than 1 gram of fat, about the same for 1 cup of canned tomato.

To peel fresh tomatoes, place them in boiling water for about 1 minute. Remove with a slotted spoon. If not yet ready to peel, give them another 15 seconds or so. Plunge them into cold water. Remove the stem and the rest of the skin should then slide off with the help of a sharp paring knife.

Tomato Salad

It certainly does not take a heck of an imagination to put tomatoes in salad! Or sandwiches! Or just about anywhere. But this is just tomatoes with seasonings and a little onion.

Preparation utensil: A large bowl

---

3 large tomatoes, thickly sliced
1 large red onion, thinly sliced
1/2 cup balsamic vinegar
1 tsp. olive oil
2 Tbs. honey
1 Tbs. Dijon mustard
1 tsp. garlic powder
1 tsp. mixed Italian seasoning
1 tsp. dried basil, crushed

---

1. Place the tomatoes on a platter; layer the onion slices on top.
2. Place all remaining ingredients in a tight-lidded jar; shake well.
3. Pour the dressing over the tomatoes and onions and serve.

YIELD: 3 cups
FAT GRAMS IN ENTIRE RECIPE: 6

BTW: This dressing does well with other vegetables and tossed salad.

Notes:

Salsa

In the last few years, salsa, the marvelous tomato concoction from Mexico, has out-paced ketchup in sales in the United States! It must be because of all the baked potatoes that salsa is now being used to top! Or maybe it's because the stuff is so satisfying.

Preparation utensil: A bowl and a large, tight-lidded jar

---

1 can (28 oz.) whole tomatoes with juice, chopped
1 can (8 oz.) tomato sauce
1 can (4 oz.) diced green chilies
1/2 cup onion, diced
1/2 cup celery, diced
1 Tbs. sugar
1 tsp. salt
1 Tbs. fresh cilantro, chopped or to taste
Pickled jalapeño peppers to taste, chopped
White vinegar to taste

---

1. Combine all ingredients in a large bowl.
2. Remove to a tight-lidded jar and refrigerate for at least 2 hours for the flavors to meld.
3. Serve cold with baked corn chips, with Mexican food, with just about any food that enjoys a robust tomato boost, like Egg Beaters omelets. The list of foods that salsa can enhance is limited only by your imagination.

YIELD: 6 cups
FAT GRAMS IN ENTIRE RECIPE: 3

BTW: Salsa is like so many basic foods, a reflection of your own tastes. Season this one to your own taste buds. If you're going to buy it ready-made, there are so many brands that are as good as home-made. Try Old El Paso, Pace or Chi Chi's.

Notes:

CHICKEN CACCIATORE

When my kids were little they called this dish, "Kitchen Cacciatore." Whatever you call it, it's delicious!

Baking utensil: An 11 x 7 baking dish or 11 inch round, treated with spray-on oil

---

4 chicken breast halves (4 oz. ea.), skinless and boneless
1 can (14 1/2 oz.) diced tomatoes with juice
8 ounces Cremini or button mushrooms, sliced
1 medium onion, chopped
1 medium carrot, shredded
1/3 cup Burgundy or other dry red wine
1 tsp. dried whole rosemary
1/4 tsp. oregano leaves, crushed
1/4 tsp. dried basil leaves, crushed
1/8 tsp. crushed red pepper flakes, optional
2 cloves garlic, minced
Salt and freshly ground pepper to taste

Preheat the oven to 350°

1. Place the chicken in the baking pan; set aside.
2. Combine all remaining ingredients in a medium-sized bowl and mix thoroughly.
3. Pour the tomato mixture over the chicken in the baking pan; bake for about 50 minutes; test the chicken for tenderness.
4. When the chicken is cut and the juices run clear, it's ready. Season with salt and pepper; serve immediately.

YIELD: About 6 cups
FAT GRAMS IN ENTIRE RECIPE: 7

Notes:

SHRIMP CREOLE

There must be hundreds of recipes for this dish. Some are very complicated, some are really simple. This one is medium-tough on the scale, because of the measuring time necessary with a number of ingredients. The one following, Shrimp Creole The Easy Way, is a different mix. It tastes good, too, so you'll have to decide which of the two you are more inclined to cook and which one tastes better to you.

Cooking utensil: A large non-stick skillet or wok

1/4 cup white wine or defatted stock
1/2 cup onion, chopped
1/2 cup green bell pepper, chopped
1/2 cup celery, diced
1 clove garlic, minced
1 can (16 oz.) whole tomatoes, crushed with a spoon, with juice
1 can (8 oz.) tomato sauce
1 Tbs. Worcestershire sauce
1 tsp. sugar
1/2 tsp. chili powder
Hot pepper sauce to taste
1 Tbs. cornstarch
1 Tbs. water
1 pound shrimp, peeled and deveined
Salt and freshly ground pepper
White or brown rice, cooked without oil or butter

---

1. Sauté the onion, bell pepper, celery and garlic in the wine or stock until tender.
2. Add all remaining ingredients, *except* the cornstarch, water, shrimp and rice; simmer, covered, for 8 minutes, stirring occasionally.
3. In the meantime, dissolve the cornstarch in the water; when the tomato mixture has cooked for 8 minutes, gradually add the dissolved cornstarch, while stirring to avoid lumping, until thickened.
4. Add the shrimp; cook over medium-low heat until the shrimp pinks and curls.
5. Season to taste; serve on steamed rice.

YIELD: About 5 cups
FAT GRAMS IN ENTIRE RECIPE: 8

Shrimp Creole, The Easy Way

The benefit of having this recipe, as an alternative to the previous Shrimp Creole, is the simplicity of the ingredients. You probably always have these products at your fingertips and with fewer ingredients to measure, you save time. Both ways the dish is delicious.

Cooking utensil: A large non-stick skillet or wok

1/4 cup white wine or defatted stock
1 medium onion, chopped
1 small green bell pepper, chopped
1 clove garlic, minced
1 can (6 oz.) tomato paste
1 can (16 oz.) whole tomatoes with juice or 1 can (14 1/2 oz.) diced
   tomatoes
1 pound medium shrimp, cleaned and deveined
Salt and freshly ground pepper to taste

---

1. Sauté the onion, bell pepper and garlic in the wine or stock until tender.
2. Mix the juice of the tomatoes with the paste (add 1/2 paste-can of water, if using the diced tomatoes); add tomatoes, juice and water to the sautéed vegetables; simmer 5 to 7 minutes.
3. Add the shrimp; cook until the shrimp are pink and cooked through.
4. Season to taste; serve immediately on white or brown cooked rice.

YIELD: About 5 cups
FAT GRAMS IN ENTIRE RECIPE: 8

BTW: This recipe will work if you have pre-cooked shrimp handy. Cook just long enough to heat the shrimp through.

Notes:

Italian Seafood Chowder

This is one of the those dishes that everyone asks for again, after they've been served it at home or at workshops. Prepare it one time and you'll be amazed at the simplicity which delivers such good eating. You combine canned products with raw seafood and you're a hero.

Cooking utensil: An 8 quart non-stick pot

1/4 cup dry white wine or defatted stock
1 large onion, chopped
1/2 green bell pepper, chopped
2 cloves garlic, minced
1 can (10 oz.) tomato soup, undiluted
1 can (14 1/2 oz.) stewed tomatoes
1 can (19 oz.) Progresso Manhattan Clam Chowder
1 Tbs. dried oregano leaves, crushed
1 tsp. chicken bouillon granules
1 pound frozen cod fillets, cut in big cubes
1 bay leaf
1 pound shrimp, cleaned and deveined
1 can (6 1/2 oz.) baby clams or chopped clams
1/4 cup white wine, additional and optional
Louisiana hot sauce

---

1. Sauté the onion, bell pepper and garlic in the 1/4 cup wine or stock.
2. Add all remaining ingredients except the clams, shrimp, additional wine and hot sauce; simmer 10 minutes, covered.
3. Add the clams, shrimp and wine; simmer 15 minutes more or until the shrimp are pink and curling.
4. Season to taste and serve.

YIELD: 8 cups
FAT GRAMS IN ENTIRE RECIPE: 18

BTW: Any additional seafood such as scallops or more clams will only enhance this particular recipe. Serving this chowder over a couple of scoops of cooked rice, brown or white, has changed the chowder to a fish stew...hearty and delicious. You can substitute another firm fish, like grouper, for the cod.

SEAFOOD VERACRUZ

The next day this seafood tastes just as good as it did the first. It takes about 45 minutes from get-go to table, during which time you can prepare the rice or pasta, if you don't have enough already frozen to defrost and serve.

Cooking utensil: A large non-stick skillet or wok

1/4 cup dry white wine or defatted chicken stock
2 cloves garlic, minced
1 can (4 1/2 oz.) diced chilies
1 pound firm, white fish (cod or haddock), cut in 1 inch cubes
3/4 pound scallops, bite size
1/2 pound medium shrimp, peeled and deveined
Salt and freshly ground pepper to taste
Pasta or rice, prepared without oil or butter

---

1. Soften the onions in the wine or stock.
2. Stir in the tomatoes, chilies and capers; bring to a boil; reduce heat to low; cook, uncovered, 15 minutes, stirring occasionally.
3. Stir in the fish, scallops and shrimp; increase heat to medium; cover and cook 10 to 12 minutes or until the fish is cooked through (will flake when prodded by a fork).
4. Season to taste; serve on rice or pasta of your choice.

YIELD: 8 cups, not including rice or pasta
FAT GRAMS IN ENTIRE RECIPE: 9, not including rice or pasta

BTW: Served with a French baguette or a hunk of sourdough bread, your guests will think you worked for hours on this dinner.

Notes:

_____

_____

_____

WINTER SQUASH

Winter squashes include acorn, butternut, hubbard and spaghetti, among others. They're firm, have a solid meat and bake well, similar to potatoes. They're used mashed and grated. Spaghetti squash, another winter squash, is totally different from any of the others because after boiling or baking, removing the seeds and stringy portion of the heart, the squash meat is "combed" with a fork, forming long spaghetti-like fibers that can be used as a veritable vegetable spaghetti.

A 2 1/2 pound winter squash will trim down to approximately 1 1/2 pounds of meat. The sizes of the different squashes vary considerably and there is no way to give you an one rule for all. 1 pound of winter squash provides about 1 gram of fat.

BAKED SQUASH

The squash can be sliced in half, either across or lengthwise.

Slice a piece of squash off the bottom of each half so it will sit securely.

Baking utensil: A baking pan with 1/4 inch water

---

1 squash
2 Tbs. Fleischmann's Fat Free Low Calorie squeeze margarine
1 Tbs. sugar (white or brown)
1 tsp. cinnamon

Preheat the oven to 400°

1. Place the halves of squash in the oven pan; set aside.
2. Combine the margarine, sugar and cinnamon; spread on the open side.
3. Bake for about 30 minutes; prick with a fork in the thickest part and when it's tender, it's done.

YIELD: 1 squash, hubbard, acorn or butternut
FAT GRAMS IN ENTIRE RECIPE: About 1

Preparing Spaghetti Squash

The squash can be baked or boiled, whole, or microwaved after slicing in half (lengthwise).

Cooking utensil: An 8 quart pot

---

1 spaghetti squash
Boiling water to cover

---

1. Place squash in the pot of boiling water; cook for about 20 to 30 minutes or until a fork goes into the flesh easily.
2. Remove from water and slice lengthwise; remove the seeds and stringy center.
3. When cool enough to handle, use your fork to "comb" the squash flesh; the strands of squash will have the appearance of spaghetti.
4. It is now ready to dress up with any of the pasta sauces or Butter Buds or Molly McButter. Grated fat free Parmesan is a very tasty add-on. Shredded fat free cheddar is another great topping for this squash.

YIELD: About 3 cups, depending on the size of the squash
FAT GRAMS IN ENTIRE RECIPE: 1

BTW: Baking the spaghetti squash takes about 1 1/2 hours. Be sure to prick the squash first with a long-pronged fork. When microwaving, slice in half, lengthwise and cover with plastic wrap. Start with about 10 minutes. The size and the power of your oven will determine the time. It should not take much longer than 15 minutes.

Notes:

_____

_____

_____

_____

ACORN SQUASH STUFFED MUSHROOMS

If you're looking for an impressive presentation for dinner, one that is hearty, attractive and different, this should fill the bill.

Cooking utensils: A baking sheet and a non-stick wok

---

3 acorn squash, halved lengthwise and seeded
1/4 cup defatted chicken stock
1 large onion, thinly sliced
2 cloves garlic, minced
1 red bell pepper, thinly sliced
1 stalk celery, finely diced
4 cups shiitake mushrooms, soaked, trimmed and thinly sliced
1/2 tsp. sesame oil
1 Tbs. ginger root, minced
3 Tbs. soy sauce
1 Tbs. rice vinegar
1 Tbs. cornstarch

Preheat the oven to 400°

1. Place the squash, cut side up, on the baking sheet; bake for 15 to 20 minutes or until tender when pierced with a fork.
2. In the meantime, heat the stock in the wok; add the onion and sauté for 3 minutes.
3. Add the garlic, bell pepper and celery; cook over high heat for 2 minutes.
4. Add the mushrooms and the sesame oil; cook for about 3 to 5 minutes, until just wilted; reduce heat to low and simmer.
5. In a separate bowl, combine the ginger root, soy sauce, vinegar and cornstarch; add this mixture to the wok; cook, stirring, until the sauce thickens.
6. Remove the squash from the oven and stuff with the mushroom mixture; serve.

YIELD: 6 squash halves, stuffed with about 4 cups of mushroom stir-fry
FAT GRAMS IN ENTIRE RECIPE: 5

BTW: The red bell pepper is sweeter than the green, but the green can be used as a substitute. If you have other mushrooms you'd like to mix with the shiitake, it will work, as well.

Zucchini And Other Summer Squash

The summer squashes include zucchini, chayote (pronounced shy-OH-tay) and yellow, crookneck squash. They have a very high water content. Keep this in mind when cooking with any of the three different squashes. They are exceedingly adaptable to almost any vegetable dish, combining well with other vegetables. This you've already recognized, since we've included so many recipes utilizing zucchini in earlier chapters of the book. It's so good in stews, ratatouilles and sliced in almost anything.

Summer squash will provide about 3 to 3 1/2 cups, sliced, to a pound. Grate the pound of squash and you get 4 cups. There is about 1 gram of fat in an untrimmed pound of squash.

Summer squash does not freeze well...it turns mushy. Consider this when preparing zucchini lasagna or a ratatouille. Eat the leftovers from the refrigerator within a week. Where zucchini is called for in a recipe, a combination of the yellow squash with the zucchini works and adds a bit of color. The chayote has a different texture and flavor, though, and is usually prepared in dishes with other vegetables and does very well with Parmesan cheese.

Always scrub the squash with a vegetable brush before using. The chayote must be peeled after boiling, whereas the zucchini and yellow squash are used with the skins on. When cooking, try to monitor the extent to which the squash has softened because they will overcook easily.

SQUASH STEW

Stews are like the weather...they change with the season. This is a great summer stew, loaded with the veggies that are plentiful at that time of year.

Cooking utensil: An 8 quart non-stick pot

---

1 pound fresh green beans, cut in 2 inch pieces
1 large potato, peeled and diced
1 large onion
1/4 cup white wine or defatted stock
4 cloves garlic, diced
1 fresh jalapeño pepper, minced
1 pound zucchini, cut in 1/2 inch pieces
1 pound yellow squash, cut in 1/2 inch pieces
1 can (14.5 oz.) diced tomatoes
Salt and pepper to taste
2 cups corn kernels, fresh off the cob or frozen

---

1. Blanch the green beans in boiling water until very crisp-tender; remove and rinse in cold water, immediately, to stop the cooking; drain and set aside.
2. Sauté the potato and onion in the wine or stock until the onion is soft.
3. Add the garlic; cook 1 minute; stir in the jalapeño pepper and the squash.
4. Add tomatoes; season with the salt and pepper; bring to a boil; reduce heat, cover, simmer for 10 to 15 minutes, until the squash is just tender.
5. Uncover, add the green beans and the corn; cook for about 5 minutes or until heated through.

YIELD: 10 cups
FAT GRAMS IN ENTIRE RECIPE: 6

BTW: Add leftover, sliced chicken or turkey breast, or other root vegetables like carrots and parsnips. The root vegetables should be added before the squash to give them plenty of time to cook thoroughly.

Notes:

ZUCCHINI, SPINACH AND RICE SOUP

The texture of this soup is soooo fine and the flavor so delicate, that it's definitely worth the extra time to shred the zucchini. We used the Salad Shooter and the effect was perfect. This can be done with the shredder on your mandolin or box grater. The ribbon cut spinach is achieved by cutting the spinach in narrow strips across the leaf. Make sure your knife is sharp or it will tear. This may be called a "chiffonade" cut in some recipes.

Cooking utensil: An 8 quart non-stick pot and a non-stick wok

---

6 cups defatted chicken stock
1/2 cup long-grain brown rice
1/2 cup onion, sliced
1/2 cup defatted chicken stock, additional
1 pound zucchini, shredded
1/2 pound spinach leaves, ribbon-cut
Salt and pepper to taste

---

1. Bring the stock to a boil; mix in the rice; simmer, covered,
2. In the meantime, sauté the onion in the additional stock in the wok until soft.
3. Add the zucchini; cook about 4 or 5 minutes, stirring frequently until tender; the zucchini will make its own juices so you needn't add any liquid.
4. Add the spinach; stir through the zucchini mixture until barely wilted.
5. As soon as the rice is done (test for tenderness), add the vegetable mixture to the rice pot; heat through.
6. Season to taste and serve.

YIELD: About 8 cups
FAT GRAMS IN ENTIRE RECIPE: 2

Btw: If you still have some folks who require flesh foods to complete a meal you can hearty this soup up. Add 4 skinned chicken breast halves, bone-in, to the 6 cups stock (before adding the rice) and cook for about 20 minutes. Remove the bones. At this point you may either return the chicken meat to the stock, add the rice, and the soup will cook the chicken until it shreds and gives a heaviness of the chicken to the soup...or you may cube the chicken breast meat, set it aside, prepare the rest of the soup according to directions and then add the chicken before serving, cooking just long enough to heat through.

ZUCCHINI CHEESE BAKE

Zucchini cooks quickly and is a natural with cheese. This dish can be a last minutes summer dinner. For color substitute one crookneck for one zucchini.

Cooking utensils: A 2 quart non-stick saucepan and a small casserole dish treated with spray-on oil

---

1/4 cup white wine or defatted stock
2 medium zucchini, sliced
1 onion, thinly sliced
1/2 pound fat free ricotta
1/2 tsp. dried basil, crushed
1 can (15 oz.) stewed tomatoes, partially drained
4 Tbs. fat free grated Parmesan

Preheat oven to 350°

1. Sauté the zucchini with the onion in the wine or stock until just crisp-tender; set aside.
2. Purée the ricotta with the basil in the blender or food processor.
3. Place single layer of squash mixture (1/2) on bottom of casserole; spoon all of the cheese mixture on top, followed by the tomatoes and then the remaining squash.
4. Top with the Parmesan; bake for about 20 to 25 minutes or until bubbly; serve immediately.

YIELD: 4 to 5 cups
FAT GRAMS IN ENTIRE RECIPE: 2

Notes:

_____

_____

_____

_____

No-Fry Squash Stix

This is a great nosh or appetizer. Make the Creole Seasoning ahead of time and keep it in a tight-lidded jar, stored in a cool dark place, for use whenever this type of seasoning is called for.

Baking utensil: A baking sheet treated with spray-on oil

CREOLE SEASONING
2 1/2 tsp. paprika
2 Tbs. garlic powder
2 Tbs. freshly ground black pepper
1 Tbs. cayenne pepper
1 Tbs. dried thyme
1 Tbs. dried oregano
1 Tbs. dried onion flakes

SQUASH STIX
3 zucchini, sliced 1/4 inch wide, by 3 inches long
1/4 cup Egg Beaters
1 tsp. Creole Seasoning
1/4 cup fat free bread crumbs
1 Tbs. fat free grated Parmesan
3 zucchini, sliced 1/4 inch wide and 3 inches long

Preheat the oven to 450°

1. Mix the Creole seasoning with the Egg Beaters in a small bowl; in a separate dish, mix the bread crumbs with the grated Parmesan.
2. Dip the squash pieces in the egg mixture and then into the crumb mixture; place in single layer on the baking sheet.
3. Bake for about 10 minutes or until golden-brown and crisp.
4. Serve immediately to keep the zucchini's natural moisture from making the stix soggy.

YIELD: About 20 to 24 stix
FAT GRAMS IN ENTIRE RECIPE: 1

BTW: If you'd like a dip to accompany these stix, serve with fat free ranch dressing or combine 1/2 cup mayonnaise with 1 tsp. horseradish (to taste) and a dash of sour cream (also, to taste), some salt and pepper to taste.

SQUASH WITH PASTA

Pasta goes well with almost any vegetable. Here, with the squash, you can add other favorites like green beans or even cannellini.

This is one of those throw-together-in-the-wok dishes.

Cooking utensil: A non-stick wok

1/4 cup dry white wine or defatted stock
1 onion, thinly sliced
1 clove garlic, minced
1 medium zucchini, thinly sliced
1 medium yellow squash, thinly sliced
1 Tbs. mixed Italian seasoning
2 or 3 fresh plum tomatoes, chopped
Freshly ground pepper to taste
1/2 pound pasta, cooked without oil
1/2 tsp. olive oil
Fat free grated Parmesan

---

1. Sauté the onion and the garlic in the wine or stock until tender.
2. Add the squash, tomato and seasonings; stir-fry over high heat, until just tender.
3. Add the pasta with the olive oil and toss until heated through.
4. Serve with the Parmesan.

YIELD: 8 cups
FAT GRAMS IN ENTIRE RECIPE: 8

Notes:

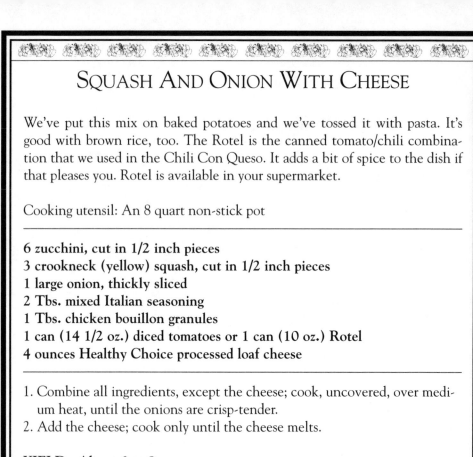

SQUASH AND ONION WITH CHEESE

We've put this mix on baked potatoes and we've tossed it with pasta. It's good with brown rice, too. The Rotel is the canned tomato/chili combination that we used in the Chili Con Queso. It adds a bit of spice to the dish if that pleases you. Rotel is available in your supermarket.

Cooking utensil: An 8 quart non-stick pot

---

6 zucchini, cut in 1/2 inch pieces
3 crookneck (yellow) squash, cut in 1/2 inch pieces
1 large onion, thickly sliced
2 Tbs. mixed Italian seasoning
1 Tbs. chicken bouillon granules
1 can (14 1/2 oz.) diced tomatoes or 1 can (10 oz.) Rotel
4 ounces Healthy Choice processed loaf cheese

---

1. Combine all ingredients, except the cheese; cook, uncovered, over medium heat, until the onions are crisp-tender.
2. Add the cheese; cook only until the cheese melts.

YIELD: About 6 to 8 cups
FAT GRAMS IN ENTIRE RECIPE: 2

Notes:

ZUCCHINI AND TOMATO BAKE

Zucchini and tomatoes are as natural a combination as carrots and peas. Here they are baked and are a tasty addition to a vegetable platter or alongside some grilled seafood or poultry.

Baking utensil: A shallow baking dish, 9 x 9, treated with spray-on oil

---

6 small zucchini, sliced 1/4 inch thick
1/2 onion, thinly sliced
1 green bell pepper, thinly sliced
2 tomatoes, peeled and thinly sliced
2 Tbs. fresh parsley, chopped
3 Tbs. fat free grated Parmesan

Preheat the oven to 350°

1. Since you're going to layer these vegetables in the baking dish, steam the zucchini, onion and pepper, without mixing the different vegetables; set each aside, separately.
2. Place the zucchini in the baking dish; then layer in the onion, then the bell pepper; top it all with the tomatoes, parsley and then sprinkle with the Parmesan.
3. Cover and bake for 15 minutes or until bubbly and heated through.

YIELD: 3 to 4 cups
FAT GRAMS IN ENTIRE RECIPE: 4

BTW: If you're a baked potato lover, this makes a grand topper.

Notes:

_____

_____

_____

_____

Zucchini Lasagna

There is a wide variety of zucchini lasagnas out there. We think this one is phenomenal. Use a large spatula when serving because this one slides.

Cooking utensils: A 3 quart non-stick saucepan and a non-stick baking pan, 9 x 12, treated with spray-on oil

---

1/2 cup dry white wine or defatted stock
1 1/2 cups onion, chopped
1 cup green bell pepper, chopped
3 cloves garlic, minced
2 1/2 cups zucchini, in 1/2 inch pieces
1 can (14 1/2 oz.) diced tomatoes
1/2 pound button or cremini mushrooms, thickly sliced
3/4 cup carrots, sliced
1 can (15 oz.) tomato sauce
1 can (6 oz.) tomato paste
2 Tbs. red wine vinegar
1 Tbs. dried Italian seasoning
3 Tbs. fresh parsley, chopped
2 tsp. chicken bouillon granules
1/4 tsp. fennel seeds
2 cups fat free ricotta
1 1/4 cup fat free mozzarella, shredded and divided
6 lasagna noodles, uncooked
2 Tbs. fat free grated Parmesan

Preheat the oven to 350°

1. Sauté the onion, pepper and garlic in the wine or stock, over medium-high heat, until tender.
2. Add the zucchini, diced tomato, mushrooms, carrot, tomato sauce, tomato paste, vinegar, Italian seasoning, bouillon, parsley and fennel; stir; bring to a boil, cover, reduce heat and simmer for about 20 minutes, stirring occasionally.
3. Remove from heat and set aside.
4. Combine ricotta and 3/4 cup mozzarella; set aside.
5. Spoon 2 cups of the vegetable mixture into the bottom of the baking pan;

arrange 3 uncooked lasagna noodles on top of the sauce; top with 1/2 the cheese mixture.
6. Repeat layers ending with vegetable mixture; cover and bake for 40 minutes.
7. Uncover and sprinkle the remaining mozzarella and the Parmesan on top; bake, uncovered, for an additional 10 minutes or until cheese is melted.
8. Allow to stand at least 10 minutes before cutting and serving.

YIELD: About 6 pounds or 6 BIG servings
FAT GRAMS IN ENTIRE RECIPE: 5

BTW: If you already have some fat free marinara handy, throw the vegetables you see in the ingredients for this recipe into the marinara, skip the seasonings, tomatoes and paste, and layer in your cheese and noodles. It will save you time and the results, crunchy veggies in a fantastic lasagna, will be the same!

Notes:

_____

_____

_____

_____

_____

_____

_____

_____

_____

_____

_____

_____

ZUCCHINI ON PASTA

Throw these ingredients together in a jiffy and here's dinner.

Cooking utensil: A non-stick wok or large skillet

1/4 cup white wine or defatted stock
1 medium onion, sliced
2 cloves garlic, minced
2 tsp. chicken or vegetable bouillon granules
2 medium zucchini, sliced in 1/4 inch sticks
1 Tbs. dried Italian seasoning
1 tsp. dried oregano, crushed
1 tsp. dried thyme, crushed
1/4 tsp. crushed red pepper flakes
2 slices fat free Swiss cheese
1/2 pound pasta of choice, cooked
Fat free grated Parmesan

---

1. Stir-fry the onion, garlic and bouillon in the wine or stock until the onion softens.
2. Add the zucchini and all the seasonings; stir-fry until the vegetables are all crisp-tender.
3. Add the Swiss cheese and continue cooking just until the cheese melts and blends through the mixture.
4. Pour over hot pasta; sprinkle Parmesan over the dish and serve.

YIELD: 6 cups
FAT GRAMS IN ENTIRE RECIPE: 5

BTW: It's oh, so easy and it's oh, so good! Heat up some French bread until crusty and enjoy!

Notes:

_____

_____

SQUASH MUFFINS

Let's not forget that zucchini bakes beautifully! And these are easy muffins that are not too sweet.

Baking utensil: A large-muffin non-stick baking tin (makes 6)

1/4 cup Egg Beaters
1 cup yellow squash, grated
1/2 cup skim milk
1/2 cup sugar
2 Tbs. applesauce
2 cups all-purpose flour
4 tsp. baking powder
1/2 tsp. salt

Preheat the oven to 425°

1. Combine the Egg Beaters, squash, milk, sugar and applesauce.
2. Sift the flour, baking powder and salt together.
3. Add the flour mixture to the squash mixture and stir.
4. Fill the muffin mold 2/3 full and bake for 20 minutes.
5. Test with a toothpick for doneness. If the toothpick comes out with moist batter on it, the muffins need more time. If sticky but baked residue is on the toothpick, they're done.

YIELD: 6 large muffins
FAT GRAMS IN ENTIRE RECIPE: 2

Notes:

PREPARATION OF CHAYOTE SQUASH

This squash demands boiling and peeling before use in any recipe.

Cooking utensil: A 4 quart non-stick saucepan

---

1 pound chayote squash, cut in half
2 quarts boiling water
1 tsp. salt

---

1. Add the squash to the boiling water; lower heat and simmer, uncovered, for about 25 minutes or until just tender.
2. Cool sufficiently to handle; remove the skin with a sharp paring knife.
3. Cut the seed from the center, along with the white spongy part around it, and discard.
4. Slice or cube the chayote for use as directed.

YIELD: 1 pound or about 3 cups
FAT GRAMS IN ENTIRE RECIPE: 1

Notes:

CHAYOTE STEW WITH SOFRITO

What is sofrito? It's a delightful, sautéed seasoning that can add an extra kick to a number of dishes.

Cooking utensil: A large non-stick skillet or wok

---

2 chayote squash, cooked, peeled and cored
1 large tomato, diced
Salt and freshly ground pepper to taste
Caribbean Sofrito:
      1/4 cup dry white wine
      1 medium onion, diced
      2 large cloves garlic, diced
      3 Tbs. fresh cilantro, chopped
      Salt and freshly ground pepper
Brown rice, cooked without oil or margarine
1 Tbs. fresh cilantro, chopped

---

1. Combine the chayote and tomato with seasonings to taste; set aside.
2. Prepare the sofrito in the wok; add the chayote mixture; stir while heating through.
3. Serve on brown rice; sprinkle chopped cilantro on top.

YIELD: 5 cups
FAT GRAMS IN ENTIRE RECIPE: 1

BTW: I mention using the Sofrito with other dishes and you may find many that would benefit from the flavor. Egg Beaters omelets folded over this mixture is one beautiful combo, and adding the sofrito to black beans or, in fact, any canned bean, in a chili sauce or not, would enhance the flavor of the beans.

Notes:

MISCELLANEOUS PUT-TOGETHERS

There are certain recipes that simply don't fit in a category dedicated to beans, grains or vegetables. Some of the seafood hors d'oeuvres that have been hailed as "can't believe they're low fat" goodies and some of the sauces or dressings that may come in handy for you from time to time.

BARI'S CLAM DIP

My daughter, Bari, is known by all her friends to be the gal who "knows" how to please a crowd with her culinary skills. You've seen some of her recipes in other parts of this book and she's a darned good cook. This is one nibbler for which she's famous.

Preparation utensil: A medium-sized bowl

---

1 container (8 oz.) fat free cream cheese
1 can (6 1/2 oz.) chopped clams, drained
1 tsp. vegetable bouillon granules
1/4 tsp. garlic powder
3 dashes Tabasco

---

1. Combine all ingredients; chill.
2. Serve with fat free crackers or baked pita triangles.

YIELD: 2 cups
FAT GRAMS IN ENTIRE RECIPE: 1

BTW: I like a little color on top so I sprinkle a bit of paprika or curry powder on it when Bari turns her back!

Notes:

TUNA CURRY ROLL-UPS

When I asked Rodney Charles which of my recipes he liked the best, this was one of them. How could I leave it out of the book?

Cooking utensil: A baking sheet treated with spray-on oil

---

1 can (6 1/2 oz.) tuna fish, packed in water, drained
1/2 cup fat free mayonnaise, plus 2 Tbs.
1/2 tsp. curry powder
1/2 tsp. onion salt
14 slices fat free whole wheat bread, crusts trimmed
Paprika

Preheat the oven to 500°

1. Combine the tuna, 1/2 cup mayonnaise, onion salt and curry powder; spread the additional 2 Tbs. mayonnaise as spread on the slices of bread.
2. Place a small amount of tuna on each slice and roll the bread around the tuna; if necessary, use toothpicks to hold the roll in place; refrigerate for 24 hours.
3. Remove the tuna rolls from the refrigerator and slice in 1/2 inch thick rounds; place on the baking sheet; bake until the bread is lightly toasted.

YIELD: About 70 to 80 rounds
FAT GRAMS IN ENTIRE RECIPE: 4

BTW:These tidbits can be enhanced with a dot of Healthy Choice loaf cheese or fat free shredded cheddar. Put the cheese on top of each round and consider them done when the cheese melts.

Notes:

SHRIMP SPREAD

Another hors d'oeuvre that's almost too easy to allow you to feel you're really entertaining.

Preparation utensil: A small bowl

---

1 can (6 1/2 oz.) baby shrimp
1 Tbs. fat free mayonnaise
Dash hot pepper sauce
1 tsp. fresh lemon juice

---

1. Remove the shrimp from the can, rinse under cold, running water, drain; refrigerate for about 20 minutes.
2. Combine the shrimp with the other ingredients; adjust lemon juice to taste.
3. Serve with Melba Rounds.

YIELD: 3/4 cup
FAT GRAMS IN ENTIRE RECIPE: 3

Notes:

BOILED SHRIMP

Most of the folks I know who eat shellfish really get into boiled shrimp. There's a way to be sure that the shrimp have a flavor that will make you proud. Following the shrimp, you'll find recipes for two favorite sauces for these morsels.

Cooking utensil: A 3 quart non-stick saucepan

---

1 pound shrimp, cleaned and deveined
1 Tbs. whole black peppercorns
1 tsp. dried oregano leaves
1/2 cup fresh parsley or 1 Tbs. dried
2 ribs fresh celery, including the tops
1 tsp. crushed red pepper flakes
1 small onion, quartered

---

1. Place shrimp in the saucepan in cold water, along with all the other ingredients; bring the water to a boil.
2. When the shrimp turn pink and start to curl, drain them in a colander or strainer and immediately rinse under cold running water to stop the cooking.
3. Remove any particles of the seasonings; refrigerate until well-chilled and serve with the Red Cocktail Sauce or Remoulade Sauce.

YIELD: 1 pound shrimp
FAT GRAMS IN ENTIRE RECIPE: 4

NOTES:

Red Cocktail Sauce

Preparation utensil: A small bowl

1 cup bottled chili sauce
2 Tbs. prepared horseradish or to taste
1 Tbs. fresh lemon juice
Tabasco or hot pepper sauce to taste

1. Combine all ingredients.
2. Refrigerate; serve chilled.

YIELD: About 1 cup
FAT GRAMS IN ENTIRE RECIPE: 0

Notes:

REMOULADE SAUCE

This sauce is one of the creations of a chef in New Orleans. It may be used as a sauce for crab, as a dip for shrimp or even as a salad dressing.

Preparation utensil: A small bowl

1 1/4 cup fat free mayonnaise
2 cup white vinegar
1/2 cup Dijon mustard
1/2 cup ketchup
3 Tbs. prepared horseradish
1 clove garlic, puréed
1 tsp. Tabasco or hot pepper sauce

1. Combine all ingredients.
2. Refrigerate.
3. Serve chilled.

YIELD: 2 1/2 cups
FAT GRAMS IN ENTIRE RECIPE: 0

Notes:

TO YOUR GOOD HEALTH

Anxiety is certain to accompany any major change in your life. If you're not already living low fat, it is awesome to consider eating a new way, not for just a limited period of time, but always. After all, you're used to living the way you have been, for all your years up till now. The obvious questions are: how difficult will this be, and, can I really stick to a major modification such as this one?

You're not alone. Others have gone before you, and they've found it has not been a difficult transition. There are more and more people, every day, who find out that living low fat is not only effortless, but, after just a short time, a more comfortable and happier way to go. I hope your adaptation is easy, if you're new to this lifestyle. If you're an old hand at the conversion of high fat to "lean and mean," you're probably keeping your eye on the new happenings in this arena.

To help you along this road, you may find my monthly newsletter, *LIVING & LOVING LOW FAT*, a journal with some answers for you. We are dedicated to bringing to those who want to (or must) live a low fat lifestyle, a simple way to face learning how, without fear; to bringing to those already well on their way to healthy eating, a source of fun, informative reading to enhance the way; and to lend to our readers up-to-date information to make the going easier. I'd love to have you visit my home page on the Internet. (www.lofat.com). Here you'll find information about my newsletter and how to order it. You'll also find low fat cooking tips and tricks, fitness and exercise information and much more. Please visit. If you have questions or comments E-Mail them to me at TStevens1@juno.com.

The phone number to order the newsletter is 800-874-7125. We accept Visa, M/C and Amex. I welcome any questions or comments you may have regarding the lifestyle, the book or the newsletter.

If you prefer to write me, the address is: Living & Loving Low Fat
P.O. Box 1017
Greenbelt, MD 20768-1017
I'm looking forward to hearing from you. Meanwhile, enjoy the lifestyle...it's elementary, my dear!

Recipe Index

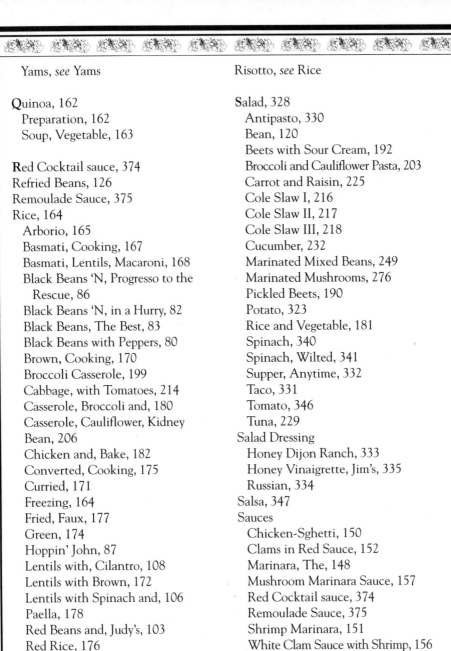